The Relations Between

Gordon Onyango Omenya

The Relations Between Asian And African Communities of Kenya

Afro-Asian Socio-Economic and Political Relations in Nyanza Province of Kenya

LAP LAMBERT Academic Publishing

Impressum / Imprint

Bibliografische Information der Deutschen Nationalbibliothek: Die Deutsche Nationalbibliothek verzeichnet diese Publikation in der Deutschen Nationalbibliografie; detaillierte bibliografische Daten sind im Internet über http://dnb.d-nb.de abrufbar.

Alle in diesem Buch genannten Marken und Produktnamen unterliegen warenzeichen-, marken- oder patentrechtlichem Schutz bzw. sind Warenzeichen oder eingetragene Warenzeichen der jeweiligen Inhaber. Die Wiedergabe von Marken, Produktnamen, Gebrauchsnamen, Handelsnamen, Warenbezeichnungen u.s.w. in diesem Werk berechtigt auch ohne besondere Kennzeichnung nicht zu der Annahme, dass solche Namen im Sinne der Warenzeichen- und Markenschutzgesetzgebung als frei zu betrachten wären und daher von jedermann benutzt werden dürften.

Bibliographic information published by the Deutsche Nationalbibliothek: The Deutsche Nationalbibliothek lists this publication in the Deutsche Nationalbibliografie; detailed bibliographic data are available in the Internet at http://dnb.d-nb.de.

Any brand names and product names mentioned in this book are subject to trademark, brand or patent protection and are trademarks or registered trademarks of their respective holders. The use of brand names, product names, common names, trade names, product descriptions etc. even without a particular marking in this work is in no way to be construed to mean that such names may be regarded as unrestricted in respect of trademark and brand protection legislation and could thus be used by anyone.

Coverbild / Cover image: www.ingimage.com

Verlag / Publisher:
LAP LAMBERT Academic Publishing
ist ein Imprint der / is a trademark of
OmniScriptum GmbH & Co. KG
Heinrich-Böcking-Str. 6-8, 66121 Saarbrücken, Deutschland / Germany
Email: info@lap-publishing.com

Herstellung: siehe letzte Seite /
Printed at: see last page
ISBN: 978-3-659-16670-9

Zugl. / Approved by: Nairobi, Kenyatta University, Diss 2010

THE RELATIONS BETWEEN THE AFRICAN AND ASIAN COMMUNITIES OF KENYA'S NYANZA REGION, 1901 – 2002

BY

OMENYA GORDON ONYANGO
Reg. No C50/50/5068/03

A THESIS SUBMITTED TO THE SCHOOL OF HUMANITIES AND SOCIAL SCIENCES IN PARTIAL FULFILMENT OF THE REQUIREMENTS FOR THE AWARD OF THE DEGREE OF MASTER OF ARTS OF KENYATTA UNIVERSITY.

MAY 2010

DECLARATION

This thesis is my original work and has not been submitted for a degree in any other university.

_____Signature   Date_____

Omenya Gordon Onyango

Department of History, Archaeology and Political Studies

We confirm that the work reported in this thesis was carried out by the candidate under our supervision.

_____ Signature   Date_____

Dr. Mildred A.J Ndeda

Department of History, Archaeology and Political Studies

_____Signature   Date_____

Dr Edward N.W. Kisiang'ani

Department of History, Archaeology and Political Studies

_____ Signature   Date_____

Dr. Samson M. Omwoyo

Department of History, Archaeology and Political Studies

2

DEDICATION

To my mother Apiyo (Nyar Okuche), maternal grandmother Dereda, my late brother Evans (dock) and fiancee Jane, as well as to all the orphaned children.

ACKNOWLEDGEMENTS

I am grateful to Kenyatta University for offering me the opportunity to undertake my Masters of Arts studies and opening my eyes to the significance of scholarship. I would like to appreciate the scholarly input of my tireless supervisors Dr Mildred Ndeda, Dr Edward W. Kisiang'ani and Dr Samson Omwoyo who initiated me into the world of research. For my thesis to take this shape, many people have made immense contributions. Without my numerous respondents I would not have had data for this study. I would also like to thank Dr F. Kiruthu, Dr G. Murunga, Dr P. Kakai, Dr P. Wekesa and Madam Susan Owino for their input and guidance which contributed to the success of this work. I cannot forget my postgraduate colleagues, Eliud Lubanda, Geoffreyson Khamala, Philip Chemelil, Martha Muraya, Isaiah Oduor and Nixon Mwangi who shared their views with me and consoled me when the going got tough at some point. My sincere thanks also go to the entire staff of History department of Kenyatta University for their moral support during my studies.

I would like to acknowledge my dad for giving me the opportunity to pursue my studies. I also acknowledge the encouragement, support and sacrifice given to me by my sisters and brothers. I am indebted to my cousins Molly and Morris for their financial support which enabled me to stay in Nairobi as I pursued my studies. I would also like to thank aunty Phoeby (Nyar Ng'iya) for ensuring a steady supply of pocket money to me. The technological support provided to me by my former roommate Orao James was invaluable and due to that I was able to type my work without incurring any extra

4

expenses. Omondi, J. of the Kenya National Archives was a great support. Mr A.D Bojana also deserves special gratitude for editing the final work. Last but not least, I would like to thank my fiancée Jane for her encouragement and long wait. It is impossible to name all the people that gave me support but to all of them I owe my greatest appreciation.

TABLE OF CONTENTS

Title page.. 1
Declaration 2
Dedication.. 3
Acknowledgement.. 4
Table of Content……… ...…………………………………...…… 6
Glossary   of   Luo   Terms.. 9
List of Abbreviation…………………………………………… 10
Abstract…………….. 11

CHAPTER ONE

1.0   INTRODUCTION... 13
    1.1 Context of the problem... 13
    1.2 Literature Review 19
    1.3 Statement of the Problem.. 32
    1.4 Objectives of the Study... 33
    1.5 Research Premises 34
    1.6 Justification and Significance of the Study.................................... 35
    1.7 Scope and Limitation of the Study 36
    1.8 Theoretical Framework... 37
    1.9 Research Methodology 50
    1.9.1 Study Locale 50
    1.9.2 A map showing Kisumu, Kendu Bay, Yala and Ndere areas of Kenya's Nyanza Region... 57
    1.9.3 Research Design 58
    1.9.4 Research Instruments and Equipments.. 59
    1.9.5 Data Collection 60
    1.9.6 Data Analysis.. 62
    1.10 Summary and Conclusion 63

CHAPTER TWO

2.0   THE   ROOTS   OF   MODERN   ASIAN   PRESENCE   IN   KENYA: SOME REFLECTIONS ON THEIR ORIGIN AND SETTLEMENT
    2.1 introduction 64
    2.2 Explaining the Asians Entry into Kenya 64
    2.3 The First Indian Settlement in Nyanza, Kibos Area 73
    2.4 The Nyando Indian Settlement in Nyanza Province....................... 87
    2.5 Summary and Conclusion 88

CHAPTER THREE

3.0   THE AFRO – ASIAN RELATIONS IN EARLY COLONIAL PERIOD 1900-1918

3.1 Introduction... 90
3.2 The Emergence of Afro-Asian Economic Interaction in Kisumu, Kendu Bay, Ndere and Yala Up to 1918…………………………………………...…….. 91
3.3 Afro-Asian Political Relations in Nyanza to 1918..................................... 114
3.4 Afro-Asian Social Relations in the Early Colonial Period to 1918................. 118
3.4.1 Education 118
3.4.2 Housing 122
3.5 Summary and Conclusion 128

CHAPTER FOUR

4.0 PERIOD THE AFRO-ASIAN RELATIONS IN THE INTERWAR AND DURING THE SECOND WORLD WAR 1919-1945

4.1 introduction 130
4.2 The Afro – Asian Economic Relations in the Interwar Period 131
4.3 Afro-Asian Relations and the Cotton Industry in the Interwar Period 142
4.4 Political Participation and Afro-Asian Relations In the Inter War and During the   Second World War Period 1919-45………………………………………… 161
4.5 Afro-Asian Social Relations During the Inter War and Second World War Period...…………………………………………………………………….. 167
4.5.1 Housing 167
4.5.2 Education 172
4.6 Summary and Conclusion 175

CHAPTER FIVE

5.0 THE AFRO-ASIAN RELATIONS IN LUO NYANZA IN THE PERIOD 1945-1963

5.1 Introduction... 177
5.2 Afro-Asian Economic Interactions in the Period 1945-1963......................... 178
5.3 Afro-Asian Relations, the Government and the Cotton Industry in Nyanza ……………………………………………………………………………... 185
5.4 Afro –Asian Interaction and Political Participation in Nyanza 1945-63 190
5.5 The Afro-Asian Social Interaction 1945-1963 206
5.5.1 Education 206
5.5.2 Housing 210
5.6 Summary and Conclusion 215

CHAPTER SIX
6.0 THE AFRO–ASIAN RELATIONS DURING THE KENYATTA AND MOI ERAS 1963-2002

6.1 Introduction... 218
6.2 Afro-Asian Relations and the Africanization Process in the Kenyatta era .. 219
6.3 Afro-Asian Political Relations in the Kenyatta Era 235

6.4 Social Participation and Afro-Asian Relations in Nyanza in the Kenyatta era 1964 -1978 240
6.4.1 Housing 240
6.4.2 Education 242
6.5 Moi-Asian Nexus and Afro-Asian Economic Relations in Nyanza Province in the Moi era 1978-2002................................... 246
6.6 Afro –Asian Social Interaction in the Moi Era 263
6.7 Summary and Conclusion 266

CHAPTER SEVEN

7.0 SUMMARY AND CONCLUSIONS 268
    Bibliography 279

GLOSSARY OF LUO TERMS

Luo Pinje	**Multilineal territories**
Nanga	**Cloth**
Nyamach	**A type of beads mostly worn by Luo women for aesthetic purposes**
Jonanga	**People who wear clothes**
Ngege	**A species of fish popularly known as Tilapia**
Mbuta	**A species of fish popularly known as Nile Perch**
Tek ateka kidi	**In this context, it is used to describe someone who is as hard as a rock**
Oluoro who	**In this context, the term is used to describe a person who fears shaving**
Jopidi	**Baby sitters**
Jokeya	**The term is used in this context as a Luo nickname for the carrier corps**
Jokarachuonyo	**People from Karachuonyo (Kendu Bay)**
Orwa	**A luo term for our son in-law**

LIST OF ABBREVIATIONS

IBEAC	Imperial British East Africa Company
DC	District Commissioner
PC	Provincial Commissioner
KTWA	Kavirondo Taxpayers Welfare Association
ITA	Indian Traders Association
CMS	Church Missionary Society
LUTATCO	Luo Thrift and Trading Corporation
LNC	Local Native Council
LEGCO	Legislative Council
YKA	Young Kavirondo Association (YKA)
RAWA	Ramogi African Welfare Association
CLSMB	Cotton Lint and Seed Marketing Board
LAC	Locational Advisory Council
KANU	African National Union
KADU	Kenya African Democratic Union
ICDC	Industrial and Commercial Development Corporation
KNTC	Kenya National Trading Company
IDB	Industrial Development Bank
KIE	Kenya Industrial Estate
DFCK	Development Finance Company of Kenya
KICOMI	Kisumu Cotton Mills
KFP	Kenya Freedom Party

ABSTRACT

This study investigates the problem of race relations between Asians and African communities in Kenya's Nyanza region. It examines the roots of Asian presence in the Nyanza region and explores the various levels of interactions between the Asian ethnicities and the Africans. Although the literature review demonstrates that some research on the Asian Question in East Africa has been undertaken by a number of scholars, there is little evidence to show Afro - Asian relations in Nyanza Province has been given scholarly attention. This hiatus makes the proposed study abundantly significant and justified. The study revolves around four fundamental premises. It proposes that forced immigration played a remarkable role in the emergence of interracial relations between Africans and Asians in Kisumu, Ndere, Kendu Bay and Yala areas of Nyanza region. Besides, it assumes that government policies were the main causes of suspicion, tension and conflict between the Asians and the African communities. Furthermore, it supposes the contest between the Africans and the Asians manifested itself in the social, political and economic spaces available in Nyanza. Finally, it proposes, racial integration and harmony have been achieved between African and Asian communities within the area of study. The study employs variants of the post-colonial theory- hybridity and plurality-to analyze data. The gist of the Postcolonial theoretical formulation is to interrogate forms of knowledge and social institutions authored and authorized by the West. Thus, the struggle against colonial values and institutions, within the postcolonial space of Nyanza, has been executed through the emerging hybridities and pluralities. What is more, the post colonial terrain of Nyanza was plural space-embracing Europeans, Africans and Asians- upon which competing racial and ethnic interests have been witnessed and negotiated. Moreover, Nyanza Province was one of the spaces, within the Kenyan postcolony, which experienced forms of knowledge and social institutions authored and authorized by the West. The study argues that the formal settlement of Asians in Nyanza and, specifically, in Kibos area was marked by contestation between the European settlers on the one hand, and the Asians. In this scheme, Asians acted as a buffer zone between the warring Luo and Nandi communities around Kibos area. While doing business, Asians employed Africans as workers in the cotton ginneries. Africans too served as domestic workers on Asian farms and in Asian residential areas. However, the study reveals that the relationship that existed between Africans and Asians was unequal. The Asians were later accused of exploiting Africans not only by inflating commodity prices but also by paying low wages. Over time, the Afro – Asian relations changed from being mutually beneficial, indifferent, to being conflictual. Towards the independence watershed of 1963, Afro-Asian relations were characterized by a lot of conflicts which led to the withdrawal of Asians from Ndere, Kendu Bay, Kibos and Yala locations of Nyanza region to other parts of Kenya or outside Kenya. During the period, 1945-1963, Africans formed such organizations as the Luo Thrift and Trading Corporation to compete with both Asians and European economic consortiums. Such developments were signs of resistance as Africans started questioning various forms of knowledge and values authored and authorized by the West. After independence, these relations took a different dimension when Asians were accused of exploiting Africans and undermining the integrity of black people. Methodologically, the study employs an elaborate scheme of oral interviews, archival investigations and library research to collect data. The data collected has been subjected to the postcolonial theoretical perspective. The study concludes that full Afro-Asian integration was not achieved in the Nyanza postcolonial space.

CHAPTER ONE

1.0 INTRODUCTION

1.1 Context of the Problem

To date, the subject matter of race relations remains a globally explosive issue. Among social and political scientists, this problem has continued to attract enormous intellectual attention and scrutiny. This is so given that any fulfilling form of human development is profoundly premised on the extent to which dependent groups can harmoniously work together while at the same time minimising conflicts that could possibly cause social stagnation and untold suffering (Bhatt, 1976). Hurd (1973) echoes similar sentiments when he argues that relationships between racial groups posed some of the most urgent problems in the world. He cites the cases of the United States of America, South Africa, Zimbabwe and many other countries, which have in the past experienced serious and often mounting racial tension.

After the collapse of formal colonialism in many parts of Africa, racial hostilities among different groups have never faded. The problem of race relations assumes even greater significance in plural societies in which the population is divided not merely on the basis of race but also by language, culture, value systems and religion. In such societies, unless there exists a common consensus or a sense of nationhood, which transcends ethnic and racial barriers, a divisive tendency may intensify, creating an atmosphere of suspicion, hate and violence (Bhatt, 1976).

In Britain, the relatively large influx of West Indians, Indians, Pakistanis and East African Asians has created a nagging racial problem.

Through her slave trading activities, her colonial adventures and industrialisation enterprises, Britain was notably involved in the development of white dominance all over the world. Yet, until the immigration of coloured people began to assume significant proportions in the 1950s, the comparative absence of a coloured population meant that there were no domestic problems of race relations in that country.

Studies of race relations in the United States of America suggest that white racism is deeply embedded in Western culture. Given its emphasis on property, order and self-control, Western culture tends to compel people to de-emphasize human relationships and to treat themselves and others as objects to be manipulated and used (Kovel, 1971). As a consequence, discrimination and the denial of equal opportunity to African- American and other non-white groups, continue to create anger, resentment and hostility. Racism has thus been regarded as the main cause of racial riots in several Euro-American societies.

In South Africa and Zimbabwe, racial hostilities have historically revolved around the quest for power as Europeans, Africans and the Coloureds attempted to outmanoeuvre each other on the social and political stage. Shortly after their arrival at the Cape in 1652, the Dutch, through superior force of arms, were able to dominate the indigenous Khoisan population. By virtue of his Calvinist religion, the Boer farmer justified both his right to expand his lands and responsibility to subjugate the 'heathen' living on that land.

Specifically, the Transvaal Republican constitution stated that there should be no equality of race in the church and the state. Upon these determinants, the psycho-sociological and historical legacies of racial conflict and fear, Afrikaner nationalism was later to build its most powerful weapon in its pursuit for the total domination of the South African society- the fierce racist ideology (Andrew, 1976).

Closer home, Uganda experienced its worst forms of racial conflicts during the reign of General Idi Amin. Upon assuming power, General Amin targeted the Asian communities for persecution and murder, blaming them for the country's economic and political problems (see O'Donnell, 1978, Siddiqi, 2004:6). Consequently, the military junta in Kampala undertook to expel Asians from Uganda in the early 1970s. Amin argued that his government was determined to make the ordinary Ugandan a master of his destiny by empowering him to enjoy the wealth of his own country (Nyanchoga, 1996; Chege, 2004.).

Between 1890 and 1895, Zanzibar, Uganda and Kenya became British protectorates while Tanganyika fell under Germany overlordship (Mungeam, 1966:1).The establishment of this British administration immediately introduced a racial issue (Dilley, 1966:3). Sir Charles Eliot, the then British Governor in charge of Kenya's colonial territory undertook to put in place the most effective administrative machinery to govern the protectorate. The real challenge that faced Sir Charles Eliot however was economic.

In Kenya, the problem of race relations is deeply embedded in the historical development of the country (Bhatt, 1976). With the establishment of colonial rule, land belonging to

15

Africans was alienated and this development excited African resentment against the Europeans. The issue of racism reached its peak between 1919 and 1923, when the Europeans and the Asians engaged themselves in bitter struggles over their respective roles in the colony. This struggle was over the occupation of the White highlands and representation in the legislative council. This crisis led to the birth of the British -crafted, Devonshire White Paper (1923) which, declared Kenya an African territory in which the interests of the African 'natives' had to be paramount (Das 1975; Bell, 1964).

In its worst form, racism could be said to have started with colonialism. It was embedded in the establishment of colonial rule. The colonial myths of European superiority were racist and European racism contributed to the establishment and maintenance of a rigid three layer caste system in Kenya, with Europeans at the top, the Asians in the middle and Africans at the bottom. Skin pigmentation, more than religion, education, culture or personal qualities became the primary determinant of a person's social status, income, occupation, place of residence and countless other aspects of life (Abuor,1972).

In their struggle against discrimination and imperial policies, some Asians expressed willingness to cross racial barriers by aligning themselves with early leaders of the African anti-colonial resistance movement (Seidenberg, 1979). The majority of the Asian traders became mercantile intermediaries who facilitated the flow of goods between foreign commercial houses and local markets.

The Asians generally opened their shops in and around areas populated by Africans and eked out a living selling basic goods such as salt, sugar, spices and, sometimes, fresh vegetables which they grew behind their shops. In the Nyanza region of Kenya, the construction and completion of the Kenya-Uganda railway in 1901 heralded the arrival of Asians in the Lake town area of Kisumu, from where they moved to areas like Yala, Kendu Bay, Kadimo Bay, Asembo Bay and the Ndere region, among other centres. After the completion of the railway, some of the Asians opted to settle permanently in these areas and undertook to open up shops (Ochieng', 1974). This study attempts to analyse the Afro-Asian relations during the evolution and analyse the development of the Kenyan postcolony.

Even though Asians denote people originating from the Asian continent such as the Chinese, Japanese and Malaysians, the terms Asian and Indian in our context are used interchangeably throughout the text to describe people originating from the Indian sub-continent. Africans in this context refer to the black Kenyans living in Nyanza province. Indeed, given that Asians have been part and parcel of the transformation of the various phases of the Kenyan postcolony, this study enhances the understanding of their crucial role in the shaping up of relations in the colonial and the post independent Kenya.

The notion of postcolony identifies, specifically, a given historical trajectory- that of societies recently emerging from the experience of colonisation and the violence which the colonial relationship involves. To be sure, the postcolony is chaotically pluralistic; it has nonetheless an internal coherence. It is a specific system of signs, a particular way of

17

fabricating simulacra or reforming of stereotypes. It is not, however, just an economy of signs in which power is mirrored and imagined self reflectively. The postcolony is characterized by a distinctive style of political improvisation, by a tendency to excess and lack of proportion, as well as by distinctive ways identities are multiplied, transformed and put into circulation (Mbembe 2001: 102).

But the postcolony is also made up of a series of corporate institutions and a political machinery that, once in place, constitute a distinctive regime of violence. In this sense, the postcolony is a particularly revealing, and rather dramatic stage on which are played out the wider problems of subjection and its corollary, discipline (Mbembe 2001:102). Kenya is thus taken as a postcolony and Nyanza as a space within the postcolony which is pluralistic and chaotic in nature and where multiple identities are transformed and various contestations and negotiations are taking place.

Loomba (1998) argues that it is now helpful to think of post colonialism not just as coming literally after colonialism and signifying its demise, but more flexible, as the contestation of colonial domination and the legacies of colonialism. Racial relation between the Asians and the Africans in Kenya's Nyanza region is studied here as one of the colonial legacies within a plural society with people having mixed and complex identities with opposing values and interest. The postcolonial theory brings questions of subjectivity to the fore. It illustrates the complexities of the postcolonial identity, particularly at a time of intense globalization. The thrust of postcolonial thinking is to recognize the existence of the otherness and dismantle formulations, which inform discourses on the otherness (Kisiang`ani, 2003).

18

In this study, the entire period 1901-2002 is treated as a postcolonial regime in Kenya's history. Linda Hutcheon (1992) and Jan Mohamed (1985) remind us that 'post' in postcolonial is taken to mean after 'because of' and even unavoidably 'inclusive' of the colonial; on the other, it signifies more explicit resistance and opposition, the anticolonial'. The postcolonial therefore, designates moments within colonialism and beyond. To be realistic, the postcolonial era in Kenya does not begin after independence in 1963. Rather, Kenya's postcolonial experience commences soon after the imposition of colonial rule in 1895. Independence therefore constituted a mere transition from the dominant phase of colonialism to the hegemonic phase of colonialism.

1.2 Literature Review

The body of literature on interracial relations in East Africa is growing by the day. However, literature on the Indian question in Kenya's Nyanza region is scanty. The Asian question in Nyanza does not assume prominence as it is tackled as an appendage of either the economy, politics or social life of Nyanza. Few scholars for example Fearn (1961), Lonsdale (1964), Ochieng (1974), Reed (1975), Obudho (1976), Anyumba (1995) among others have just mentioned this relationship briefly in their works. In the history of Nyanza, this study would be the first of its kind. This therefore indicates a gap in scholarship that requires attention.

Although the roots of the Asian – African mercantile activities ran deep in the history of the East African littoral, it was not until the advent of British colonial domination in the area that a more structured presence of the Asian community began to be felt. Asian political activities during Kenya's early colonial period were conditioned by the colonial economic structure in which they were placed. The lure of trade, prospects for a better life and the 'protection ´ of the British Empire accelerated the migration of various peoples of different classes, castes and religions from different regions of the Indian-sub continent to East Africa. On arrival, they were quickly separated from the Africans and the Europeans by the colonial regime through colonial policies, which could not allow them to settle and stay in one place. Indeed, the British colonial authorities encouraged the allocation of economic functions by race rather than visible skills (Seidenberg, 1979).

Looking at the issue of race relations, Baker (1983) argues that European nations conquered, controlled and settled in the vast areas of the Americas, Asia, Africa and the Middle East, thereby bringing indigenous people under their rule. Whatever the initial motivation, colonialism was invariably justified by notions of white racial superiority. Europeans were persuaded that they had a duty to 'civilise' 'native' populations in conquered areas. Though not directly related to our current study, Baker's work is relevant as it provides the basis for analysing and understanding some of the critical causes of racial disharmony. This study has appropriated Baker's arguments by subjecting his conclusions to Kenya's racial theatre in the Nyanza region.

Contributing on the role of culture in nation building, Mazrui (1972) contends that the problem confronting African countries generally was the crisis of national integration. It arose because different clusters of citizens did not accept each other as compatriots. It could, therefore, be seen that a process of cultural fusion leading to an enlarged empathy, a shared language, or a shared lifestyle was a contribution toward the integrative process. Further, Mazrui says that the commitment to indigenize what is foreign, idealise what is indigenous, nationalise what is sectional and emphasising what is African is central to the process of cultural fusion in the African condition. Mazrui's arguments enrich our efforts to appreciate racial tension between Asians and Africans in Nyanza.

Ghai (1965, 1971) contends that the most important contribution of the Asians to the East African economies had been the extension of the monetary economy into the subsistence areas- a prerequisite for any economic development. Their function was essentially the introduction of attractive imported consumer goods to large sections of the rural population throughout East Africa. Until recently, Asian traders acted as main outlets for produce from the indigenous rural economies. But unfortunately, Asian dominance in the distribution sector of the economy tended to lay them open to charges of exploitation. Ghai too observes that Asians continued to perform the old but vital function of introducing and extending the money economy in many African countries. This work is significant as it sheds light on the Asian economic interaction with the Africans. Lemoosa (1996), Musalia (1996) and Murunga (1998) also interrogate the Asian question in a similar fashion as Ghai's.

Focussing on Asian political activities in Kenya, Uganda and Tanzania to 1945, Mangat (1969, 1975) states that some indentured Indian labourers (workers on contract) were settled at Kibos in the Nyanza region in 1903. This settlement was meant to engage the

21

Indian community in farming and in irrigating the areas around the Kibos River. The settlement at Kibos, however, gradually made progress by 1908 when 1000 acres were put under the cultivation and production of cotton, sugarcane, chillies and corn. Most of the Asian indentured workers who stayed behind after the end of the railway construction exercise, in fact, took to work for the railway company, while others became market gardeners, itinerant traders, carpenters and masons. Besides, some of the Indian labourers spread into Uganda, Tanganyika and Zanzibar. However, Mangat's work focuses mainly on Indian agricultural settlement and does not explain in detail how these Indian railway workers related and integrated with the local people at Kibos. The current study attempts to address this hiatus.

On migration, Mangat (1975) contends that both the Indian Office and Foreign Office in East Africa were involved in negotiations with a view to amending the Emigration Act to permit the emigration of indentured Indian servants to East Africa for the purpose of constructing the railway line. The Indian Office also undertook to encourage railway workers whose contracts had expired to settle as agriculturists in the colonies. This settlement would later set the stage for Afro-Asian interaction in Kenya's Nyanza region.

Lofchie (1973) avers that Asians in Zanzibar were primarily a middle class group that virtually monopolised trade, commerce and the clerical levels of the civil service. Some Asians were extremely wealthy and those who owned the large import and export firms were by far the richest Zanzibaris. However, Lofchie observes that as a community, Asians were politically ineffectual. This work outlines some of the political and economic spaces upon which the Asians interacted with the Africans. Using Lofchie's arguments as the basis, the current study explores the extent to which the Kenyan experience was similar or probably different from that of Zanzibar.

Bharati (1972) demonstrates that Africans were ungrateful even after Asians had 'taught' them nationalism, which eventually brought about the African independence. He further observes that Asians supported all the nationalist endeavours of the African leadership financially and ideologically. Although this study only looks at the general feelings of the Asians toward Africans after independence, the current study utilises Bharati's work to explore the dynamics of the Afro-Asian relations in Kenya's post-independent space in Nyanza.

Makhan Singh (1972) asserts that, alongside the Kenya African Union (KAU) and the East Africa Indian National Congress, the East Africa Trade Union Congress (EATUC) was instrumental in the struggle for Kenya's independence. Through these organs, both the Asians and Africans were united politically against British imperialism. However, it is also significant to establish the relationship between Asians and Africans not only politically but also in social and economic fields in the Nyanza region which Makhan did not cover.

Contributing to the issue of race relations in East Africa, Nanjira (1976) demonstrates that race relations have always been influenced by many factors such as politics, religion, race, skin colour and cultures. He argues that the main influence on these relations comes from two forces: economics and law. From the economic standpoint, Nanjira observes that problems of interracial relations arose whenever movements of population occurred from one part of the world to another. He further asserts that in post-independent East Africa, the main contribution of Asians has been in the economic field.

Thus, despite outcries against Asian 'exploitation' and despite government efforts to transfer the instruments of the economies to the Africans, Asians continued to play vital roles in the commercial fields in the post independence period. This problem of race relations was so huge, he argues, that it culminated in the expulsion of Asians particularly from Uganda. The big issue is: Do Africans feel exploited and do Asians think they have been exploiting Africans? This study explores this question

Looking at the racialization of political thought in colonial Zanzibar and how racial identities were reproduced, Glassman (2004) observes that the Arab Association in Zanzibar stresses the inherent difference between islanders and mainlanders. Whereas Islanders have become 'sufficiently Arabianized ' to have lost most of the qualities of 'African barbarism', Mainlanders were but 'primitive' natives whose culture and history were in the process of formation only then. He stresses that there was a bitter conflict between the Indians and the mainland Africans over the issue of clove crop most of which was purchased by Indian merchants. Although Glassman studied race relations in the Zanzibarian context, his work provides the parameters upon which the current study interrogates the Afro-Asian conflict in the Nyanza region of study.

Gregory (1971) looks at the Asian question in both South Africa and Uganda. He notes that in 1885, the government of the Republic of South Africa enacted legislation which denied all persons of Asian origin the right to citizenship including the right to own property. The government also restricted their residence to designated locations and required them to register and pay a fee of 25 dollars as registration fee.

On Uganda, Gregory observes that although harmonious relations prevailed between the Africans and the Asians, Africans showed some resentment against the dominant economic position of the Indians. Resentment by Africans against the overwhelming influence of Asians leading to local fights in Kenya's business transactions between 1890-1939 have also been captured in Gregory's work. This study has utilised Gregory's rich historiographical data to interrogate segregative colonial policies that fuelled racial rivalry between Asians and Africans.

Rothchild (1973) focuses on the racial bargaining in independent Kenya. He provides a demographic breakdown and a brief social history of Asians in the country during the colonial period. He notes that from the beginning, the Africans refused to accommodate themselves to foreign power and reacted aggressively towards any European and Asian pretensions of superiority.

Such rejections took the form of isolations or open protests and rebellions. With the advent of independence, African protests and rebellion gave way to African power. This study has been significant in that it explores the racial structure of the colonial government and how the colonial structures determined Afro-Asian relations in the post-independent Kenya.

Frost (1997) argues that the existence of a small, educated and economically prosperous European community among an African population, a hundred times larger was certain to produce many problems. The situation was further complicated by the presence of an Indian community three times the size of European community. The contribution of the Indians to the development of Kenya was of enormous value, but their success brought on them the jealousy of both Africans and Europeans. The latter feared the competition of the richer Indians and the possibility of their being granted land in that part of the highlands which they were determined to keep 'White'.

The Africans, Frost notes, became jealous of not only Indian presence in small trading and craft enterprises but also their capacity to take up junior office jobs. However, sometimes Africans and Indians made common cause against the Europeans. The European social exclusiveness without doubt gave impetus to such collaborations. Since Frost looks at the multi-racial relations between the three communities, his study is useful to our current study as it helps us in exploring the changing social, economic and political dynamics of Afro-Asian relations in the Kenya's Nyanza region.

Contributing to the problematic of Asian immigrants in East Africa under British colonialism, Rai (1979) argues that segregation rules were extremely humiliating to Indians in the Kenya colony. None of them, however wealthy or respectable, could live or carry on business in certain designated localities. For example, colonial legislation

26

barred Indians from establishing business enterprises along the Government Road (now Moi Avenue in Nairobi). He observes that some of the hostility carried by the Africans against Indians was largely a legacy of the British regime in East Africa. It thus appears pertinent for us to investigate the extent to which this discriminatory policy affected racial integration.

Seidenberg's study (1979) on the role of a minority community in Kenya's politics takes a necessarily limited view of the Asian community. He focuses primarily on the Asian activities in political associations, the press and trade unions. The work excludes certain aspects of the Asian history that could be critical in understanding the Afro-Asian relations in Kenya, such as trade and education. The present study has attempted to go beyond Seidenberg by delving into such issues as education and housing.

Mbae (1996) contends that in their political struggle and when sorting out their relationship with other races, Asians were inconsistent and the struggle for their own racial supremacy did put them in perpetual misunderstanding with Africans. Nevertheless, the outcome of the Devonshire White Paper of 1923 gave paramountcy to African interest against other races. Therefore, the fear of a possible European leadership and the Asians desperation in a foreign land made them to pattern their struggle with the Africans. This move was aimed at transcending racism and buying safety in the presumed African goodwill. The foregoing observation is relevant to the present study. This is because it sheds light on whether or not the outcome of the Devonshire White Paper affected Afro-Asian relations later in the post-independent period. Works raising related issues include Ngare (1996) and Ogot (1968).

Maxon (1995) and Nabende (1996), argue that racially stratified social structure was particularly evident in the areas of occupation, income and education. Educational inequality formed an obvious and important indicator of the racial caste structure. Such arguments are important since they guide us in exploring how the colonial education system laid the foundation for social interaction between the Asians and Africans in the Nyanza region of study.

With regard to periodic markets, urbanisation and regional planning in Western Kenya, Obudho (1976) argues that in the main townships in Nyanza the population of Asiatic people increased very steadily. The same source reports that Asians were behind the building of a cotton ginnery and oil refinery at Kisumu. Asians too were responsible for the evolution of the sugar refinery jaggeries at Kibos. This study utilises the rich data provided by Obudho to interrogate the various forms of relations which developed between the African and the Asian communities in the Nyanza region of Kenya.

Fearn's study (1961) highlights the response of the African peoples of Nyanza to the new economic problems and opportunities created by European settlement and administration. He argues that the Nyanza economy was based upon the agrarian and fishing enterprise of the Africans. This economy was facilitated by the marketing opportunities provided, during the mid 1930s, through the financial, technical and organisational contribution of the immigrant races.

Thus, to Fearn, the stimulation of the developing economy of Nyanza came from the European sources but aided by Asian enterprises in marketing and trade. The above arguments are relevant to the present study since apart from explaining the backbone of the Nyanza economy, Fearn's work also credits Asians and Europeans with the development of the region. This study utilizes the arguments in Fearn's work in exploring the Afro-Asian relations, which developed as a result of the Indian participation in the commercial activities of the region.

Lonsdale (1964) explains that the weight of anthropological opinion supports the view that normal political leadership in Nyanza was founded on lineage loyalty with the advantages of genealogical seniority being tampered by the need for leadership qualities. He contends that while the government programme of economic and political development institutionalised tribal division, education and migrant labour, the general modernisation processes associated with colonial rule were to cut across clan and tribal loyalties. The tension between tribal values and the colonial modernisation instruments became a constant feature of Nyanza political history. The foregoing work is relevant to the present study as it provides some insights on the involvement of Asians in the political activities in Nyanza region.

Anyumba (1995) states that, the independent Kenyan government came up with the Trade Licensing Act of 1969 as a policy which restricted Asians from doing business along some major streets within the town centres and the Africanization programme which was to ensure that Africans controlled the economy of the country. These policies impacted negatively on the economy of Kisumu. He observes that in mid- 1970s, complaints about Asians were still common in the press. Official government warnings were still being issued from time to time to Africans who secretly resold business premises to Asians.

The overall image of Asians was so negative that Kisumu was referred to as the 'Bombay of Kenya' on the account of the Indian domination of commerce in the town. This work has been important to the present study because it sheds light on the government policies, which formed the basis of Afro-Asian relations in the post-independent Kenya's Nyanza region. Did these official warnings arouse any kind of suspicion, hostility or tension between the Africans and the Asians, and if so, how was this tension contained? This is one of the gaps that this study sought to address.

Reed (1975) observes that in 1901 commercial cultivation of cotton was introduced into Kenya's Nyanza province by the British government. It was expected that cotton production would produce results similar to the cotton industry in Uganda. However, during the period 1901-1923, it became clear that Kenyans had not enthusiastically embraced cotton growing and that it would not become the major cash crop of Nyanza Province. He observes that Asians were involved in the buying of cotton from the African

30

growers. Even though Reed deals with the introduction of cotton production in Nyanza, his work is relevant as it provides the basis for analysing the dynamics of Afro –Asian economic interactions in Nyanza Province.

Mbembe (2001) is precise in describing the postcolony as a place marked by the colonial domination and which is trying to reconceptualize itself. He argues that the postcolony is characterized by multiple identities and that under colonial rule and beyond, a constellation of distinctively indigenous interests came into being. It played a key role in the transformation of ancestral systems of power and in the realignment of alliances, including economic ones, between 'natives' and colonizers.

Other postcolonial thinkers like Edward Said (1998) in his work *Orientalism* examines the Western academic field of ' Oriental Studies' in terms of how its discourses have shaped and structured a fictionalized and exoticized 'Orient' that serves as the subaltern Other for the West. It states that Orientalist academic discourse served political and imperialist ends, despite its claims to 'objective' neutrality. In short Orientalism is a Western style for dominating, restructuring, authorising views and having authority over the Orient (Said, 1978:3).

In exploring the question of race and African identity, Kwame Antony Appiah (1992:ix-xi) argues that there is plenty of room in Africa for all sorts and conditions of men and women; and that at each level, Africa is various with people of multiple identities.

31

Kwame's observations will therefore, be useful in helping us understand how different identities (ethnic and racial) can exist within the chaotic plural space of a postcolony.

The literature reviewed indicates that some studies have been undertaken on the Asian question. However, there are several gaps which the review has identified and which require scholarly attention. This study therefore addresses some of these gaps by looking at the Afro-Asian economic, social and political relations in Kisumu, Ndere, Kendu Bay and Yala areas of Kenya's Nyanza region, as well as assessing whether these relations have been mutually beneficial or conflictual. Indeed, the works, which have been reviewed above are just a selected few. There is thus little doubt that, from the foregoing reviews, very little research has been undertaken to interrogate the Afro-Asian relations in Nyanza region. This study utilizes the numerous sources in related fields to harness relevant data in order to address this hiatus. In addition to the failure by scholars to seriously address the Afro-Asian relations in Nyanza, none has given these relations a postcolonial theoretical interrogation. This is also a gap which this study intends to fill.

1.3 Statement of the Problem

The significance of the Asian question in Nyanza cannot be ignored. The contribution of the Asian presence to Nyanza economy, social life and politics warrants a study. The relationship between the Africans and the Asians particularly in the rural areas and their contribution to colonial entrenchment has also not been undertaken and this needs to be addressed.

Given the existing gap in scholarship in the study of race relations between the Asians and the Africans in the Nyanza region, this study undertakes a historical analysis of the relations between the Asians and Africans in specific locations of Kendu Bay, Yala, Ndere and Kisumu in the Nyanza region from 1901-2002. Its focus is on such crucial issues as interracial integration, discrimination, tension and their social, political and economic impact on Africans. It also interrogates the ownership and use of resources, the causes and management of interracial conflicts. The study addresses the following questions:

i.   What are the roots of the Asian presence in Kenya's Nyanza region?

ii. What are the historical causes of suspicion, tension, and conflict between Asians and Africans in Kisumu, Ndere, Kendu Bay and Yala areas of Nyanza?

iii. How have the Afro-Asian relations manifested themselves in the social, cultural, political and economic spaces of Kisumu, Ndere, Kendu Bay and Yala areas of Nyanza and with what impact?

iv What were the major attempts to resolve the racial tensions between Africans and Asians? To what extent were they successful in Kisumu, Ndere, Kendu Bay and Yala?

1.4 Objectives of the Study

i.   To examine the roots of the Asian presence in Kenya's Nyanza region

ii. To trace the historical causes of suspicion, tension and conflict as well as the overal impact of interracial tensions between the Asians and Africans on the socio-economic and political practices of Nyanza.

33

iii.   To investigate the role played by Asians and Africans in the socio-economic and political activities in Kisumu, Ndere, Kendu Bay and Yala areas of Nyanza and how these influenced their relations with Africans .

iv.   To analyse the outcomes and extent of interracial integration and harmony between the Asians and Africans in Kisumu, Ndere, Kendu Bay and Yala areas of Nyanza.

1.5 Research Premises

The study revolves around four fundamental premises.

i. Forced immigration played a remarkable role in the emergence of interracial relations between Africans and Asians in Kisumu, Ndere, Kendu Bay and Yala areas of Nyanza.

ii. Government policies were the main cause of suspicion, tension and conflict between the Asians and the Africans in Kisumu, Ndere, Kendu Bay and Yala areas of Nyanza.

iii. The contest between the Africans and the Asians manifested itself in the social, political and economic space.

iv. Racial integration and harmony have been achieved between Africans and Asians in Kisumu, Ndere, Kendu Bay and Yala areas of Nyanza.

1.6 Justification and Significance of the Study

As the literature review has demonstrated historical documentation on interracial relations between the Africans and the Asians in the Nyanza region has not received serious scholarly attention. Thus, the study is necessitated by the fact that it deviates from the nationalistic analysis of interracial relations by embracing localized investigations into the study area. At such levels, it is possible to uncover certain dynamics and features, which might have been assumed or overlooked by the all –embracing nationalist discourses on interracial relations. Being aliens in this setup, Asians need to be studied so as to see how they have and continue to relate with the Africans socially, economically and politically in the study locale which is foreign to them.

Kisumu is particularly crucial to this study because it offers an entry point for Asians to penetrate into the areas under study. Furthermore, the study intends to improve relations between the African and the Asian communities not just in the region under study but also in the entire nation. Findings from this study would be helpful to members of other races too (race is used here in a broad social sense to designate ethnic groups of various sorts e;g religion and nationality among others) who may want to invest in Nyanza region moreso, Kisumu, Yala, Ndere and Kendu Bay. The study also suggests possible solutions to the causes of suspicion, tension and conflict in areas where they occurred between the two communities.

35

Given the crucial role that the Asians played in the socio-economic transformation of the Kenyan postcolony, it is important for scholars to delve deeper into their relationships with the African communities with whom they interacted. The few studies available look generally at multi-racial relations between Europeans, Africans, and Asians at the national level. Historical documentation on the relations between Africans and the Asians in the Nyanza region of study is extremely scarce. This makes this study not just crucial but significant.

This study is thus significant in that, apart from enriching the historiography of the Afro-Asian relations in East Africa, it also provides new methodological and theoretical tools to interrogate the problematic in the Nyanza region. It also expands the historical studies of Afro-Asian relations in Nyanza region.

1.7 Scope and Limitation of the Study

The study has examined and analysed the dynamics of the Afro-Asian relations in Kenya's Nyanza region from the period 1901 –2002. The term relations in this study refers to interaction, connection or contact between Asians and Africans. The year 1901 provides a good starting point for this study because it marks the beginning of the Asian occupation and settlement within the study locale. However, this does not mean that the study will not look at the period before 1901. The year 2002 provides a good historical period to end the study as it marked the end of Moi's rule. Moi's relationship with some

Asian personalities at the national level affected the community's relationship with the Africans at the local level in Nyanza province. The year 2002 was also the year of political transition in the country that raised peoples's expectations for change in the government.

The focus of study was, however, limited to only selected areas in Kenya's Nyanza region. These included Kisumu town, Kendu Bay, Yala and Ndere. These were areas where the Asian presence was high in Nyanza province. They also constituted spots where Asians owned businesses, houses, plots, built schools and participated in the political processes. The study also looks at the social (education, housing), economic (trade and industry) and political (representation, governance and elections) aspects of the two communities under review. This work does not cover Asian religion, relationships between different Asian communities among themselves and their settlement in other parts of Kenya as a topic of study, but leaves these areas for further research.

1.8 Theoretical Framework

The original theory of socio economic development that accompanied the post-1945 decolonisation of Asia and Africa rested on the idea of modern society as the goal of development. Modern society supposedly had typical social patterns of demography, urbanisation and literacy, economic patterns of production and consumption, investment, trade and government, finance and typical psychological attributes of rationality, ascriptive identity and achievement motivation. The process of development consisted, in this theory, the moving from traditional society, which was taken as the polar opposite of the modern type, through a series of stages of development – derived essentially from the history of Europe, North America and Japan- to modernity, that is, approximately the United States of the 1950s (Toye, 1995:43)

Proponents of this theory such as Rostow (1960) and Myrdal (1968) for instance recommended that development in Africa would only be achieved through the simultaneous transfer of Western political, social and cultural structures together with the diffusion of the economic and technological complex from the West (Hoogvelt 1978). Therefore, the logic behind this theory was that, Africa could not make any meaningful progress in its social, political and economic fields until it espoused the principles of Western modernity, science and rationalism. This was seen as the only universal truth that would rescue Africans from their state of hopelessness.

A few years into independence, new African states began to confirm the reality that the modernisation theory presented a general framework for development toward modern statehood conceived mainly within the Western mould of thinking. Similarly, critics of this theory had pointed out that the principal terms of the theory- the 'traditional' and the 'modern' were much too vague to be of use as classifications of distinct societies.

The two terms did not give any indication of the great variety of societies that have and do exist; instead, the 'traditional' label was offered as a blanket term to cover a range of pre-industrial societies that had exceedingly different socio-economic and political structures such as feudal, tribal and bureaucratic empires. A much more careful historical analysis was, therefore, required of these pre-industrial forms in order to have any hope of understanding the subsequent processes of social change they underwent (Webster, 1995:114). African nation states had to come to terms with the irrelevance of modernisation to the African conditions because this project had overlooked the African reality and achievements (Kisiang'ani, 2003).

Marxist, neo-marxist and dependency schools analysed development and underdevelopment in the context of the international capitalist system. According to Marx, the development of society is the result of the continual productive interaction between men and nature (Giddens, 1971:35). Classes emerge where the relations of production involve a differentiated division of labour which allows for the accumulation of surplus production that can be appropriated by a minority grouping which thus stands in an exploitative relationship to the mass of producers. In Marx's conception therefore, classes form the main linkage between the relations of production and the rest of society, or 'superstructure' (Ibid 39).

In his understanding of social life, Marx freely admitted that individuals are 'personifications of economic categories and embodiments of particular class-relations and class-interest'. What stands out in Marx's argument is that the mode of production is socially primary because it shapes class struggle and encompasses the development of the productive forces (Gottlieb, 1992:11).

While other thinkers focus on how people understand themselves in terms of religion, nationality or personal life, Marx believed that the mode of production naturally divides social life into antagonistic classes and groups determined by relations to the mode of production. In all but the most primitive societies, an exploited class performs the bulk of the productive labour; and a ruling class controls or owns the forces of production, decides how much of the economic surplus will be distributed, and/or controls the process of production. Class actions, in turn, shape the overall development of social life. Hence Marx claimed that 'the history of hitherto existing society is the history of class struggles (Marx and Engels, 1954:13, Gottlieb, 1992:11). Classical Marxism therefore, looked at society only in terms of economic class consciousness. All other forms of consciousness as racism, ethnicity, religion were considered false consciousness.

The neo-Marxist thinking was against African dependence on foreign capital, which did not invest its surplus in the underdeveloped nations (Rodney, 1976). Thus development would require the elimination of foreign penetration, which supports the status quo, and the creation of a socialist context of development (Chilcote & Edelestein 1974:28).

Like its forerunner, Marxism, neo Marxism was permanently transfixed on economic determinism as if economics had the capacity to explain all the diverse aspects of humanity (Kisian'gani, 2003:40). Neo- Marxism recognises the analytical tool of classical Marxism which highlights the domination of the haves by the have-nots. However, in a specific third world space, Neo-Marxism acknowledges that certain variables, for example means of production, classes, workers and peasants, had never developed strictly on the lines envisaged in the 18th and 19th century Europe. Two, exploitation in Africa was not just on class lines but also on racial, ethnic and even religious lines. The inadequacies of both classical and neo Marxism as a useful theoretical tool, therefore, lay in its failure to interrogate post-colonial realities in Afro-Asian relations which goes beyond class relations.

Paul Baran (1957) who spearheaded the emerging school of neo-Marxism provided the first major analysis of the effects of imperialism from the point of view of the less developed countries. Baran explains underdevelopment not as 'an original state of affairs' but as the result of a particular historical process. In this process, developed countries became so by exploiting and colonising the less developed countries and that independent industrialisation was blocked by an alliance between local (comprador) elites and the metropolitan states (Ayres, 1995:101).

The analysis by Andre Gunder Frank (1967) suggested that underdevelopment was part of the process of development itself. There were several other versions of neo colonialism but the common logic was that capitalism was the impediment for development. The central political message was, therefore, the need for revolutionary national liberation (Ayres, 1995:101).

From the early 1980s, the African condition deteriorated despite the continent being rigorously forced to embrace the Western ideologies of development, within the parameters of capitalism and socialism. This state of hopelessness raised new challenges for scholars. Given the need to explain and find a solution to problems associated with this reality, African scholars continued to search for paradigms of analysis that could best explain the problem of the Third World. These challenges began to be tackled through emergent postmodernist and postcolonial thinking. Thus, from the 1980s, these theoretical formulations received a great deal of attention from Africa and Africanist scholars (Kisiang'ani, 2003)

The postcolonial theory deals with the reading and writing of literature written in previously or currently colonized countries. It also denotes the intellectual production of formerly colonized peoples after colonization. It focuses particularly on the way in which literature by the colonizing culture distorts the experience and realities of the colonized people and shows how, through the same literature, colonial subjects have been condemned to an inferior status.

In addition, the postcolonial theory demonstrates that literature by the colonized people should articulate their identity so that they could possibly reclaim their past in the face of that past's inevitable otherness (Lye, 1998). This theory is based on the concept of subversive resistance against the tyrannies of Western forms of knowledge and cultural institutions. It is thus a counter-discourse of formerly colonized others against the cultural hegemony of the West with all its imperial structures of feeling and knowledge (Xie, 1997). In many ways, therefore, postcolonialism signifies an attempt by the formerly colonized peoples to re-evaluate, rediscover and reconstruct their own histories and cultures. It is also an act of rethinking the history of the world against the inadequacy of

42

terms and conceptual frames invented by the West. It represents an urgent need and determination to dismantle imperial structures in the realm of culture (Xie, 1997).

On the other hand, it is worth noting that postcolonial relationship is not primarily a relationship of resistance or of collaboration but can be characterized as illicit cohabitation, a relationship made fraught by the very fact of the colonial authority and its 'subject' having to share the same living space. The post colony is made out of one single 'public space' but of several sub-spaces, each having its own separate logic yet nonetheless liable to be entangled with other logics when operating in certain specific contexts. Thus, the postcolonial subject has had to learn to bargain in this conceptual market.

Furthermore, subjects in the postcolony have also had to have a marked ability to manage not just a single identity for themselves but several, which are flexible enough for them to negotiate as and when required (Mbembe, 1992). The relation between the Africans and the Asians could possibly be viewed within the context of the various forms of contestations over values, and interests on the plural postcolonial space. The theoretical perceptions posed by Mbembe have given this study a crucial analytical tool with which to analyze the diverse Afro-Asian relations in Kenya that, by and large, carries significant bearings on the struggles by the different communities within the Kenyan postcolony.

This study adopts two variants of postcolonial theory to interrogate its data. Variants of the postcolonial theory such as the concept of 'Plurality', and 'Hybridity' as put forth by Achille Mbembe and Homi Bhabha respectively have been used to assess the Afro-Asian relations in the study locale. This is because the crisis of race relations has to be understood in the context of the crisis of the postcolonial state in Africa. Such a crisis is reflected in the conflict over power sharing, identity and access to resources; in the incapacity of the state to provide for and protect its citizenry, in the collapse of the social and economic structures in the rural areas (Honwana, 1999).

In his book Orientalism Edward Said (1978) argues that Orientalism is a study of how Western academia has represented the Orient over the last two centuries. Inspired by Michael Foucault, Edward Said constructed Orientalism as a manifestation of power and knowledge. Examining Orientals as a discourse, Edward Said argues that the western academia is responsible for the creation of the 'Other' the Orientals, who are significantly different from those in the Occident (Ahluwalia, 1996). Edward Said alludes to a collective of identifying 'Us' European as against all 'those' non-Europeans and indeed it can be argued that the major component in European culture is precisely what made that culture hegemonic both in and outside Europe: the idea of European identity as a superior one in comparison to all the non-European peoples and cultures (which were seen as backward). To him, therefore, the relationship between the Occident and the Orient is a relationship of power, dominion, of varying degrees of a complex hegemony (Said, 1994).

Said's methodology is embedded in what he calls textualism. This allows him to envisage the Orient as textual creation. Textualism entails concern with authority and positioning in Oriental discourse. This produces the West as a locality of power and centre distinctly demarcated, the 'other' as the object of knowledge and inevitable subordination (Ahluwalia, 1996).

This juxtaposition of Us/Them, We/Other, central to Said's work is instructive when we examine African studies and the manner in which it has chosen to identify, describe, characterize and represent a continent that has been marginalized particularly in the last century. Said's Orientalism as a variant of postcolonial theory allows Africans to be represented as the 'other' and ensures that they continue to be marginalized. But Hommi Bhabha does not think these strict divisions vividly describe the true arrangements of the postcolonial space.

Bhabha (1994) raises concern over the failure of the postcolonial discourse to deliver stable and fixed identities. He describes colonial identities as almost the same but not quite. He argues that, the grim polarities of the colonial encounter are necessarily bridged by a 'third space' of communication, negotiation and, by implication, translation. It is in this indeterminate zone or 'place of hybridity' where anti-colonial politics first begins to articulate its agenda and where the 'construction of a political object that is new, *neither the one nor the other*, properly alienates our political expectations, and changes, as it must, the very forms of our recognition of the moment of politics'(Bhabha 1994).

This is because the explosion of European dominance and the age of empire, coupled with the massive movement of peoples since the advent of both the slave trade and indentured labour as well as the mass migrations of the twentieth century mean that postcolonial identities and locations are now highly intertwined, intermixed and complex. The corollary to the ambivalence of colonial authority, of stereotypical modes of

45

representation is, for Bhabha, the hybridities of colonial and postcolonial condition (Zeleza, 1997).

Based on Bhabha's criticism, Edward Said revised his concept of the We/*Other* binarism captured in *Orientalism*, by admitting that such intellectual rigidity was untenable in a situation where relations and identities are temporary, fluid, and constantly changing. As is evident in many colonial discourses authored in the West, the colonized have been given the identity of the other, the inferior, and the savage (Said, 1994).

Notably, African identities are complex and rooted in the postcolonial experience. This is because there exist long standing and populous Arab, Asian, European and Middle Eastern Diasporas in Africa, which play critical roles in the ongoing evolution of African societies and to the formation of African identities. Historical and contemporary interactions between the African populations and other people, including the Europeans have created multiple and sophisticated cultural hybrids, which defy and, in fact, transcend the simple binarism of the *We/Other* (Mwangi, 2002).

According to Loomba (1998), the term hybridity in postcolonial discourse refers to the integration or mingling of cultural signs and practices from the coloniser and the colonized. In this regard, the *We* would have some elements of the *Other* and vice versa. It, therefore, becomes difficult to differentiate between the *We* and the *Other*. In the Afro-Asian relations, there are certain values which the Asians borrowed from Africans and vice versa. This makes Said's variant of We/Other inadequate as a tool of analysis in this study. This inadequacy of the We/Other as a variant of postcolonial theory puts hybridity

46

and plurality in a better position as a theoretical tool of analysis to interogate Afro-Asian relations

Ahluwalia (2001) points out that those concepts as hybridity, which in postcolonial studies we have come to see, as proposed by Bhabha, have always been intrinsic to African identity formation. In the African context, multiple identities are part of the very fabric of society. The variant of hybridity has been used therefore, to determine whether the relationship between the Asians and the Africans who were colonial identities has been influenced by the hybridity of their cultures in the Nyanza region of study or their interaction created hybrid identities beyond the known identities of black and Asian.

The concept of plurality as a variant of the postcolonial theory has been employed to interrogate the Afro –Asian relations within the postcolonial space of Kenya's Nyanza region. Recognising the plurality of the postcolonial space which also signifies opposing values and interest, Achille Mbembe (1992) observes that the African postcolony is chaotically pluralistic and that it is in practice impossible to create a single, permanently stable system out of all the signs, images and markers in that disposition. That, in Mbembe's view is the reason why everything in the postcolony is constantly being shaped and reshaped, as much by the rulers and the ruled, in attempts to rewrite the mythologies of power. In a sense, Achille Mbembe echoes, in a different way, what Bhabha states.

In this study, Nyanza is treated as a postcolonial sub-space, which is grappling with imperial hegemony and legacy. The subject of race relations assumes even greater significance in such plural sub-spaces as the Nyanza region in which the population is divided not merely on the basis of race, but also by language, culture, value system and religion. In such societies, unless a common consensus exists or a sense of nationhood is developed, divisive tendencies may intensify creating an atmosphere of suspicion, hate, and violence (Bhatt, 1976).

Like any other theory, the postcolonial theory has been criticized and characterized as being epistemologically indebted to both post structuralism and postmodernism. Such a reading denigrates the authenticity of postcolonial theory and renders it subservient and theoretically vulnerable to charges levelled at post structuralism and post modernism (Ahluwalia, 2001).

Nevertheless, it is important to note the position articulated by Ashcroft and Tiffin et, al. (1995) who point out that the confusion between post colonialism, post structuralism and postmodernism is caused because, a key aspect of postmodernism is the deconstruction of the logocentric metanarratives of European culture which is much like the postcolonial project of breaking down the binaries of imperial discourse. For them, the conflation between post colonialism and postmodernism arises because of their concerns such as decentering of the discourse, the focus on the significance of language and writing in the construction of experience. It also arises because of the use of subversive strategies of mimicry, parody, and irony (Ahluwalia 2001).

True, postcolonialism owes most of its sophisticated conceptual language to postmodernism, but it emerges as a distinct discourse with a set of problematics different from those of postmodernism. Indeed, postmodernism is a tool for critiquing modernity from the European standpoint while postcolonialism is an instrument of interrogating modernity from the point of view of the *Other*, the colonized. Thus post colonialism looks at the specific effects of modernity, propagated by colonialism on people who were never part and parcel of European culture (Kisiang'ani, 2003).

All postcolonial societies are still subject, in one way or another, to overt or subtle forms of neo-colonial domination, and independence has not solved this problem. The development of new elites within independent societies often buttressed by neo-colonial institutions; the development of internal divisions based on racial, linguistic or religious discriminations, the continuing unequal treatment of indigenous peoples in settler/invader society- all these testify to the fact that post colonialism is a continuous process of resistance and reconstruction. This does not imply that postcolonial practices are seamless and homogenous but indicates the impossibility of dealing with any part of the colonial process without considering its antecedent and consequences (Rabaka, 2003).

This study has employed the postcolonial variants of hybridity and plurality to investigate the various ways in which African and Asian communities in the Nyanza region have struggled to curve out meaningful spaces through the ever-continuing contestations that are a permanent feature of every postcolony. This theory represents a deliberate effort to put in the spotlight non-European cultures, political systems, economic programs, educational policies, scientific knowledge and social values as it looks at the Afro-Asian relations both during the formal and informal colonisation period within Kenya's Nyanza region.

1.9 Research Methodology

1.9.1 Study Locale

This study was carried out in Kisumu town, Kendu Bay, Ndere, and Yala areas of Kenya's Nyanza region. Nyanza province of Kenya is one of Kenya's seven administrative provinces outside Nairobi; it is in the southwest corner of Kenya. It includes parts of the eastern edge of Lake Victoria and is inhabited predominantly by the Luo. There are also Bantu speaking groups such as the Gusii, the Kuria and a few Luhya. Initially, this province comprised of North Nyanza, Central Nyanza and South Nyanza which formed the greater Nyanza and was also known as Kavirondo (Barker,1958).

However, this study was carried out specifically on the areas (Kisumu, Ndere, Yala and Kendu Bay) which were majorly inhabited by the Luo speaking people and which were parts of central and South Nyanza, respectively. These areas were chosen because they represent areas which had a high concentration of Asians in Nyanza Province. The Asians also owned plots and ginneries in these areas which acted as sites where Afro-Asian socio-economic and political interactions and contestations took place. Kisumu was particularly chosen because of its being the provincial headquarters of Nyanza Province and because all the formal Asian settlements occurred within the district. It therefore offered a cosmopolitan and plural space upon which Afro-Asian relations were interrogated.

50

Ndere, Yala and Kendu Bay are adjacent to Kisumu town (which is the headquarters of Nyanza province) even though they lie in different administrative districts. For instance, while Kisumu town lies in modern Kisumu District, Kendu Bay is part of Rachuonyo District. However, both Ndere and Yala are enclaves of Siaya district. All these areas are located within range of Lake Victoria and could have attracted the Asians either because of trade in goods or fish. In addition, the construction and completion of the Kenya-Uganda railway in 1901 heralded the arrival of Asians in the lake town area of Kisumu (Port Florence), from where they moved to areas like Yala, Kendu Bay, Kadimo Bay, Asembo Bay and Ndere among others.

Rachuonyo District where Kendu Bay is situated was carved from Homa Bay District and was declared a full-fledged district on the 1st of July 1996. The district is located in south western part of Kenya bordering the Lake Victoria. It is one of the nine districts of Nyanza province. It shares a common border with Kisumu to the north, Kisii and Nyamira to the south, Homa Bay to the west and Kericho to the east. It is located between longitudes 34 degrees 25' East and 35 degrees East and latitude 0 degrees 15' South and 45' South. The district covers an area of 931 square Km which includes 365 square Km of water. It is divided into four divisions namely Kabondo, Kasipul, East Karachuonyo and West Karachuonyo. Kasipul Division has the largest, that is, 368 square Km, followed by East karachuonyo with 249 square Km while West Karachuonyo and Kabondo Divisions are the smallest (Rachuonyo District Development Plan 1997-2001).

51

The district has an inland equatorial climate which is however modified by the effect of altitude and the proximity to Lake Victoria which makes local temperatures comparatively low. The temperature in the lower parts of the district (1,135- 1,300 above sea level) range from a minimum of 17 degrees centigrade to a mean maximum of about 20 degrees centigrade. In the higher eastern part (1,300-1,600 metres above sea level), the mean minimum and maximum temperatures vary between 14 degrees centigrade and 25 degrees centigrade (Rachuonyo District Development Plan 1997-2001).

The rainfall received is caused by the convergence of the westerlies and south easterly winds which result in high downpour with frequent thunderstorms especially in the afternoons. The district has two rainy seasons, the long rains start from late February to March and range from 500mm-1000mm, and is 60% reliable. The short rains start as early as August and continue to November ranging from 250mm-700mm. Kasipul and parts Kabondo Divisions receive reliable rainfall while the rest of the district has varying and unreliable rainfall. The dry season is between December to February and June to September when there is very little agricultural activity (Rachuonyo District development Plan 1997-2001).

The district is divided into four administrative divisions namely; Kasipul, Kabondo, East Karachuonyo and West Karachuonyo. The divisions are further sub divided into 34 locations and 92 sub locations. The district has two parliamentary constituencies, namely Karachuonyo Constituency and Kasipul Kabondo Constituency. Karachuonyo

Constituency comprises East and West Karachuonyo Divisions while Kasipul Kabondo Constituency comprises of Kasipul and Kabondo Divisions. The district has three local authorities namely Rachuonyo County Council, Oyugis Town Council and Kendu Urban Council with a total of 28 electoral wards. Of the 28 electoral wards, 12 wards are under Karachuonyo Constituency and the remaining 16 fall under the Kasipul Kabondo Constituency. The growth of Kendu Bay Town is attributed to its importance as a port on Lake Victoria. It is the second largest urban centre in the district. Other urban centres with considerable population include Kosele (District headquarters), Chabera, Ringa, Oriang', Mawego, Pala and Rakwaro (Rachuonyo District Development Plan 1997-2001).

Kisumu District lies within longitude 33 20'E and Latitude 0 20'S and 0 50'S. The district covers a total area of 918.5 square Km and has four administrative divisions namely, Winam, Maseno, Kombewa and Kadibo. The district has three parliamentary constituencies namely: Kisumu Town East, Kisumu Town West and Kisumu Rural. Kisumu Town West covers Kadibo division and part of Maseno division while the Kisumu Rural constituency covers Kombewa and part of Maseno divison. The topography of the district is divided into zones: The Kano plains and the midland areas of Maseno and Kombewa. There are some notable physical features such as the scarps in the north, east and south. The Kano plains have historically been vulnerable to flooding during the rainy seasons (Kisumu District Development Plan 2002-2008).

The district has a long shoreline along Lake Victoria. This shoreline is 80 km long, has more than thirteen beaches all of which are fish landing bays. The mean annual rainfall varies with altitude and proximity to the highlands along the Nandi escarpment and Tinderet. Maseno has a mean annual rainfall of 1630mm, Kisumu1280mm, Kibos 1290mm and Koru 1103mm (Kisumu District Development Plan 2002-2008).The lowland area forms a trough of low rainfall, receiving a mean annual rainfall of between 1000mm and 1800mm. This area has two rain seasons, with the long rains occurring in between March and June.

During the short rains which occur between October through November, the average annual rainfall ranges between 450mm and 600mm. The reliability is low and the rains are distributed over a long period, making the cultivation of second crops difficult. Although there is entirely no dry month, the peak generally falls between March and May with a second peak in September to November. The mean annual temperature ranges from 20 degrees to 30 degrees centigrade (Kisumu District Development Plan 2002-2008).

On the other hand, Siaya District where Ndere and Yala lie is one of the twelve districts that comprise Nyanza Province. It is bordered by Busia District to the north, Vihiga and Butere-Mumias to the South East. The total area of the district is approximately 1520 km squared. The district lies between latitude 0 degrees 26' to 0 degrees 18' north and longitude 33 degrees 58' East and 34 degrees 33' west. Siaya district is divided into seven administrative divisions namely: Yala, Wagai, Karemo, Ugunja, Boro, Uranga and

Ukwala. These divisions are further divided into 30 locations and 128 sub-locations. There are 5 local authorities in the district with Yala town council being one of them (Siaya District Development Plan 2002-8). Ndere is situated in North Alego location, Komolo sub-location, Siaya District.

The district experiences abundant rainfall. The relief and the altitude influence its distribution and amount. The district is drier in the western part towards Bondo District and is wetter towards the higher altitudes in the eastern part. On the highlands, the rainfall ranges between 800mm-2000mm. The lower areas receive rainfall ranging from 800-1600mm. The long rains fall between March and June while the peak is realized in April and May. The short rains occur between August and November. Temperature varies with altitude too. The mean minimum temperature is 15 degrees centigrade while the mean maximum temperature is 30 degrees centigrade. The humidity is relatively high with mean evaporation being between 1800mm to 2000mm per annum (Siaya District Development Plan 2002-2008).

The district has three major geomorphological areas namely: dissected uplands, moderate lowlands and Yala swamp. These have different relief, soils and landuse. The altitude of the district rises from 1140m in the eastern parts to 1400m above sea level in the west. There are few hills found in the district namely Mbaga, Odindo, Akala, Regea and Nyambare. Rivers Nzoia and Yala traverse the district and enter Lake Victoria through the Yala swamp. These physical features have a bearing on overall development potential

55

of the district. High altitude areas forming Yala, Ukwala and Ugunja divisions have higher rainfall and are hence suitable for agriculture and livestock keeping.

Rivers Nzoia and Yala and Lake Kanyaboli have great potential for irrigation. The low altitude areas of Boro, Uranga and Wagai receive less rainfall and thus are suitable for growing of cotton (Siaya District Development Plan 2002-8). These ecological features influenced patterns of Afro-Asian activities since Asians established cotton ginneries in areas where cotton was grown.

1.9.2 A MAP SHOWING KISUMU, KENDU BAY, YALA AND NDERE AREAS OF KENYA'S NYANZA REGION

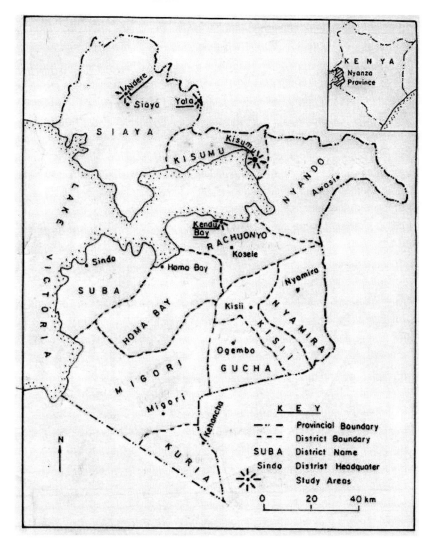

SOURCE: KENYA ADMINISTRATIVE BOUNDARIES: SURVEY OF KENYA 1998

1.9.3 Research Design

To execute the interviews, a purposive sampling procedure was employed. In this method of sampling, the researcher selected people to participate in the research for a given reason. Though the method is subjective, the information derived from this procedure was ably counter-balanced. This technique also helped in drawing up a temporary list of key informants. Informants were drawn from both Asian and African businessmen and women, and residents of the particular areas of study. The choice of key informants was based on both Asians and Africans mentioned by other oral informants during the interview, people who were normally acknowledged and respected by the rest of the community on the basis of being able to recall certain issues of the history of the people concerned.

Other people interviewed included both Africans and Asians engaged in trade and business activities as well as Africans working for Asians as houseboys and girls and as shop and supermarket attendants. Local leaders such as chiefs, both Asian and African students in public and private schools (primary and secondary schools) owned by Asians as well as school teachers in Asian owned schools and public schools were also interviewed. Information relating to their interaction was sought ranging from social, economic and political, from both men and women of varying ages.

58

1.9.4 Research Instruments and Equipments

A question guideline (see appendix A) which embraced information on the interaction of both Asians and Africans, as well as the social, political and economic institutions which informed their interaction from 1901 to 2002 was used. The interviews were to a large extent, informal as the researcher was not bound to follow

the question guideline strictly. The questions formulated were not treated rigidly but flexibly posed to harness as much information as possible. They were flexible depending on the knowledgeability of and the patience of respondents.

The discussions were based on themes such as the settlement of Asians in Nyanza, Afro-Asian involvement in local politics, trade between Africans and Asians, Afro-Asian social interaction on housing and education, African response to the Asian presence in their areas since these were the frontiers on which their interaction could be found and interrogated.

This approach gave the reseacher room for posing further questions as the discussion progressed. Occassionally, the researcher intervened to ensure that the respondents did not go out of the major themes of discussion. The respondents were questioned about their own activities and experiences as far as Afro-Asian relations were concerned. The study investigated whether this relationship was mutually supportive, beneficial, conflictual or indifferent.

In some cases, a tape recorder was used to collect and store information which was transcribed later from *Dholuo* and Kiswahili into English. Given that the field research covered a wide geographical area, it was neccessary to use some research guides or assistants to assist in the process of research operations. To counter problems of refusal to divulge pertinent information, the researcher used assistants within the region who are well-known by the locals to guide and introduce him.

This aided in easy collection of oral data. The information obtained from such oral research was corroborated with other data for validity and reliability. It is from these data that we formed the basis for analysing and interpreting the relations between the African and Asian communities of Kenya's Nyanza region.

1.9.5 Data Collection

Primary and Secondary Sources

This study relied on two complementary sources, viz : primary and secondary sources of data. To harness secondary information, written sources such as books, journals, thesis, magazine articles, dissertations and periodicals relevant to the study were consulted. These were obtained from several libraries including the Kenyatta University's Moi library, University of Nairobi's Jomo Kenyatta library, Macmillan library, Institute of African Studies library and IFRA library among others. The written materials from these libraries constituted important secondary data for the research.

Primary sources included archival data and oral interviews. Archival research was conducted at the Kenya National Archives, Provincial archives and archives belonging to the Municpal Council of Kisumu. The main documents which were scrutinised included Provincial(Nyanza) and District (Kisumu, Siaya and South Nyanza) annual and quarterly reports, political record books, intelligence reports, minutes of the Local Native Councils, confidential reports, correspondences on matters such as education, trade, cotton industry, housing and local politics.

These are first-hand records from participants and observers that have been passed down to posterity. These sources yielded information on the operations of Asians in Nyanza as well as their interactions with the indigenous Africans. Information obtained from archival materials enhanced the later discussions with the respondents during oral interviews.

To check on the reliability and validity of the archival information, it became neccessary to corroborate such information with other data especially that obtained through oral sources to minimize any subjectivity. The documents were critically evaluated and counter-checked to establish their veracity and reconcile the information elicited. The documents were also scrutinized against both secondary and oral sources.

Oral Interview

Another source of primary data was oral interview. Oral interviews were conducted to collect oral histories and experiences of participants in relation to their interaction both

61

with Asians and Africans who were considered appropriate by the researcher were consulted and interviewed in order to get more relevant information.

1.9.6 Data Analysis

In analysing and interpreting the data, the historical method was used. It is the application of this method that leads us to knowledge that is uniquely historical (Wafula 2000). The logical historical method entails the analysis and explanation of harnessed data both historically and logically (Onimode, 1985). It involves a critical investigation of events, developments and experiences of the past; the careful weighing of evidence and the validity of sources of information on the past and the interpretation of the weighed evidence. The historical method is neccesitated by the fact that the historical inquiry into social phenomenon needs more than a mere knowledge of facts and events in their chronological order. Facts must be applied to establish the historical specificity of social phenomenon in terms of its constituent elements and of the relations between these elements which determines the structure of the phenomenon and give it a coherence (Aseka, 1989 :66).

Historical data collected during fieldwork may have had their biases given that all forms of narrative (archival or oral) is not completely free from an element of subjectivity. However, the study engaged procedures of historical investigation and analysis of data to bring about a corroboration of the diverse data. This was to minimise prejudice and exaggeration during the process of analysing data. Most of the data was presented in a qualitative form, which is descriptive in nature. Overall, all the data was analyzed within the postcolonial theoretical framework.

1.10 Summary and Conclusion

In this chapter, an attempt has been made to problematise the Afro-Asian relations in Nyanza province. It has been argued that the issue of race relations has not been given attention at a local level by scholars, which therefore makes this study not only important but also urgent.This chapter demonstrates that theoretical formulations such as Marxism and neo-marxism have failed to address the realities of Africans and as such a postcolonial theoretical framework has been adopted to interrogate race relations which go beyond class interests.

The study has adopted hybridity and plurality as variants of postcolonial theory to interrogate Afro-Asian relations. This is because Africa's problems are unique and the postcolonial plural space is a space which is charaterised by contestations and negotiations. This chapter has also embraced primary and secondary methods of data collection in order to gather, analyze and present data. In Chapter Two, we discuss the roots of Asian settlement in Kenya's Nyanza Province.

CHAPTER TWO

2.0 THE ROOTS OF MODERN ASIAN PRESENCE IN KENYA: SOME REFLECTIONS ON THEIR ORIGIN AND SETTLEMENT

2.1 Introduction

In Chapter One, we problematized the Afro-Asian relations within the postcolonial space of Nyanza and demonstrated that there was intellectual need for using the tools outlined to delve deeper into these relations. In this chapter, an attempt is thus made to trace the historical roots of the Asian presence and settlement in Kenya, particularly in Nyanza by looking at their origin and subsequent settlement in this region. Moreover, the various settlement schemes and plans which were put in place to ensure the settlement of the Asian community in Nyanza are explored.

Specifically, an explanation on why the Asian settlement in the Nyanza region was rather expansive and how this settlement laid the foundation for Afro-Asian relations in Nyanza Province is also undertaken. This study adopts two variants of postcolonial theory to guide in its analysis. These are the concept of 'Plurality' and 'Hybridity' as put forth by Achille Mbembe and Homi Bhabha respectively.

2.2 Explaining the Asians Entry into Kenya

The popular image that all Asians arrived in Kenya with the construction of the railways is false and misleading because Asians arrived in East Africa much earlier. Given that Kenya, Tanzania and Zanzibar lie on the Indian Ocean, they had hosted a pool of sea

64

faring traders some of whom came from as far as China. The first European explorers were possibly the Greek and Roman traders as well as the Portuguese who built Fort Jesus at Mombasa in 1593. However, they never ventured into the hinterland. Asians arrived at different times and in different capacities. Significantly, there were Asian merchants who traded with the East African coast before the advent of British colonialism in the 19th century. When the first British arrived, they found well-established Asian communities from India and Pakistan doing business under the protection of the Sultan of Zanzibar (Van Zwanenberg & King, 1975).

Ancient Indian literature makes frequent reference to sea voyages and sea borne trade, while countless representations of ships in early Indian art are a clear testimony to the use of the ocean as a highway for international commerce. Some historians have suggested that Egyptians, Phoenicians, Persians and others may have come to the East Coast centuries before the birth of Christ; Herodotus, the Greek scholar, gave a brief account of the circumnavigation of Africa by Phoenicians (Bhatt, 1976). The earliest available historical reference to the trade between India and East Africa is found in the *Periplus of the Erythrean Sea* attributed to the first century.

There are frequent references in this work to large Hindu ships in the ports of East Africa, Arabia and the Persian Gulf, and the existence of Indian settlements at the coast. These ships brought cotton cloth, beads and sesame oil. It is thus evident that as early as the first century, there existed a trading connection between Western India and the East Coast of Africa (Chittick, 1974).

The presence of Indian traders and merchants on the coast was also mentioned by many travellers, sailors and adventurers who visited East Africa from the twelfth century onwards. In his *Nuzhat-al-mustag* ('the pleasure of travelling'), Al Idrisi mentions that Indians served as financiers and intermediaries. The trade links between India and Africa also feature in the writings of the Venetian Marco Polo (1948). In his writings, which date back to the late 13th Century, Marco Polo mentions the ships from Malabar which visited Madagascar and Zanzibar, while in his description of Kilwa in the 14th Century, Ibn-Battuta alludes to the large number of Indians settled there.

It was also an Indian pilot Ibn Majid who guided Vasco Da Gama across the Indian Ocean to Malindi near Mombasa in 1498. Duarte Barbosa, a Portuguese official who served in India between 1500 and 1516 wrote that the ships from Bombay, the great seaport of Gujarat, were to be seen in the harbours of Mombasa, Malindi, and Mogadishu and that the Arabs purchased cloth, spices and wheat from Indian merchants in exchange for gold, ivory and gum. Trade between India and the East Coast of Africa has thus been flourishing for several centuries and the presence of Indian merchants and their settlement on the coast before the advent of European colonizers cannot be disputed (Bhatt, 1976).

Early contacts between Indian traders and East Africa that go back over centuries were however sporadic. But, the major influx of Indians in East Africa came with colonization when they were brought in as indentured labourers to build the railway from Mombasa at the coast to Uganda (Tandon, 1973). It was argued that since some indigeneous people had not as yet been initiated into a labour and money economy as their Asian counterparts had been, the latter were ready targets to provide labour for the railway construction (Bennet 1966:4). It is observed that the first major and organized immigration of the Indians to East Africa was at the behest of colonialism and as its unwilling tool to aid imperial expansion as indentured labour to build the railways (Tandon: 1973:1).

The year 1840 when Seyyid Said transferred his court to Zanzibar and made it the new capital of Oman began a new era in the history of East Africa and its association with India. He had a liberal fiscal policy and benevolent attitude toward Indians. He encouraged commerce by a policy of free trade. There were no excise taxes on internal production, no export duties and no harbour duties, pilot fee or other shipping or navigation charges nor were monopolies permitted. Seyyid Said's benevolent treatment of Asians combined with forces in the mid 19th century to stimulate a great revival of Indian commercial enterprise. He also put Indians in charge of government finances and always kept Indians as collector of customs which was one of the most important posts.

Because of this favoured treatment and Said's unusually liberal fiscal policy, Indians were attracted to Zanzibar and its dependencies in large numbers (Gregory, 1971:18). The use of Indians as collector of customs in Zanzibar and Seyyid Said's benevolent attitude towards them was therefore a major impetus to Indian immigration to East Africa before colonialism.

By the beginning of the 1880s, as the imperial net widened to encompass East Africa, growing numbers of Indians arrived as potential shopkeepers, indentured labourers or low-grade civil servants in the colonial government (Seidenberg: 1996:1). Indian immigration was accelerated by colonial state intervention in the form of Indian Emigration Act of 1883, permitting Indians to travel without any restrictions to East Africa and elsewhere (Nanjira 1976:51).

Asian immigration into the interior was facilitated by the British colonizers when the Imperial British East Africa Company (IBEAC) was founded at Mombasa in 1888 by Sir William Mackinon, a Bombay based British shipping tycoon. The company utilized the laws and personnel of the Government of India as well as Indian indentured labour to help in the construction of the Uganda railway. The company imported from India old guards and police, clerks and accountants to help in the running of its affairs (Gregory, 1971).

In May 1891, Sir Guilford Molesworth, consulting engineer for railways to the Government of India who had been engaged to make the first of several reports on the proposed railway, stated that it probably would be necessary to depend on imported labour. Within the same year Capt J. R. L. Macdonald, who had been employed for seven years in India on railway construction and frontier defence was appointed Chief Engineer, and to survey the route for the railway. He brought with him from India not only several European officers of the Royal Engineers, but also 37 India *Kalasis* (riggers) and four Indian *jemadars* (Army officers). In March 1893, after the survey, Macdonald recommended the employment of Indian labourers.

People from Madras and south of India generally, he advised, would be best employed on the coastal section of the line between Mombasa and Kibwezi; while Punjabis, Pathans and natives of Northern India would do well at the higher altitudes and that, the Indian commercial body, would help solve the problem of obtaining African labour (Gregory, 1971:49). Looking at this development within the imperial lens, we see an attempt by the British to entrench their imperialism within the country by establishing the railway that was meant to open up the interior parts of the territory as well as to ease British administration. As Mungeam (1966:124-130) puts it, once built, the railway had to be made to pay for itself. This objective could only be achieved through the imposition of hut tax and by the judicious introduction of settlers.

Later, the company found itself unable to administer the country successfully. Only at the eleventh hour did the British Government step in, and in 1894, on the Company's withdrawal, a British protectorate was declared over Uganda. Later in July 1895, a British protectorate over Kenya was formally proclaimed (Mungeam, 1966: 7). The establishment of this British administration immediately introduced a racial issue (Dilley, 1966:3).

Soon after this declaration, economic and strategic issues took a central position in the minds of those British politicians concerned with the handling of colonial matters in East

Africa. In the European scramble for Africa, the need to control the headwaters of the Nile was strategically crucial to the British imperial interests in East and Northern Africa.

Further, there was the feeling that the hinterland of the present Kenya coast could be economically exploited to enhance the British imperial power. These twin factors led to the construction of the railway from Mombasa to Kisumu. In general, the railway symbolized the beginning of a permanent connection between Kenya and the rest of the world. But more importantly, it laid the foundation upon which European capitalists were ruthlessly going to colonize and exploit Kenya for many years to come (Kisiang'ani, 2003).

In October 1895, a Uganda Railway Committee under the chairmanship of Sir Percy Anderson was appointed, and in 1896, a bill authorizing construction was introduced in the British Parliament. During the debate on the bill, the proponents of the railway stressed the need to overcome the financial difficulties that had plagued the company (IBEAC), the desirability of striking the Germans in a race to the great lakes and the necessity of striking the slave trade at its source (Gregory, 1971: 50).

While seeking the necessary financial aid at home, the British Foreign Office approached the colonial government of India (Indian Office) for the essential labour. The need to recruit workers in India had become apparent with the failure of efforts to attract and retain sufficient African labour. John Kirk, who in the 1890s was the vice chairman of the Railway Committee, explained that his group had initially tried native labour but the Africans had proved scarce and insufficient. He argued that when the rains began, the

Africans had to go back to cultivate their farms. During famine, owing to want of rain, it was almost impossible to get labour. But the Indian government response to the labour crisis in East Africa was hardly encouraging due to the fact that the past experience of exporting Indian labourers to other parts of the British Empire had often been disastrous.

After long deliberations, however, the government of India conceded to the request but only on condition that every emigrant leaves labour service at the end of three years of service. This was besides the fact that the labourers could be given the option to renew the contract before returning to their homeland. Further, on completion of contract a labourer was to return home with full compensation for his labour (Gregory, 1971:51).

By 1896 with the planning of the Uganda railway under way, the Emigration Act was amended further legalizing and encouraging Indian emigration to East Africa particularly for the construction of the Uganda railway under three-year contract terms (Nanjira: 1976:51). In January 1896, the first indentured servants of 350 arrived at Mombasa, and early in 1897, they laid the first rails. Less than five years later, in December 1901, the track of 582 miles to Kisumu on the shores of Lake Victoria was completed (Gregory, 1971:51).

With the arrival of the Asians during this time, a plural colonial space with competing interests and cultures had already been established, and the entire region had a collection of African ethnicities, Europeans and the Asians. This condition would later form the basis and space upon which the Afro-Asian relations were to be contested and negotiated.

71

The main reasons behind the Asian immigration into Kenya and specifically Nyanza was to work as indentured labourers on the Kenya-Uganda railway, as artisans to help build the colonial administration structures and as traders because the economic activities were important aspects of colonialism.

Having been introduced to the monetary economy, Asians were quite handy to the colonizing administration. Finally, the Asian community immigrated as military and police personnel to beef up the British forces and help in the protection of IBEAC's property in Mombasa and along the railway lines (Finance, May 1997:8). From the word go the colonizers had embarked on an imperial and capitalist mission within the newly acquired protectorate.

The importation of indentured Indians did not cease with the completion of the Kenya-Uganda Railway in 1901. The majority among them chose to return to India after completing their contracts. Only about six thousand chose to remain in the country. Of those who stayed behind, many became traders while others became market gardeners (Bhatt, 1976, Shah, O.I 2005). Those who stayed were allowed to engage in any activity that was not only beneficial to them, but also to the newly established colonial government. Apart from labour and commerce, the British administration considered the Asian as an important agent of colonial change (Dilley, 1966:3).

A majority of the Asians set up shops and bazaars at key points along the railway. They also applied for land to set up shops and do business with Africans at key points along the railway line (Mungeam, 1966:62). The heavy costs incurred in the building of the railway had been borne by the British taxpayers. As it neared completion, the British government and the officials searched for a way by which the railway would pay for its own costs.

It was generally conceded that the rapid economic development of the country would facilitate this task and bring in the necessary revenue. The Foreign Office and the British administration were fully aware of the benefits of the Indian presence in the Protectorate. The Indian traders had successfully extended the frontiers of trade to remote areas in the country. They were also aware that the Indian had played a vital role in the early economic development of the country. As a result, various schemes for settlement, both for the Europeans and Indians, were suggested by the colonial government (Bhatt, 1976).

2.3 The First Indian Settlement in Nyanza, Kibos Area

There were several inquiries on the possibility of acquiring land in the British East Africa territory for both Asian and European settlement. The founders of the IBEAC and the proponents of the Uganda railway, as already mentioned, envisaged such a settlement. From 1900, Lords Salisbury and Lansdowne, successive British Secretaries of State for Foreign Affairs, repeatedly urged the Protectorate commissioners to consider the promotion of Indian immigration.

Because the white highlands were reserved for the European settlers, schemes for settlement of Indians in and outside the highlands were submitted by George Mackenzie, former director of the IBEAC, General W. H Manning, former acting commissioner of

73

the British Central Africa Protectorate and George Whitehouse, Chief Engineer of the Uganda Railway (Gregory 1971:67; Kalaine 1998).

Sir Harry Johnston, Special Commissioner in Uganda (from 1899-1901), was one of the earliest proponents of this idea of Indian settlement. He believed firmly that both the Indian and Indian agriculturalists were needed in Central and East Africa. In Sir Harry Johnstone's opinion:

> The yellow man was just as much needed in Africa as the white man and the black because he would inevitably occupy 'a middle place' between the two other races. Moreover, not only would Indians stimulate trade in backward areas but, if encouraged to settle as farmers, they would also introduce Africans to 'better system of Agriculture (Hollingsworth, 1960: 51).

Sir Harry Johnston hoped that new agricultural experiments within the area would enable the Africans to learn how to carry out irrigation from the Indians and to cultivate sugarcane and cotton. He stated that 'Indian trade, enterprise, and emigration require a suitable outlet' and that East Africa was and should be from every point of view 'the America of Hindu'. Similar views were expressed by top British politician Winston Churchill who wrote that 'The mighty continent of tropical Africa lies open to colonizing and organizing capacities of the East' (Mungeam 1966:102, Churchill, 1908). Such remarks represented the imperial and capitalist nature of colonialism.

The general view of the European settlers on the Indian settlement was negative. There was a concerted effort by the European settlers to exclude the Indians from highland areas. The settler members of the Land Board, a colonial institution, had no misgivings as to how the problem should be solved. One of them moved a resolution and another seconded 'that Indian immigration be discouraged as much as possible for the purpose of settlement and that no government land be allotted to them' (Ross, 1968:309). They also recommended that all future farm leases should insist on occupation by a whiteman so that even if an Indian did possess a farm, he would be forced to employ a white manager or resident. The official members did not go so far, but they agreed upon an amendment that:

> The definition of 'Highlands' be extended, that Indian close settlement in limited areas should be allowed in the lowlands but that Indian settlement should not be encouraged by the government (Ibid :309).

The East Africa (Land Acquisition) Order in Council of 1901 authorized the Commissioner to sell, grant, lease or otherwise dispose of land. Specific terms for this were laid down in the Crown Lands Ordinance of 1902, though the Commissioner was further limited in his discretion by instructions to refer grants above a certain size to the Foreign Office for approval (Bennet, 1966:9).

With the creation of such institutions as Lands Department, Public Works, Land office and other ordinances, it was very easy for the colonial agents, the Asians, to continue to penetrate and acquire land for settlement, while helping in the expansion of imperialism. Because the British had already colonized India, they had created hybrid Asian agents who glorified British values and civilizations. Further, some British administrators had supported Asians entering into East Africa because many years of living together had created a hybrid European who appreciated some Asian values. In this case, the British trusted Asians more than they trusted Africans in building the postcolonial space.

75

Statements on grants of land for Asians were reiterated in correspondence between the Indians and government officials in Nyanza on issues concerning land acquisition and also between the government officials themselves regarding application for lease of land and registration by the Asians in Kibos area (KNA, PC/NZA/3/22/11-12, 1908/10).

Sir Charles Eliot, the Commissioner of the East Africa Protectorate was initially favourably inclined towards the scheme of Indian settlement. In practice, Eliot himself was fast coming round to the view that European rather than Indian settlement should be encouraged. Admittedly, Sir Eliot had given guarded support to the idea of Indian agriculturalists entering the country, and in January 1902, he told Lord Lansdowne that he was prepared to begin the experiment of settling one hundred Indian families on low lying land at Kibos, near Kisumu (Mungeam,1966). But he emphasised that, in his view, Indians should be confined to the low-lying parts of the Protectorate and added:

> Believing as I do that the East African highlands are for the most a white man's country, and hoping that they will be taken up by white colonists in the near future, I doubt the expediency of settling large bodies of Indians in them as even in Mombasa there is considerable friction between the European and Indian traders (Mungeam 1966:103).

Sir Charles Eliot was determined to find a "White Man's Country" over the whole highland area from Mount Elgon to the border of Tanganyika. He stated:

> … the interior of the Protectorate is a white man's country and so I think it is mere hypocrisy not to admit that white interest must be paramount, and that the main object of our policy and legislation should be to find a white colony (Frost, 1978:8).

76

The British attitude here emphasizes the superiority of the English to the Indian, the Indian to African. This is the policy which governed racial relations during the formal colonization. The problems which were to face the new territory were thus the problems of a plural society. The settlers' frontier established a community which acquired power and privileges and, largely to support its position, discrimination grew up in the colony (Frost, 1978:10). The political spaces were also racial spaces. This heightened tension and competition in the postcolony.

The British imposed many conditions on the Indian settlement to restrict them from moving close to the so-called White highlands. Despite the restrictions, the British government still wanted Indians to act as a reserve army in case of any African uprising, an indication of the ambivalence on the attitude of the colonial government.

This was because from the very start, many Africans resisted foreign occupation of their land. So there was also fear of contestation and war as evidenced by plans that were put in place for the creation of the Kibos settlement whose purpose was twofold: One, the Asians were to provide a military buffer between the Luo of Kajulu Location who were in conflict with the Nandi community.

Asians were therefore to form a buffer between the victorious Luo who occupied Kajulu location and their defeated Nandi neighbours. Asians who were armed by the Protectorate government, were deployed by the Protectorate government to deter any Nandi attempts to reopen hostilities and regain their lost territory after part of their land was alienated by

77

the Europeans and from vandalizing the railway line. Two, the community was to engage in farming and in irrigating the areas around the Kibos River.

It was envisaged that Asians, would be innovators, ostensibly introducing new crops and techniques and thereby creating an impetus for change in the surrounding African community (Reed, 1975, King, O.I., 2005). So the Asians had several identities including being traders, soldiers on hire, railway builders and farmers. They had multiple identities on a plural postcolonial space. Each identity they exhibited had different consequences when applied to their Afro-Asian and Afro-European relations.

In 1903, at the instigation of D.D. Waller, Acting Paymaster of the King's African Rifles in the Treasury Department, the Protectorate established a settlement of Indian agriculturists at Kibos, which was the second railway stop north of Kisumu. This, was the first authorized Indian settlement in Kenya.

The site was in the lowlands of the lakeshore, the Nyanza basin, and was not considered within the highlands. Waller, who had lived many years in Calcutta, was relieved of his duties as paymaster and given charge of the project as the protector of immigrants. He collected about thirty Indians who were former employees of the Uganda Railways and helped them to settle   in Kibos (Gregory, 1971:69). At Kibos they planted rice, cotton, sesame and linseed on the excellent black soil (Kalaine 1998:17). Kalaine quoting Eliot states that:

At Kibos, the Indian coolies have set up vegetable gardens
and are doing a good trade at the neighbouring stations. Small
experiments have also been made in wheat, rice, and
sugarcane, which grew with great success. Between 800 and
900 acres in Kibos have been cleared up and planted with
cotton, wheat, rice, oats, grams, sugarcane, Indian corn, and
vegetables. The Kavirondo (African) people are imitating the
methods of Indian and are growing various things, the cotton
being most successful' (Kalaine, 1998:17).

With so many alien crops introduced, the eating habits also reflected powerful hybridity

of cultures between Asians, Europeans and Africans. Contextualized within the rubric of

imperialism and capitalism, it is evident that colonial crops ranged beyond cotton, from

sugarcane and sisal, to rubber and coffee, all of them tropical agricultural products and

their significance was either strategic or simply economic. As early as 1904, the cotton

question had become sufficiently important to be included in the King's (His Majesty)

speech when he stated that:

The insufficiency of the supply of raw material upon which
the great cotton industry depends has inspired me with deep
concern…I trust that the efforts which are being made in
various parts of the Empire to increase the area under
cultivation may be attended with a large measure of success
(Mamdani, 1996:37)

The King's statement was in favour of colonization and imperialism. However, it should

be noted that since African farmers around Kibos had not been approached regarding this

Indian settlement and its intentions from the beginning, they felt under no real obligation

during the first days to follow the new practices of the Asian community.

79

Seldom did Africans inquire about or even go to observe the new techniques or crops at the experimental stations in Kibos. Later, Asians started to interact with Africans within Kibos trading centre where Africans bought goods from them and started imitating their agricultural techniques (Reed, 1975, Odingo; O.I., 2005). Refusal by Africans at first to learn new practices could mean protest against the chemistry and nature of the postcolony. This was also an aspect of Afro-Asian relations in Nyanza's Kibos area.

The idea of a settlement scheme was never totally abandoned and was reviewed from time to time. An official report on the possibilities of cotton cultivation in the Protectorate, published in 1904 categorically stated that great benefit would accrue from the settlement of Indians, for the latter were keen to cultivate cotton. The report observed that the 'development' of the richest districts of East Africa depended on the introduction of Indian farmers.

Another report published in 1905 referred to the success of the Kibos settlement and praised the efforts of the Indian agriculturists who were producing large quantities of maize and cotton which were some forms of Western knowledge. The mimicry by Africans of the Asian agricultural activities influenced their relations with the Asians.

The scheme to import Indian cultivators to expedite the development of agriculture in the East Africa Protectorate was once again revived in 1905 with the strong recommendation of Sir Edward Buck who toured the protectorate in the same year. He recommended the multiplication of the pioneer settlement in the larger uninhabited areas around Kibos. Sir

Edward Buck pointed out that the country was ideally suited for the products of the East and the extensive experience acquired in India should be fully utilized (Bhatt 1976).

Because of the success at Kibos and the interest in extending Indian settlement, the Protectorate took further steps to promote Indian immigration. It appointed a committee on Indian immigration under the chairmanship of J.A. L. Montgomery, Commissioner of Lands, with D.D. Waller as one of the four members. In its report of July 1906, the committee recommended that the government facilitates Indian settlement in the lowland between the Coast and Kiu and between Fort Ternan and Lake Victoria. It also outlined a comprehensive scheme for settlement (Mangat, 1969:68;Gregory, 1971:70).

As a first step towards implementing the report, the Governor sent D.D. Waller to India in late 1906 to recruit fifteen more Indian families for Kibos. D.D. Waller tried to recruit in Bihar, Madras, Bombay, and the central provinces, but he found that suitable Indians were very reluctant to leave India, and he met opposition from some administrators, especially Sir Denzil C. Ibbetson, Lieutenant- Governor of the Punjab, who felt that his province could not spare any agriculturists. From the arguments above, it was evident that the postcolonial space of India was in conflict with the British postcolonial space of Kenya. After his return to Africa without a single Indian family, Waller was convinced that the only recourse was to import indentured labourers who might eventually be induced to settle. In 1907, Kibos consisted of only four Punjabi families, who grazed cattle and grew cotton, sugarcane, chillies and maize on 600 acres (Kalaine, 1998; Gregory, 1971).

81

Since Kibos was the first Indian settlement initiated by the British Government, there were more inquiries within and outside British East Africa about its success. An application was written by an overseer of Uganda railway at Port Florence (Kisumu), requesting Lord Curzon, the Viceroy of India to intercede so that Indians could get free grants of land at Kibos. The letter partly stated:

> Having heard that Sir Charles Eliot, Her Majesty's commissioner has left for India to arrange with you to allow Indians to migrate to British East Africa, I therefore beg to enclose notice for free grants of land between miles 0 and 19 and 534 to 584, which portion assigned for Indians and they be given land promised at 15/- Rupees for 100 acres per year, 2/- Rupees per acre. For freehold and not Rs 100 for 100 acres as is now being given to us Indian cultivators at Kibos where the Indian settlement is to be formed (Kalaine, 1998:19)

These Indians embarked mainly on sugarcane production, an activity that later created what remains currently as the sugar belt region in Nyanza. The Kibos Indian scheme therefore, merits special attention since it contained several of the elements involved in transforming territories into viable economic entities. The Indians in this settlement were thus seen as a vehicle for the entrenchment and development of colonialism.

Although the Africans imitated Asian agricultural techniques in Kibos area, the Indians residing along the Indian settlement bordering on all sides of Kibos, Kajulu and Kano reserves later complained about the Africans from these reserves who came in batches and groups and took away with them sugarcane, maize cobs and small ploughs. There was also increased theft of cattle owned by Asians in Kibos area (KNA, PC/NZA/3/15/145, 1943).

However, this problem was solved through the construction of a fence as a cattle theft preventive measure. But these acts of theft and attacks should be viewed as a resistance by the dispossessed Africans within the colonial space against forms of knowledge and institutions authored and authorized by the West through the Asian agents. Such activities enhanced suspicion and conflict among the two races.

In his many *safaris* (trips) in Nyanza Province, Odera Ulalo, a colonial chief of several Luo *pinje* (multilineal territories) would normally go to 'Dagamoyo' the present Kibos near Kisumu, where Indian retail traders had established a market centre. The porters, soldiers and leaders who had been on *safari* with him were paid in kind with goods provided by these Indian traders (Ogot, 2003:7).

These goods included different types of cloth (known then as Japan, because they were imported from Japan) ready made clothes and beads. The most popular beads were the blue ones known in Dholuo as 'nyamach'. These beads were worn mostly by women for aesthetic purposes. Africans were therefore encouraged to wear clothes in order to embrace modernity. It was through this arrangement that the practice of 'nanga' that is the practice of wearing clothes started in Luoland. Soon 'jonanga' that is, people who wear clothes, became a social class apart from the other people, the naked ones in society (Ogot, 2003:7)

Other Asians who settled and owned land through government lease, leasehold in Kibos were Bosawaram, son to Kalooram, Gulam Mohammed, Inder Singh, Munshiram, Dewa Singh, and Sodeagar Singh. Jumna Dass Karami who owned a piece of land in the same area sold his plot to Allidina Visram (KNA, PC/3/22/1/2-9, 1910-12).

Most of the farmers in Kibos were Sikhs who included, Chanan Singh, Kisan Singh, and Kala Singh. Kala Singh means 'Black Singh' as *Kala* is the word for Black in Gujerati language. The Africans called all Sikhs *Kalasinga* (Devji, O.I., 2006) a merger of *Kala* and *Singh*. This name is neither African nor Asian but a hybrid of the two which was accepted by both the Asians and Africans. This was probably an African way of deconstructing Asian names in order to fit into the African situations. Such were the linguistic hybridity which characterized Afro-Asian relations as they settled in Nyanza.

Continued Indian acquisition of land and settlement in Kibos was also enhanced by what would be considered as local demand. Increased demand for African grain flour all over the country created a big necessity of more flourmills in this district to cope with demands. Due to this increased demand, Alibhai and Rahimtulla, both Asians, erected more flourmills around Kibos. This was facilitated by the two obtaining a Temporary Occupation Licence from the Lands Department. This necessity therefore ensured mutually beneficial Afro-Asian relations as Africans used the Asian posho mills to grind their cereals (KNA, PC\NZA\3\22\1\13, 1915).

The Asians in Kibos also acquired land by public auction. Plot number 111 of 25 acres owned by Ramchand and Labchand located in Kibos was sold to Ram Ghasita, who later sold this piece of land to Chawdri Ram Jawaya by public auction on the 17th May 1909 (KNA, PC\NZA\3\22\1\6, 1910-15). Hence, transfer of land took place by sale, government lease, or public auction. Since the Asians had acquired wealth, whenever plots were auctioned, it was almost impossible for an African to outbid them (Kings, O.I., 2006). The idea of auctioning African land was to raise revenue for the colonial government.

It is evident, that the colonial government used the Indian institution to exploit and open up the Kenyan reserve at Kibos and other areas. Acquisition of land was meant to create the notion that Africans did not know how to use the land. It was also to justify the fact that since they could not put land to good use, somebody else, the Indian and Europeans should.

Salvadori (1996:171) asserts that the histories of many Asian communities in Kenya could be traced to their few original immigrants, who settled, succeeded and then sent back to India for members of their own communities to join them. It is reiterated that this strong corporate spirit, integral to the traditional Indian socio- economic system was strengthened by the immigrants' position as immigrants in a strange land.

Forbidden (with a few exceptions) by law from owning farmlands, Asians settled in the townships and villages (in many cases they built the towns) and became increasingly urbanized. According to one informant (Ajay Gosh, O.I., 2006), his grand father who worked for the railway as a clerk, got freehold land near the Kibos

River to farm. After getting a settlement, he invited his wife from India. He later invited and welcomed his brothers and other kinsmen interested in settling in Kenya. Initially, they planted local crops like *wimbi, mtama* (type of millet) very effectively. They also planted maize and vegetables but when they tried to plant wheat, it was not successful.

The family too had a very reliable labour supply from the Luo people. Luo labourers stayed on the same compound as their Indian employers (Kings, O.I., 2006). Therefore, we see a situation where Asians also planted local crops thereby suggesting that there were some African agricultural values that the Asians acquired and adopted. By employing Africans as labourers, the postcolonial space of Nyanza was set for Afro-Asian labour relations which formed one of the major aspects of their relations.

There is evidence, therefore, of a relationship which is not primarily that of resistance or of collaboration, but one, which is made fraught by the very fact of the colonial authority and its 'subject' having to share the same living space. In this situation, Nyanza is a postcolonial space made out of one single space but of several sub spaces. The Indian settlement scheme at Kibos, was therefore, created out of contestations between the Luo and the Nandi and also between the Asians and the Europeans over the occupation of the white highlands. The colonial system thus created a new space within the Nyanza postcolonial space. In this space, Asians were settled and used as colonial agents of capitalism and imperialism. This space also laid the foundation upon which Afro-Asian relations were to be established.

2.4 The Nyando Indian Settlement in Nyanza Province

The second Indian settlement was established at the Nyando valley, which extended to Fort Ternan and Muhoroni areas and not very far from Kibos later in 1903 (Abuor, 1972:67). There were fertile soils and favourable climate and irrigation was undertaken from River Nyando. At the beginning, 250 Indians settled here. Mr. C.W Hobley, the Assistant Deputy Commissioner for the East Africa Protectorate reported on this agricultural settlement as follows:

> The Nyando valley has been selected as a suitable location for the Indian immigration experiment and a fair start has now been made. About a year ago, before the scheme was mooted, I had allowed several agriculturalists to take up plots of land in the vicinity of the river Kibos and these original plantations have served as nucleus for those now being settled under the auspices of the scheme. There are in the vicinity some 16 settlers holding all together about 340 acres of land. They have already brought upwards about 80 acres under cultivation, some 20 of which are planted with cotton, part of the remaining 260 acres has been broken and will be planted when the rainy season breaks. The chief products of the settlements are cotton, rice, wheat oil-bearing seeds of various kinds and Indigo, to say nothing of various indigenous African cereals. Some of the settlers too are anxious to experiment with opium culture (Kalaine, 1998:21).

Similar to the Kibos settlement scheme, the Nyando scheme was an experimental scheme created by the British government later in 1903 in order to test their capitalist ideas by introducing plantation farms. By extending these schemes, it was hoped that the Africans within the interior parts would come under the influence of the British rule.

In the Nyando agricultural settlement scheme, a number of fruits from the coastal areas such as oranges, pineapples, mangoes, and *papayi* (Pawpaw) were grown on experimental basis. The seeds for these fruits were distributed free of charge by the British administrators. The aim was to have them grown on plantation farms to ensure a constant supply of fruits for the residents of Kisumu.

With time, more and more Indians were settled on the Nyando scheme. All these settlement schemes were in close proximity to the railway line and since there were many Indians working on the railway, they provided additional market for the farm produce (Kalaine, 1998:22). The Indian community thus played a crucial role in the colonial agricultural development within the region. The predominant plantation crops were mainly cotton, coffee and sugarcane. The ideas behind the Nyando Indian settlement scheme were the same as those that set up the Kibos settlement scheme. Asians were used as the colonial agents to exploit the interior reserves and to introduce the rural economies to western forms of capitalism and imperialism.

2.5 Summary and Conclusion

It was the objective of this chapter to examine the roots of modern Asian presence in Kenya by looking at their origin and settlement specifically in the Nyanza province of Kenya. We have demonstrated that contact between Asians and Africans started way back in the first century and not with the construction of the Kenya – Uganda Railway.

It has been demonstrated that Kibos Indian settlement scheme was the first authorized formal Asian settlement scheme in the colony to come up in 1903. This settlement scheme was as a result of a contested and negotiated space within the Nyanza postcolonial sub-space between Asians and Europeans on one hand and different African communities on the other. This contestation was over the white highlands. The Kibos settlement scheme as a space for contestation was, therefore, to form a buffer zone between the Luo and the Nandi communities. The Asians, therefore, occupied a middle place which Bhabha calls an indeterminate zone between the Luo and Nandi communities as they engaged Africans in their daily activities. The establishment of the Nyando scheme in the area brought to two, the number of Asians' settlement schemes in Nyanza.

The chapter concluded that by settling Asians in the lowlands, the colonial government laid the foundation upon which Afro-Asian relations and interaction was to be built. The rural economy of Nyanza was exploited to the fullest by Asians who penetrated these areas and introduced Western values which the Africans imitated.

Although the Asian settlement in Nyanza was characterized by Africans imitating their agricultural techniques, there were also instances where Africans attacked Asians. This was a sign of protest or resistance which formed part of relations within the postcolonial space of Nyanza. Although some aspects of economic relations featured briefly in this chapter, this aspect alongside Afro-Asian social and political relations in the early colonial period will be explored properly in the next chapter.

CHAPTER THREE

3.0 THE AFRO – ASIAN RELATIONS IN EARLY COLONIAL PERIOD 1900-1918

3.1 Introduction

In Chapter Two we discussed the initial settlement of the Asian community in Kenya and argued that the formal Asian settlers specifically in Nyanza came with the construction of Kenya Uganda Railway as indentured labourers. We concluded that the formal Asian settlement was a contested and negotiated space within the Nyanza postcolonial space. The current chapter interrogates the Afro- Asian relations in the early colonial period (1900-1918). These relationships are issues of trade, education, and politics.

The chapter examines the emergence of Afro-Asian economic interaction in Kisumu, Kendu Bay, Ndere and Yala up to the end of World War 1 in 1918. It also examines the Afro-Asian social relations in the early colonial period to 1918 by exploring how these relations were shaped despite the racial prejudices which were common at that time. It concludes that the Nyanza postcolonial space was chaotic and plural with different people fighting for the same space. Although there were some forms of knowledge stereotyping which made Africans feel inferior to Asians, there were some African values which the Asians borrowed from Africans and vice versa. This chapter therefore explores the emergence of Afro-Asian economic relations in Nyanza and analyses how trading activities shaped their relations.

3.2 The Emergence of Afro-Asian Economic Interaction in Kisumu, Kendu Bay, Ndere and Yala Up to 1918

Kisumu was founded in 1893 when the chief engineer and a railway surveyor agreed to make it the terminus of the railway and named it Port Florence after his wife. This name indicates a move by the colonialist to westernize some African values. A food depot was then established to feed forward survey parties. Telegraph lines, roads and other means of communication were immediately constructed to connect the new port with other settlements (Obudho, 1976).

As the Uganda railways steadily approached Lake Victoria, C.W Hobley, a British administrator, was ordered to move from Mumias to establish the new headquarters for Nyanza Province. In 1900, he appointed Odera Ulalo, chief of several *Luo pinje* (multilineal territories) including Asembo, Sakwa, Uyoma, Yimbo, Gem, Seme and Kisumu. The appointment of Odera Ulalo as a chief witnessed the introduction of some forms of Western knowledge which informed the administration of Nyanza province. Together with Hobley, they established a new administrative station, which later developed into the Kisumu town of today (Ogot, 2003:6).

Right from the start of the Asian immigration into Kenya, the colonial administration was determined to keep them from any political engagement and from any respectable income-generating activities. By limiting them to trade in the colonial administration, the Asians were destined to the towns and trading centres where they met Africans in the context of formal interaction as merchant/customer and as junior officers in the colonial administration setup (Finance, 1997:9).

Asian involvement in trade, in contrast to African participation, was supported by the colonial state from the word go. They were encouraged to follow British military expeditions into the interior, and permitted to build shops at the military garrisons which later became administrative headquarters and also near the railhead as the railway advanced from Mombasa to Kisumu (Fearn 1961: 108). And so Africans saw Asians as extensions of Western discourses and narratives about Africa. These narratives so much captured in Western literature and values presented Africans as inferior beings. Thus from the beginning Africans viewed Asians with a lot of suspicion.

The government ban or restriction of Asian engagement in estate agriculture and their exclusion from senior administrative posts encouraged them to concentrate their energies on commerce with insular aggressiveness and racial cohesiveness. Unlike the Africans, the Indians were not subjected to tight restrictions on sources of capital investment in small-scale activities (Ndege 1992:211, Opondo, 1998). With this advantage, they were able to get capital to manage their businesses unlike Africans. Even in the plural postcolonial space, relations were unequal with Africans being treated as sub human. The white man's stereotypes about African were quickly domesticated by Asians in their daily dealings with Africans.

They were encouraged by the colonial state as a means of stimulating commerce and the monetarization of exchange relations with Africans in the rural areas. Asian traders thus became a major vehicle for the marketing of peasant produce. Not only were Indians heavily involved in produce buying from Africans but also set themselves up in general retail and wholesale trade as well where they sold certain goods to the Africans. At first, many engaged in itinerant trade, but by the end of the first decade of the 20th century, most had settled in the country's townships or urban areas (Maxon, 1992:69, Kenyanchui, 1992:112).

The colonial administration's 'encouragement' of trade was undertaken within a broad economic policy framework which assigned the different races in Kenya and fractions of merchant capital specific roles. Occupying the highest rank on the commercial ladder were European importers and exporters. Asians occupied a middle position while Africans formed the lowest chain in the marketing system. The colonial government also employed indirect and direct compulsion to 'encourage' trade. For instance, in addition to raising revenue, the imposition of the hut tax early in 1902, was also intended to induce Africans to grow and sell surplus produce if they were to be able to meet the tax obligation (Ndege, 1992:204). In such situations, Africans were compelled to engage in exchange of goods in Kisumu, Ndere, Yala and Kendu Bay with the Asians so as to raise money to pay for their tax (Wasonga, O.I., 2005).

With the Township Ordinance of 1903, a myriad of townships and trading centres such as Kendu Bay and Kibos were established all over Western Kenya (Memon 1976:133, Obudho, 1976:13). These towns, therefore, marked the systematic installation of Western modernity and the eventual displacement of African institutions.

According to Memon (1976:133), the chief reasons behind the establishment of these towns were: To be centres of colonial authority and rule, from which the colonial administrators could bring under effective control the surrounding people. The establishment and growth of trading centres in Kenya was closely tied up with the then prevailing colonial policy for stimulating production of saleable crops in African reserves through development of trade. This, according to Memon, had the twin objectives of integrating the African subsistence economy into the colonial mercantile system and deriving increased government revenue through the institution of the hut tax to support the expanding colonial establishment.

So the postcolonial space was developing several subspaces with Africans suffering the brunt of oppression and marginalization. Memon further argues that the imposition of the hut tax was supposed to have a chain effect on the traditional African economy. To pay the tax, the African peasant would have to produce more crops for sale which would subsequently increase trade between themselves and Asians. Increased trade meant a greater dependence on imported goods which would force a person to produce even more crops for sale and so on.

Trading in the reserves was monopolized by Indian traders (Okech, O.I., 2005). The Indian traders not only purchased local produce and sold manufactured goods and determined local prices, but also sponsored many pioneer African traders by providing them with stock usually on credit since these aspiring traders rarely had the necessary capital, contacts or credit standing to purchase directly from wholesalers in Nairobi and Mombasa.

During these early decades of colonial capitalism, the position of Indian traders was directly facilitated by the colonial state policy towards gazetting of trade centres. The Indian traders were seen by the state as invaluable economic 'middlemen' who could stimulate trade and the consumption of imported commodities among Africans, which would then lead to increased production and the general monetization of rural economies, a necessary precondition for the integration of those areas into the colonial and wider mercantile networks (Zeleza 1982:92).

As early as 1902, Jamal Hasham an Asian trader stationed in Kisumu, dealt in *Amerikani* (American) cotton, importing his own brand- on which at every yard, his picture was printed. His relationship with the local people in Kisumu was so good and he was well-known for his fair dealing that he acquired the nickname '*Bwana mzuri*' (Good man) (Salvadori, 1996:149). This means that in this hybrid arrangement and plural space not everything was conflictual. There were certain things that the Africans had internalized from Asians and vice versa. So the postcolony was not just about conflicts.

95

By 1903, the Asians were generally concentrated in doing business in their *Dukas*, (Kiswahili word for shops) which functioned as retail stores, depots and living quarters. The postcolonial subjects therefore, had to learn to bargain in this market place. The Asian traders brought exotic goods into the indigenous market. These were bicycles, blankets and clothes, which they sold from their shops in Ndere, Kadimo, and Yala to the Africans (Ochieng 1974:86).

With this kind of trade, the traditional barter system was gradually replaced by the money economy in which the Indian rupee was the medium of exchange. In this Afro-Asian interaction, rupee acquired a new local name. The term rupee linguistically became known locally as *rupia*. *Rupia* was neither an Indian nor an African term but a hybrid of both. However, when mentioned, it referred to the same thing for both the Asian and the Africans who were engaged in trade (Owiyo, O.I., 2007). Later, *rupia* applied to every form of money including the British shillings.

Thus, the Africans in Nyanza began to grow surplus food like sweet potatoes, bananas and vegetables, which they sold to the Asians in order to meet their taxes. The administration encouraged peasant production in Nyanza simply to generate cash income for Africans fro m which they could pay their taxes (Kabong, O.I., 2006, Zeleza, 1989: 46). Grains, beans and eggs would be sold to Asian traders in exchange for imported manufactures (Ndege 1992:210). With this kind of trade going on, roads were built to connect Port Florence (Kisumu), Port Victoria, Kendu Bay, Karungu and Homa Bay.

Through this Afro- Asian interaction, African trading skills were improved. This is because both Asians and Africans got involved in trade activities which initially were not African or Asian. For instance, the Asians ventured in trading in dry fish which was exclusively African. On the other hand, some Asians gave Africans exotic wares such as blankets or clothes to sell on their behalf to fellow Africans sometimes on credit. The nature of relationship was, therefore, not primarily that of resistance or of collaboration but could best be characterized as convivial, a relationship fraught by the fact that the colonial subjects, Asians and Africans had to share the same living space (Mbembe, 2001:104). The trade was however unequal since some of these wares were sometimes sold to Africans expensively.

It is important to note that during 1903, there was neither mechanical (car) transport nor road systems but in spite of this, Indian traders were engaged in trading in even the remotest parts of Nyanza Province especially in Ndere and Kendu Bay. The goods were transported by African porters and Indian traders travelled on hammocks or on mule backs. Later on, they (Asians) introduced ox-cart transport between Kisumu and Yala (Opondo, 1989:43). The Asians also used dhows to sail to lake ports where they had businesses in such areas as Asembo, Homa Bay, or Kendu Bay and Kisumu.

On these dhows, they employed the local Africans mostly the Luo. Before the Indian *Badalas* (workers of the railway steamers) came, the Africans had small boats. It was the Indian *Badalas* who taught them how to make and sail dhows (Salvadori, 1996:151). This interaction led to a mutually beneficial relationship between the Asians and Africans. This is because they relied on these dhows for their fish supply. Asians involved in the trade also took the opportunity to learn the local names of the species of fish such as *Ngege/Nyamami* (Tilapia), *Omena* (Restrineobola argentea) and *Mbuta* (Lates Niloticus). It is therefore evident that the two communities learnt and borrowed some cultural values from each other which they viewed to be important as far as their relation was concerned. There was therefore some form of cultural hybridity between the two communities.

In 1906, the Acting Nyanza Provincial Commissioner (PC) H.B Partington reported that there was scarcity of food due to failure of the November rains (KNA,PC/NZA/ AR 1906-7). By the time Partington was writing his annual report, the whole of the immediate lakeland was already in the grip of a terrible famine known locally as *Nyangori*. Africans travelled extensively from Kisumu District to Mumias to purchase food. The Nyanza Indian traders took advantage of the famine and bought all the food they could lay their hands on and sold it expensively to the Africans living in Kisumu and other parts of Nyanza (Cokumu, 2000:85). There were also other African traders who bought soap and salt from Indians and sold these items to the people at local market places like Yala, Lwanda (Kamang'ongo) Kamito and Siaya (Ndeda, 1991:129).

With the food shortage persisting into 1907, Africans found it necessary to sell their cattle to Indian traders in order to raise money to pay tax. This economic interaction was characterized by unequal exchange of goods between Asians and Africans because Asians bought cattle from Africans cheaply (KNA, PC/NZA/1/3 1907/8). This is how the postcolony was initially conceived. Some people benefited by exploiting others. Indeed that is why the theoretical basis of postcolonialism is to disaggregate this exploitation not only on the cultural terrain but also on the political and economic fronts.

The Western building materials such as the popular *mabati* (corrugated iron sheet) which the Asians sold to the Africans would gradually replace the not permanent thatch for roofing mud walled African homes. The popular highly coloured cotton textiles known as *kitenge* and *kanga,* originally imported from Holland, and noted for their appealing Indonesian influential prints became a popular wear for the great majority of African women. The importation and distribution of the fabrics were also to be the work of Asian traders (Seidenberg, 1996:47).

At first, Africans were suspicious of exotic ware, but they soon found that the clothes and blankets were warmer and less cumbersome than their traditional wares. Besides clothes and blankets, other merchandise like oil, salt, sugar, tea, basins, lamps among others were introduced to the people of Nyanza for the first time. The Asians also bought certain amounts of skins, cattle, cotton and sisal and all these products were sold to Asians by Africans who in turn distributed them in the country (Ochieng': 1974:86). What the Asian merchants brought changed the consuming habits of the local inhabitants forever.

Their dressing habits began to change as they moved from the wearing of hides and skins to a dutch-manufactured *kanga* with deep Indonesian influence. Initially, the Nyanza people's reception of these foreign cultures and forms of knowledge seemed ambivalent

99

but later, they embraced them. Nevertheless, in Bhabha's (1994) argument, cultural production is most productive when it is also most ambivalent, and indeed, the Africans fully embraced exotic wares brought by the Asians at the expense of their traditional wares. Postcolonial thinking is thus not to go back to the past and discard everything European or Asian but to dismantle those values and institutions that perpetuate our marginalization. Indeed some values and institutions were positive.

From the economic interaction above, there is evidence of the spread of Western forms of knowledge in the form of Western merchandise through the Asians, who were a colonial construct. The utilization of such kinds of knowledge, which was part of Western culture, enhanced cultural domination of the African people at the expense of African traditional values. This move was both negative and positive at the same time, there was the entrenchment of European imperialism at a very unique level where African clothings and food were replaced by Western types of clothing and food. The Asian traders in this sense exhibited a mimicry of the colonial presence which Bhabha (1994:86) views as the partial representation and the recognition of the colonial object.

The other class of urban centre was the trading centre. Trading centres in Kenya were established under the Outlying District Ordinance of 1908 (Memon, 1976:133). To handle increased traffic from the new and central administrative centre at Kisii, a new port was opened at Kongo (Now Kendu Bay) in 1908, with the construction of a jetty, a warehouse, and certain administrative offices.

100

Such Asian traders as Mohammed Hassan (locally known as Madassan) and Nasoor, who arrived in Kendu Bay through Wagwe (Miti Mbili), would later play an important role in the establishment of Kendu Bay as a trading centre, since they were the first traders in the area dealing in hides and skins which they bought from their African agents like Odieny Nyariro. The local Africans frequently referred to Kendu Bay as *Kanyasooro* which locally means place of Nasoor (Malit O.I., 2006, Ojijo O.I., 2007).

Business also increased at Homa Bay trading centre because more *dukas* (Kiswahili word for shop/general stores) were built and port facilities were improved to accommodate rich hinterlands in Karachuonyo, Kanyada, Gem, and North Nyokal Locations (Obudho 1976:13). *Dukas* for the Asians functioned as retail stores, depots, and living quarters from where they bought African produce and stimulated demand for manufactured goods. Afro –Asian relations at this early period was based on trade. Also the Asians employed some Africans as domestic workers. Suffice it to say that the postcolonial space was a plurality of people and activities, some of them competing while others working in harmony.

Similarly, through the Outlying District Ordinance of 1908, trading centres were established in places like Yala in 1908 and Asembo Bay (Schiller, 1982:283). The Indian Bazaar (an oriental market place or market that usually consists of rows of shops or stalls where all kinds of goods are offered for sale) established at Yala by 1908 at the Yala River developed as an important trade centre because it was a great collection centre for grain and produce of the country (KNA, PC/NZA/1/4 Annual Report 1909).

101

In Kendu Bay and Yala, the Asians bought hides, sweet potatoes, beans, groundnuts, and milk from the Africans. The milk was used for making tea and the cream (*samul*) which was taken to Kisumu for sale by the Asians such as Abdo Salah (O.I., Ojijo, 2006). Asian traders like Abdunam gave out free samples of sugar to his African agents who traded in hides and skin to taste and tell the rest that the item was sweet. Through these samples, the Africans in Kendu Bay started using sugar, which was distributed by the Asians.

The hides bought from Africans by Asians in Kendu Bay were exported to areas like Uganda and Tanzania and ultimately to Europe and the United States of America, while some were taken to Kisumu (Malit, O.I., 2005). This commercial interaction was characterized by a situation whereby there were some African items which were needed and valued by the Asians and some items from the Asians which were needed and valued by the Africans, thereby making this relationship as one which was mutually beneficial.

The remainder of 1909 saw rapid urban growth due to a newly adopted policy, which empowered the Provincial Commissioner to establish trading centres and *bomas* at suitable points in the province to foster trade among Africans. This policy was adopted as a result of an increased demand by Africans and Asians to establish *dukas* all over the province (Obudho 1997).

Opening up the province by 1909 to traders and establishing trading centres for Indian traders was thus viewed by John Ainsworth (Sub-Commissioner for Nyanza) as essential not only to economic development but also to social change. Not surprisingly, he fostered close cooperation between government and traders.

When District Commissioners or District Officers made extensive trips, Indian traders were invited to accompany them and show off their wares during meetings. Asians were therefore, being used by whites to paint the postcolonial space with Western values to show Africans that Asians were better off because they had long ago embraced Western civilization. Shortly after the province had been opened up to traders, mostly Indians with few restrictions, Ainsworth summed up his imperialistic thinking thus:

> The throwing open of the country generally to trade has had very marked results. It has increased the industry of the 'natives' and has improved their attitude to aliens, and has brought considerable wealth to the people. As a civilizing agency amongst these 'pagan' tribes, trade has an undoubted advancing tendency, and has assisted very considerably the administrative effort (Maxon, 1980:218).

The trading activities in Nyanza Province were given an impetus by a system in which Indians and other shopkeepers in the province were allowed to accompany the government officers on their monthly journeys to various parts of the province. This privileged position that the Asians enjoyed above Africans would later be resisted by Africans as they contested Asian dominance in trade. Therefore, the Asians took advantage of their privileged position within the colonial system to exploit Africans and also help in entrenching colonial imperialism and capitalism. The traders took with them cheap goods that the Africans were encouraged to buy. The purpose was to create wants on the part of the Africans and to induce them to invest their money in imported goods instead of in cattle and sheep and to supply them with improved agricultural implements. This method stimulated trade within the province (DC South Kavirondo District, AR 1913 \1914).

Indeed, the remarkable tenacity and courage of the Indian trader had mainly been responsible for stimulating the wants of the indigenous people even in the remotest areas, by opening to them a window to the 'modern' world and for collecting for sale elsewhere, whatever small surpluses that were available for disposal (Obudho, 1976:37). By moving together with the Asian traders, this was an evidence of the hegemonic phase of colonialism in the Nyanza postcolonial sub space. But this combination of Asian traders and government officers depicts the domineering and hegemonic phase of colonialism in the Nyanza postcolonial sub-space.

The Asian contribution in Nyanza, therefore, derived from the fact that as they related with Africans 'as willing purchasers of their (African) products, they created and continuously widened those markets in Nyanza upon which development in trade was fundamentally dependent. As sellers of trade goods, they both satisfied existing needs and created new incentives for further production. Their transaction injected a stream of cash crop into the economy.

However, the rapid multiplication of trading centres and the African periodic markets was not received well by Indian traders as it meant competition, which consequently shortened their area of influence and therefore reduced the frequency and capacity of Afro-Asian economic relations (Obudho 1976:13). Evidently, none of the African and Asian communities was independent of the other as both went beyond racial issues to engage in trade together. The consequent growth of the Nyanza economy sustained the colonial government's activities in the province.

Between 1910 and 1920, Kisumu was an important commercial centre. It was a major axis where goods imported from outside British East Africa and destined for Nyanza Province could be taxed (KNA, PC/NZA/1/4, 1908/9, Anyumba, 1995:80). For the Asians, Kisumu was a depot for the distribution of imported goods throughout Nyanza Province and Eastern Uganda. It was also the place where raw materials gathered from African periodic rural markets in the hinterland by the Asians were assembled for export to places like Mersailles, Somaliland and Arabia.

These collections and distribution functions attracted more Africans to reside in the town and in the peri – urban areas. It also enhanced their relations with the Asians (KNA, PC/NZA Annual Report, 1928, Obudho, 1976). Trade was on the increase and this led to the expansion of trade at various centres such as Yala, Kendu Bay and Ndere among others. However, racial segregation in towns, unequal business opportunities and taxation, import and export trade (involving both exotic and local produce) as well as colonial industries like the cotton industry, all these promoted the growth and expansion of British imperialism.

In the centres, the Africans sold their produce mainly beans, simsim, ghee, eggs, millet, hides and skins, groundnuts and fish to the Indians and European traders who exported them out of the province. In particular, simsim added more value to Kenya's export trade than any other single produce between 1911 and 1913 (Ndeda, 1991). When there was demand for any particular local produce, the colonial authorities, by virtue of its capitalistic interest, enforced its production.

Because of the increased trade on simsim, Allidina Visram had to start operating two motor wagons on Gem -Yala road. In return for what the Asians sold in the shop, Africans got wire, blankets, knives, cups, umbrellas, beads, pipes, and second-hand clothes. Asians sold these items for cash and bought imported goods for cash. In Central Kavirondo, simsim was produced in Asembo, Seme, Gem, Sakwa, and Uyoma (KNA, PC\NZA\1\5, Annual Report 1910). Conclusively, the Afro-Asian interaction led to the introduction and expansion of the money economy in the Nyanza postcolonial sub-space.

The enterprises of some of the pioneer Indian traders in the interior expanded on the foundations laid in the early years. The most notable in this respect were the achievements of Allidina Visram, who built up an extensive East African –wide business network. Various contemporary accounts describe the expansion of his *duka*-based enterprise in different parts of the colony such as Kisumu, Yala among other areas (Mangat, 1969: 77).

Allidina's firm employed over 500 Indians and many more African assistants as well as African traders who acted as his agents (KNA, PC/NZA/1/2 Annual Report 1906\7, KNA, PC/NZA1/3 AR 1907/8). However, the growing role of the petty Indian trader and middleman was to expose him to frequent abuse for resorting to sharp practice and dishonest business methods- mainly in respect to unfair price dealings (Mangat 1969: 94). This capitalistic tendency ensured that Africans were exploited fully. In these trade relations, therefore, the level of Afro-Asian economic exchange was unequal.

The Asian prices of goods were not controlled and in spite of this they were protected by the British government (Ochoko, O.I., 2006). The postcolony was, therefore, commercially chaotic and it was hard to fix acceptable prices By 1912, Lord Cranworth stated that Indians were draining the resources of the country and there was hardly a crime among Africans, which was not directly traceable to the Indians. He included economic exploitation and cheating among those evils committed by the Asian community (Finance 1997:14). As early as 1914, cases of Asian exploitation and cheating had already emerged.

Africans involved in the production of simsim in areas such as Yala and Asembo complained that they were exploited by the Indian traders who only paid them 60 per cent of the 1914 price (KNA , PC/3/3/20 1914). This made the Africans withhold simsim.

This cheating showed how Asians felt racially superior to the Africans. This is because they treated African adults as children who could not detect any anomaly. By withholding simsim Africans were determined to protest against Indian exploitative and capitalistic tendencies. This shows evidence of early instances of conflictual relations between the Africans and the Asians.

The outbreak of World War I in 1914 upset and restricted Afro-Asian trade. But trade recovered the following year. Business in produce was strong in response to military demands, and prices also rose sharply during the war by as much as 100 percent (Zeleza, 1989:57). Over 200 Indian artisans and other Asians left Kisumu town for war service. During this time, the Asians increased prices of the commodities they sold to the Africans and made handsome profits (KNA, PC/NZA/1/2 Annual report 1917).

The issue of labour requirements during the war which made Africans to fight alongside the British in the World War also remodelled Afro-Asian relations as Africans were forcefully recruited from the reserves to go and serve in the army. People feared loitering because chiefs were conscripting able bodied men into the army (Ogada, O.I., 2006). On the other hand, some Asian businesses were also temporarily closed. This made the frequency of interaction between the Asians who remained in Ndere and other parts of the Province minimal.

It should be noted that during the World War 1, there were new demands for African produce and prices went up. As the trading sector became more attractive, more women income seekers moved into trade. Many of the new traders were women whose husbands were recruited into war, forcing them to assume the roles of family heads (Ngesa, 1996:45). This role would later put more women in direct contact and interaction with the Asians.

The Indian bazaar in Kisumu, established from the early days of the colonial period, grew in importance as a local centre of Indian trade (KNA, PC\NZA1\2, AR 1910\14). In a 1915 report, that included a reference to trade at Yala near Kisumu Simpson, the expert advisor of the Colonial Office avered:

> Yala is the great collecting centre for the grain and produce of the country north of the Yala River. To this station, the natives bring their baskets of grain and sell it to the Indians, who store it ... until it is convenient to send it in bags or carts to Kisumu. The road between Yala and Kisumu is thronged with carts passing to and fro. Those from Yala are loaded, according to the season of the year, with sim sim, maize, beans, hides and skin and those from Kisumu with rice.... Clothes etc' (As quoted in Mangat, 1969:87)

Elsewhere, Mangat (1969:87) explains that the Indian traders in the interior of Kenya built steadily on the foundations of Indian commercial enterprise towards the close of the 19th Century. Their competitiveness and the general absence of local agency to perform similar economic functions further facilitated their enterprise (Mangat 1969:87). It is, therefore, worth noting that with the absence of many African players within the plural setup as far as trade was concerned the Asians capitalized on this and curved a niche, which later helped them to survive in the Nyanza economic environment.

The gradual extension of the commercial frontier by the Indian traders contributed to greater local production in various areas, and thereby set into motion the whole process of modern economic development in the countryside. As one contemporary Kenyan official later commented,

> If an abrupt clearance of the Indians could have been effected ... One certain result would have been that the 'native' tribes would suddenly cease to receive many supplies to which they were becoming accustomed, and still is the Indian who delivers the goods and pushed trade in the interior of Kenya' (Ross 1927:416).

The above statement justifies the fact that Asians dominated trade in the African reserves. This domination ensured exploitation which was a central theme of British colonialism in Kenya (Kisiang'ani, 2003:100). But also, another aspect of the relations is that the gradual extension of the commercial frontier by the Indian traders created a dependency syndrome whereby Africans could hardly operate without Asians. The reason is Africans' trading activities and production system had been destroyed or realigned to European and Asian systems making Africans overly dependent.

After the war, increasing numbers of Indian traders reduced their engagement in produce buying and concentrated primarily on retail trade. It was during these years that large Indian wholesalers began making their impact felt in the import-export trade (Zeleza 1989:57).

Towards the end of World War 1, another famine hit Nyanza Province between 1918 and 1919 (Maxon 1980:266). However, the colonial government responded to this famine by encouraging trade. Indian traders were allowed to import food into the province and sell it to the Africans (Cokumu, 2000:101). Famine conditions were very instrumental in enhancing Afro-Asian interaction in Nyanza Province.

Schiller (1982:62) argues that in times of famine, exchange intensified as large numbers of people looked for food. Besides, the more severe the famine, the wider people looked for food for sustenance and the more they looked for these foodstuff beyond their extended families. It was during these times that the market place system expanded to include a number of famine markets operating only during these periods. These market places in both normal and famine times not only fulfilled the 'economic' function of providing for the needs of the household but also provided a forum for social contacts between normally antagonistic Afro-Asian groups.

Afro- Asian relations in Nyanza Province were not centred on trade in food items alone. Many of the skilled immigrants such as Rehmat Khan, Hayer Bishan Singh in Kisumu, Abdul Kassam, and Mohamud Khan in Kendu Bay, among others, were to launch a variety of business enterprises as contractors, outfitters, builders and mechanics. They also helped to supplement the activities of the Indian commercial population, which also witnessed a steady expansion during this period (Mboya, O.I., 2006).

With their skills in various fields, Asian artisans imparted to Africans invaluable vocational skills in making furniture, repairing bicycle, printing magazines and books, stocking shops, crafting leather shoes and handbags and teaching so many other income-generating occupations. Through such trainings, there emerged a permanent skilled class of African artisans and technicians within the region and especially in Kisumu. Within the chaotic plural space there are losses and benefits.

So helpful were the Asian artisans that they gained the endorsement of the ordinary African people (Seidenberg, 1996: 37). The brave, heavily bearded and turbaned *Kalasinghas* (Sikhs) were the most helpful as they were not afraid of mixing and sharing beer with the Africans (Mbudi, O.I., 2005, Seidenberg 1996). These were some of the values propagated by the Asians which the Africans adopted.

From this Afro-Asian interaction, several nicknames also emerged to describe the nature of the two peoples within the economic realm. For instance in Kendu Bay, Abdo Hassan was nicknamed as *tek ateka kidi* which in *dholuo* meant as hard as a rock. This was because Hassan had fixed prices of commodities in his shop and was unwilling to yield to any bargain. Another one was called Abib Okore. Okore (from the root word *Kor*) is a Luo name for the chest. Abib was named Okore because he coughed frequently. This habit forced the locals to assume that he had a bad chest (*Kore*). *Oluoro liedo,* a Luo word for someone who fears shaving was also given to a certain Indian shopkeeper because he had a lot of hair on his head and he kept a bushy beard.

112

Gulamali (Ghulam Ali) was nicknamed Ogola Amali. Another Asian trader was also locally known as *Adharaum (Ume ochot)* because his nose was cut,(*Um* is a Luo word for nose). Faraj Ojijo states that 'we were born and found when these people were being called so, that is, Adharaum, Oluoro Liedo, Ogola Amali, Abib Okore and so forth and children were directed to go to their shops according to those identifications to buy sugar, soap and oil (Ojijo, O.I 2006). These Asians were given local names by the natives to easily identify them. Some of these names signified ridicule while others (*Ume Ochot, Oluoro liedo*) signified humour for the Africans within the plural space of Nyanza.

But we also see hybridization in the way some of these names were constructed by the Africans. For instance, Ghulam Ali was locally pronounced as *Ogola Amali* which is neither purely Asian nor African. Some of these names were Luonised for humour but some represented certain forms of protest against a continuously coughing person, a shopkeeper who does not lower prices or one who keeps long hair and beards.

Similarly in Ndere, the Asians were given nicknames by the locals. The names were either pronounced as the locals heard them or they were given local names and the locals never bothered to ascertain their names. For instance, Ashur was nicknamed Oyugi, the other who dealt in cotton was called Ogolla Mzee and the one who brought bicycles, and other wares to the Africans of Ndere was called Omollo. Other Asians who interacted with the Africans in Ndere were Jamnadass, Mithur and Leeila.

113

On the other hand, the Asians locally refered to their African counterparts by their physical appearance for instance *kijana* (Young person), *kadogo*,(small) *and mrefu* (tall) and so on (Ondiallo, O.I., 2006). The use of such words gave Africans a demeaning status and dignity. However, such were the dynamics of relations which characterized the lives of Asians and Africans in the area of study. Africans thus lost their identity by being renamed from, for example, Ogolla to *Kijana* or *Kadogo*. A new culture was thus evolving both for the Asians and Africans.

3.3 Afro-Asian Political Relations in Nyanza to 1918

Elsewhere in this chapter, we observed that by December 1901 after the railway line reached the town, Kisumu's future position as a regional administrative centre and a port had been established. However, between 1901 and 1903 Nyanza Province had no effective government control and was regarded as a mere supply zone for the route to Uganda (Obudho, 1976). In 1907, John Ainsworth arrived in Kisumu and embarked on the administration of the Nyanza Province.

Soon after his arrival, John Ainsworth found that the existing administrative structure lacked guidance and consistency. In his eyes, the system of administration in the province's five districts Elgon (Mt Elgon), Ugenya (Siaya), Nandi, Kisumu, and Lumbwa (Kericho) was tending toward chaos. In contrast to his predecessor as Sub-Commissioner, S.S Bagge, Ainsworth saw much that was wrong. He stated that:

> There were many matters, which required considerable
> attention and settlement, also that in consequence of an almost
> absolute lack of any policy or application of general procedure
> matters generally were subjected to a process of drift (As
> quoted in Maxon,1980:176).

In Elgon (Mt Elgon), Kisumu and Ugenya (Siaya) districts, it was practically impossible to know who the chiefs and headmen were (KNA, PC/NZA.1/4 Nyanza Provincial Special Report 1909). The headmen refused to recognize the authority of chiefs. Individuals set themselves up as rivals to those who held political power and influence before the onset of colonial rule, reinforcing their claims by their problems direct to European officers. Ainsworth proceeded to say:

> The people, in turn, when so inclined, refused to recognize their chiefs or any headman and made a practice of coming in daily to the Provincial Commissioner or the District Commissioner, or to the police, or indeed, to anyone who would listen to them and so enable them to get the better of somebody else. Affrays and disturbances were common. Government armed police wandered from village to village and added to the general state of disorder (As quoted in Maxon, 1980).

The problem of administration as described by Ainsworth was not however due to the poor calibre of officials, their constant switches in posting and a lack of policy. It lay also, and perhaps most importantly, with the Nyanza people. The Africans of Nyanza were organized into many clans, most of which had their own heads or leaders and were independent of and competed with others. This is how the postcolony was plural.

Most clans were gathered in territorial clusters and shared traditions of descent and links created by marriage with other clans in their cluster or ethnic group. In some of these clusters, a chief recognized by the various clans had achieved a position of leadership, but in most parts of Nyanza, there existed what Lonsdale described as 'mutually competitive leaderships rather than discrete leaderships (Ogot, 1999: 29). The problem of introducing executive rule in such a society was immense, and Ainsworth himself was to be severely

tried by it. As Mr T.A Watts, a former District Commissioner of Central Nyanza

observed:

> The administration has had a long experience of Luo
> segmentary units within the Native Authority. Forever
> multiplying, forever jealous of each other, each and every unit
> has been in dispute, quick to demand at the cost of a rival the
> promotion of their own interests. Successive generations of
> Administrative officers from the earliest days have
> complained bitterly of the 'clan jealousies' of the tribe and
> their disruptive effects on the social life (As quoted in Ogot,
> 1999:29).

This stereotype is part of the forms of knowledge authored and authorized by the West

which has to be dismantled within the postcolonial framework. Given the above

framework, it is evident that the Nyanza postcolony was chaotically pluralistic.

Mbembe (1992) observes that in such a situation, it is in practice impossible to create a

single, permanently stable system out of all the signs, images and markers in that

disposition. The African community was in itself as plural as the Asians, with various

clans jostling for power and recognition of their own headmen and chiefs. On the other

hand, the other players, the Asians and the Europeans as will be seen later continued to

make the postcolony even more pluralistic with each other engaging in contestations.

In 1909, despite the enormous settlers' opposition, merchant prince A.M Jeevanje was

handpicked by Governor Sir Percy Girouard as the first Indian representative to the

legislative council (Seidenberg, 1996:123). By 1913, Asians saw the need for a communitywide political organization to protect and promulgate what they considered their own separate and identifiable rights.

The various attempts to organize themselves politically culminated in the formation, in March 1914, of the East Africa Indian National Congress. At a meeting held in Mombasa to inaugurate the movement, Indian representatives from all over East Africa attended (Mangat, 1969). Asians continued to confront the state on the voting rights. However, during the World War 1, Asian political activists were generally quiescent as almost everyone was preoccupied with the war.

The point to note here is that Afro-Asian political interaction was not achieved during this early colonial period in Ndere, Yala, Kendu Bay and Kisumu. This is because Asians were not keen on local politics. Their major concern was about settlement in white highlands and recognition of their fundamental rights by the colonial government. They were also keen on trade.

But this could also be attributed to the plurality of the Asian community which developed along sectarian lines, each, with its own interest. For instance, the Goans with their own Goan Institute, the Hindus with their Guru Singh Sabha and the Shia Ismaili with their Jamat Khana – none of these were purposively political and none served the interests of the whole community. This arrangement could not allow for Afro-Asian political interaction as each community had its unique problems at the local level in Ndere, Yala, Kendu Bay and Kisumu.

3.4 Afro-Asian Social Relations in the Early Colonial Period to 1918

3.4.1 Education

Education was one of the most important ideological apparatus through which   colonial governments maintained their control (Rodney, 1989:264). Colonial education had the double task of incorporating the colonized people into the Western capitalist system and reproducing the emerging capitalist relations of production in each colony. Kinyanjui (1979) avers that at the time the colonial economic system was being imposed, colonial schools were vehicles for the transmission of metropolitan cultural capital, a view which is also supported by Rodney.

For Rodney, colonial education had an economic function in the colonial division of labour. It was a vehicle for implanting and encouraging capitalist individualism, and an instrument of cultural imperialism. 'Colonial schooling', he argued, 'was education for subordination, exploitation, the creation of mental confusion and the development of underdevelopment' (Rodney, 1989:264, Zeleza, 1989:60).

In Kenya, three parties controlled African education namely, the mission, the government and the settlers. Almost unanimously, the three parties agreed that vocational, industrial, and religious instructions, all forms of Western knowledge, should constitute the African curriculum. Imbued with racial feelings of superiority, most whites considered spiritual, vocational and industrial education as best suited for Africans (Berman 1975a).

At the mission schools in Nyanza, pupils learnt religious knowledge, reading, writing, arithmetic, hygiene, gardening and drill. It should be noted that apart from gardening, more emphasis was placed on literary subjects which were all taught in Dholuo (Ogot, 2003:22). To be able to meet its obligation of preparing the Africans to fit into European civilization, the Church Missionary Society (CMS) submitted that all education was to be based on spiritual foundations (Odwako, 1975:50).

In 1909, (Professor) J.Nelson Frazer, an education adviser to the British East Africa Protectorate produced a report for consideration by the authorities in which he suggested the establishment of three educational systems to cater for the three major racial groups in the country; Europeans, Asians and Africans (Osogo, 1969). Frazer also advised the colonial authorities: "....not (to) put forward plans for literary education for Negroes but to consider the possibilities of developing industries among them." (Osogo, 1969:104)

In the spirit of the Frazer recommendations, Africans were denied literary education because it was considered too superior for the black intellect. Accordingly, the British authorities embarked on aggressive projects to train Africans in basic skills with regard to smelting, carpentry, agriculture, tailoring, and typing (Kisiang'ani 2003:94). Apart from being designed to prove blackmans inferiority, colonial education aimed at training individuals for the service of the colonial society (Nyerere 1968:268).

Traditional African education emphasized human relations and behaviour. It also stressed the importance of communal activities. While traditional education taught individuals to be members of a cohesive society, Western education was based on individualism and had little relation to society (Kenyatta 1968:12). These were forms of knowledge authored and authorized by the West which Africans resisted and formed the basis of African nationalism. Generally, colonial education was used to reshape the postcolony by not only giving inferior instructions to Africans but by dismantling African values and education institutions and replacing them with those authored and authorized by the West. This created a new African person who felt inferior and incapable of participating in progressive endevours. Segregate education meant that Africans were different from either Asians or Europeans. This psychological arrangement defined the relation between Asians and Africans in all aspects of their interaction.

The Asians of the Ismailia sect in Kendu Bay started their school at *Sanatan,* their place of worship within the compound of a mosque known locally as Khoja Ismailia. Next to the *Sanatan* was the Aga Khan School. Only the Ismaili children and the Punjabi Muslim children schooled there and after standard four, they proceeded to Kisumu to continue with their education. The Ismaili also employed various Gujarati Hindus to teach secular subjects (Salvadori, 1996:173, Faraj, O.I., 2007). Emphasis on teaching in Gujerati showed confidence in Indian cultural values, which, the Asians felt were superior to African cultural values. Therefore, their children were to be introduced to these values at a very early stage.

120

In Ndere, the Asian children were also taught separately from the Africans, near the Ndere old trading centre in a small block building, which was later to become the site for Oseno Primary School. The Indians of Yala also built a school in Yala. This was a one-roomed building all made of corrugated iron sheets. The colonial government encouraged such schools and catered for the teachers' salaries. The Asian school in Yala was known as Yala Government Aided Indian School (Shah, O.I., 2006). In these schools, the syllabus was Indian and there was no way the African children could attend such schools and benefit (Mzungu, O.I, 2006, Mboya, O.I., 2006).

The issue of segregation was more prominent in the urban parts of Nyanza with Kisumu being more affected than Ndere, Yala and Kendu Bay as far as socialization was concerned. In Kisumu, as would be seen later, both Asians and Africans attended separate schools. During the first decade of colonialism, Afro-Asian relations in schools were non-existent because of the strong segregation policy which rendered Afro-Asian interaction and mixing impossible. As one Asian stated, 'We children did not have anything to do with African children. The African children were 'illiterate' in those days' (Shah, O.I., 2006).

This segregation could not, however, be entirely blamed on the Europeans but also on the Asian cultural practices which thrived on caste system where members of a certain caste were superior to the other. Their sects also encouraged each community to run their schools separately. But also the management of African education by the missionaries

121

also ensured that Africans and Asians attended different schools thereby affecting their interactions in schools.

This recommendation gave the missionaries a firm grip on the fate of African children whom they taught. It also meant that the Department of Education had to define its relationship with different missionary organizations (Ogutu, 1981:127). This situation therefore affected Afro-Asian interaction and relations within the school system in Nyanza province.

3.4.2 Housing

For many years Africans were regarded as temporary inhabitants of the towns in which they worked as unskilled labourers. They lived in traditional huts either inside or outside the township boundaries, and when urban authorities found it necessary to provide them with accommodation, it was on the assumption that they would work in towns for short periods unaccompanied by their families, and would then return to their areas of origin. They were regarded socially and financially as liabilities for whose housing and welfare the urban authorities were responsible (Olumwullah 1986:132). Therefore, Africans were generally given the identity of rural folks. These stereotypes are what defines and stabilizes relations on the postcolonial terrain as everybody is forced to accept their status defined by the dominant culture. Liberation begins when people reject their status and begin to question the stereotypes.

Upon his arrival in Nyanza in 1907, Ainsworth found that the bubonic plague was endemic in the site (Maxon, 1980:176). He made every effort to contain the situation specifically by the introduction of inoculations, rat killing, and the destruction of infected buildings. Ainsworth planned to alter the character of the township so as to protect railway, port installations and European residential areas better. His plan involved the establishment of a more rigid system of segregation than had previously existed. Ainsworth's plan would result in three distinct areas.

The first zone included the port, town, official residences and offices, and the European quarters and well to do Indians. Zone two contained petty Indian and Somali traders as well as Africans outside the township. Zone three was the uninhabited area around the township which would serve as a buffer. It was never possible to move all petty traders out of the township. Although Ainsworth was able to move African labourers out to the outskirts of the town, this was the origin of the strictly segregated residential pattern for Africans, Asians and Europeans that was to characterize Kisumu throughout colonial rule (Maxon, 1980:176, KNA, PC/NZA/1/4 KPAR 1908-09).

While Indian indentured labourers were technically the responsibility of the railway administration, Murunga (2007:10) argues that the Chief Engineer George Whitehouse and Engineer Colonel Peterson "only took into consideration the European employees of the railway and the European and Asian traders who were expected to come" along with the railway and completely neglected the Asian labourers and Africans. This forced the neglected groups to seek their own shelter, to build a symbiotic relationship with each other and with the Africans who supplied them with essential foodstuff.

In other words, their choice of settlement and the social milieu that emanated from the settlement reflected their experience of neglect and adjustment to marginalization. This neglect had also to do with the Indian caste system which was replicating itself in the Nyanza postcolonial space. As neglected groups, the Asian labourers and Africans were led into engaging with each other by the sheer force of necessity.

The commercial success of the Indian was not commensurate with his accommodation in Nyanza. The position regarding the housing of Asian clerical staff in Kisumu was reported to be most unsatisfactory and scandalous due to overcrowding. The type of housing favoured by the Asian community and which had been evolving (The shop cum residence) found its most mature development in this period as either the single storey front shop and shop residence with walled backyard or the two storey town house with shops on the ground floor, stores, a walled backyard and residence upstairs (Anyumba, 1995). These types of houses suited the long hours of business transactions and those were and still are typical of the community. This structure too suited the exclusiveness and security needs of the extended Asian family.

The issue of their security wherever they stayed affected their interaction with Africans. However, within their houses, their relationship was only limited to the Africans whom they employed as house servants or *ayahs*. House servants were employed to do the cleaning and cooking and *ayahs* to look after the children (Ondiallo, O.I., 2006). The Asian women in these houses continued speaking the vernaculars of India while learning

124

some elementary 'kitchen' Swahili to communicate with the African house help/servants. Some went ahead and learnt the local Luo language from the African househelps whom they employed. Inter home visits between Asians and Africans was however minimal. In Ndere, Yala and Kendu bay, the Asian community was housed in the trading centres where they used their shops for both commercial and residential purposes (Ondiallo, Faraji, Ochoko, O.I., 2006).

Apart from the government and railway owned residential houses for the Asians in Nyanza, interaction between the Asians and Africans within the residential areas was also minimal. This is because the Asians stayed in isolated and well-fenced residences where Africans could not access. This fencing of Asian premises was probably a defence mechanism to protect themselves from perceived African attacks, a kind of African protest against their presence in some of these areas.

After a day's work, the Asians would go back to their houses where some would pray and relax with their families (Orenda, O.I., 2006). The popular discourse was that Africans were wild. In Kendu Bay, for example, the Asians stayed in some houses made of iron sheets within the old Kendu town almost close to the current Kendu Muslim Secondary School. Each plot in Kendu Bay had a building with two or three shops in the front and some living quarters behind.

In Ndere area, the Asians stayed in the living quarters at the back of the shops. This pattern of housing was also the same in Yala where the Asians stayed behind their shops in the old Yala trading centre (Odhiambo, Akinyi, Orenda, O.I., 2006). In the Asian residential premises, African *Askaris* (watchmen) were under firm instructions from their employers not to allow in any 'strangers' in. Watchmen were instructed to tell those who wanted to see these Asians to meet them at their places of work (Ondiallo, O.I., 2006). The African guards (Askaris) therefore bailed Asians out for fear of burglary and other related cases of theft. This segregation marked an uneasy relationship between Asians and Africans.

Afro-Asian relations that existed within the residences were that of a master/servant relationship, whereby some Africans were employed as *boyi (shamba boys/houseboys)* and *ayahs/yaya (housegirls)*. The African servants refered to their Indian masters as *mzee, mama* (respected man or woman, respectively) or madam. Such colonial names as *ayahs* (housegirls) and *boy*i (houseboys), often aimed at fixing rigid class categories between the Asians and Africans.

Reverential status was conferred upon the Asians (ruling classes) by such words as *mzee, memsahib* (respected man's wife) which the local Africans pronounced as *mamsap*. Some of these words were incorporated into Swahili language as well as English. However, the word *boyi* was transformed into *bayi* by Africans in Kisumu, Ndere, Kendu Bay and Yala. This word was neither Asian nor African, however, it became a common term which Africans used to refer to all the Asians regardless of their status in the course of their relationships.

126

Some of these African employees occupied servants quarters inside the Asian compounds, while other servants worked and went back to their respective homes in the evening. It should be noted that for an African to be employed by the Asians to work in their residential areas, he had to be well known enough by the Asians. This is because, generally, Asians perceived all Africans as 'thieves' which was a form of knowledge stereotyping. This notion caused Asians in Ndere to close their shops as early as six O'clock to avoid any attacks from local Africans. This is why they fenced and fortified their residential areas and did not allow any African to visit them in their residences.

However, once they trusted an individual, they maintained a favourable and cordial relationship and could even leave such person(s) in charge of their homesteads while they were away doing business (Odhiambo, O.I., 2006, Ogallo, O.I., 2006). African protests and resistance to some forms of Asian domination and exploitation was evidenced in certain aspects of their social lives when Africans made jokes out of the word *boyi* (boy). In cases where one was given a lot of work to do in the African household, one could be heard saying *ok an boch muindi* (am not an Indian boyi) to be given such amount of work load denoting that working for an Asian was actually exploitative. These linguistic coinages served various purposes in the postcolony.

The housing situation in Nyanza and especially Kisumu during the early colonial period 1900-1918, was generally not good since the Asian residences were very crowded. The same condition applied to the Indian *landies* (residential plots where railway employees and their families lived). A few plots in the Indian bazaar had been taken up by the

127

Indians and new business premises erected. Two Indian residences were in the process of construction. Several other plots which were bought by the Indian community at the sale of plots, were not yet developed. This was because of the money market and the high cost of building materials (KNA, PC/NZA/1/16, Annual Report 1920-21). Afro-Asian interaction which took place in the residential areas was therefore between Africans employed by Asians in their houses and also those Africans who went to buy goods from Asian shops which served as their places of work and residence.

3.5 Summary and Conclusion

It was the objective of this chapter to examine the Afro-Asian relations upto 1918. We have demonstrated that these relations were diverse and included such issues as trade, cultural and social relations which described the postcolony. We have concluded that these relations changed the African lifestyles. The Africans' eating habit changed as they started eating exotic foods. Their dressing habits began to change as they moved from wearing of hides and skin to a Dutch manufactured Kanga with deep Indonesian influence thereby introducing a class of people known as *jonanga* (cloth wearers). Asians too borrowed some positive values from the Africans. The study has also demonstrated that some Asian names were Luonised within the chaotic commercial plural space of Nyanza.

Such linguistic hybridity was also a common feature which characterized Afro-Asian relations in Nyanza province. We have concluded that education and housing followed a racial pattern. But because of sheer force of necessity, the Asians were forced to hire and stay with Africans as domestic servants. Because of differences in political agendas which were also pursued along racial lines by the two communities, it was not possible for Afro-Asian political relations to flourish during this early period. In the next chapter we examine the Afro-Asian relations during the interwar period.

CHAPTER FOUR

4.0 THE AFRO-ASIAN RELATIONS IN THE INTERWAR AND DURING THE SECOND WORLD WAR PERIOD, 1919-1945

4.1 Introduction

In Chapter Three, we interrogated Afro-Asian relations in the early colonial period and argued that Afro-Asian relations were diverse. These relations also changed the lifestyles of Africans. We have concluded that there were some Asian values which the Africans borrowed and vice versa. However, political and social relations followed a racial pattern. The current chapter examines Afro-Asian relations in the interwar and during the Second World War period. The year 1919 marked the beginning of the interwar period while 1945 marked the end of the Second World War. The Great depression, widespread drought in Nyanza as well as the rise of protest movements characterised the interwar and Second World War period.

This chapter focuses on the Afro-Asian economic, political and social relations that developed especially with the emergent class of African traders. It also examines the role of Asians in the cotton industry amid concerted government effort to promote the planting of this crop and how the cotton industry shaped Afro-Asian relations in Nyanza province. The postcolonial theory is used in this chapter to analyse the various contestations emerging within the plural space of Nyanza. The chapter concludes that the position of Asians in this

130

relationship was ambivalent and that the colonial institution like the office of the chief was widely used to marginalize Africans.

4.2 The Afro – Asian Economic Relations in the Interwar Period

The years immediately after the First World War were not very good for the Luo of Central Nyanza. A severe food shortage occasioned by the 1918 and 1919 drought had made the people of Nyakach, Kadimo and Uyoma sell a lot of their stock to purchase food. People reacted variously to these circumstances. While quite a large number left the reserves to seek work, others decided to migrate permanently from their homes to settle in other places like Lumbwa (Kericho District) or South Nyanza. The total number of labourers registered from Central Nyanza between March 1919 and March 1920 was about 6,021; in addition there were 3,123 recruits for the government departments. The Uganda Railway, some government departments, European and Indian farmers also recruited a large number without recording (Ndeda, 1991).

When Kenya was declared a British colony in 1920, it was already clearly established policy that commerce and industry should be in the hands of the Asians. To their credit, the Asians exploited to the full this paternalism extending their commercial roots to practically all the emerging settlements in Kenya. The Asian economic position was firmly secure. Africans, the colonized people, were not rivals because of their limited experience in the monetary economy.

Right from the start of the Asian immigration into Kenya, the colonial administration was determined to keep them away from any political engagement. By limiting him to trade in the colonial administration, the Asian was destined to the towns and trading centres where he met Africans in the context of formal interaction as merchant/customer and as juniors in the colonial administration setup. Such a policy could not endure for long. The Asian successes in business, even if eventuated would soon or later bring the issue of his political standing on a racial basis. This political dimension was intensified by the increasing number of Africans in the fields previously reserved for Asians as a result of enlarged opportunities and further experiences (Finance, 1997:9).

In the early 1920s, the general character of the Indian role had to a large extent been determined by the policies adopted towards them. These policies had a combined result both of greatly increasing Indian participation in the 'development' of the region and, at the same time, of restricting the Indian role within the well-defined limits. These policies affected Afro-Asian relations in Nyanza in different ways. At the same time it was reported that African traders were gradually able to compete here and there with their Indian counterparts (Memon, 1976:209). The groundwork was being laid for the emergence of an indigenous trading class whose interests tended to conflict with those of the immigrant Asian traders thus making Afro –Asian relationship a relationship fraught with antagonism and tension.

The Asian economic role underwent certain subtle changes during this period which shaped their relations with the Africans. On the one hand, there was a marked increase in

132

the number of Asians engaged in large-scale business operations. They also continued to play their role as shopkeepers, traders and artisans. Their role in this respect was increasingly challenged by the growth of African competition and hostility towards their (Asian) predominance in the middle ranks of the economic ladder. This had the additional effect of accelerating the diversification of Asian enterprises into new fields of secondary manufacturing industries or where possible into agriculture.

Slowly, Indian businessmen moved out of the wholesale and retail business into industry, while artisans and clerks transformed themselves into successful entrepreneurs and managers (Van Zwanenberg, 1977:126 Seidenberg, 1996:39). With the acceleration of local industry, a permanent labour force was also created and stabilized (Shivji, 1976:36). The presence of African competition began to make itself felt among small retail stores, especially in the villages and other small centres and resulted in a drift of some Asian traders to the towns and cities (Ghai, 1965:44). More significant also was the gradual transition in their economic activities from small-scale enterprise of early years to larger business undertakings.

As this transition took shape, the bulk of the trade was still in the hands of Indians. By 1926/27, the Africans bought small quantities of goods from Indians and then sold at a profit in the reserve (KNA, PC\NZA\1\27, AR 1927). The ordinary Indian trader would willingly give credit to Africans. The Indian traders, in whose hands most of the African retail trade rested, used their takings to renew their stock and expand their businesses (KNA, PC\NZA\ 1\23, AR 1928\29).

133

The African traders in Ndere for instance, could take goods on credit from the Asian shops to sell and then pay later. However, this depended on the trust bestowed upon such people by the Asians. This gesture by the Asians was to gradually create a paternal and capitalist relationship between the two communities to ensure that this economic relation was sustained for a longer period. Africans sold local produce such as cassava, sweet potatoes, *ododo* (a particular type of local vegetables), pepper (*pilipili*), pawpaw and unripe bananas to the Indians (Odindo, O.I., 2005).

The Africans also developed a lot of interest in the Asian Jaggery, which they bought and utilized to prepare local gin known as the Nubian gin (African brew). The preparation of Nubian gin was very common in Kibos area. In fact, some Asians also frequented the African settlement houses to take this drink. This was a sign of the emerging inter-racial relations between the Afro-Asian communities. However, this act by the Asians could be viewed as a marketing strategy of the Asian products (KNA, PC\NZA\3\15\142, 1931-50).

On the consumer side, the activities of the Kavirondo Taxpayers Welfare Association (KTWA), the first African political organization in Nyanza in the 1920s, among other things, stimulated co-operative self-help schemes, particularly in grain milling by waterpower thus competing with the Asians in the processing of local produce. The formation of KTWA thus informed the African protest and resistance to bad trade practices which emerged between the Asians and the Africans on this plural and hybrid postcolonial space of Nyanza.

Yet, the significant features of the cash economy during this period were the Asian commercial initiatives and the limited consumer needs of the Africans. The government allowed the chiefs to open up their own markets. Here, they became middlemen for the Asian traders. In this process, the chiefs also secured positions in the trading line for their own kinsmen as hoteliers and hawkers. Thus, the Asian thrust into the Nyanza area through the cooperation of the chiefs, such as Odindo in Asembo, Muganda in Ugenya, Amoth in Alego, and Odera Akang'o in Gem Yala (Atieno-Odhiambo, 1976:226 Omoro, O.I., 2005). The chiefs were therefore used by the colonial government to consolidate their control of Africans.

While Asians in Ndere enjoyed harmonious trade relations with Africans, in Yala area, the Asian merchants complained of crimes committed by Africans. They notified the DC Central Kavirondo that, during the last few months of 1928, a dozen houses had been broken into in Yala town and consequently a number of merchants had suffered. They, therefore, appealed to the government to arrange to station *askaris* there to protect their lives and property (KNA, PC/NZA/3/39/1, 1927). These criminal acts by Africans could be viewed as representing their resistance and protests against Asians who were seen as an appendage of European rule in Kenya. Their appeal to the government to station *askaris* symbolized the ruthless and brutal way in which colonialism manifested itself in

135

the colony. These acts were, therefore, meant to dismantle the unequal economic relations which existed between the Africans and Asians.

In a correspondence with the DC Kisumu, Hon. Desai, the Secretary of Indian Association complained concerning the lawlessness and rowdiness of the Africans in the trading centers of Nyanza Province and particularly in the Yala and Sio districts. Due to lack of quick response from the government, the Africans had become bolder by the day and considered that the authority had condoned their aggressive actions (KNA, PC/NZA/3/39/1 1927).

Due to the laxity of the chiefs and headmen regarding the individual complaints of the Indians concerning African aggression, the Indian traders believed that the irresponsible Africans were encouraged by them. The chiefs' failure to act could have had a double meaning within the postcolonial thinking. First, this could be construed as a tactical retreat with some racial connotations on the part of the African chiefs.

On the other hand, it also symbolized a resistance by African chiefs aimed at dismantling the colonial racial structure where Asians were superior to Africans. The African lawlessness was, therefore, an effort by Africans to protest and dismantle colonial structures and forms of knowledge which the Indians partly represented. But also one should see the lawlessness and rowdiness of the Africans in the trading centres, as Furedi (1974) puts it, in terms of the growing conflict between the aspirations of the African trading class and the powerful Asian monopoly over trade.

The Africans in Yala and Luanda frequently said that the trading centers were their 'Communal Reserve' and the Indians were only allowed to stay there at the will of the chiefs and headmen. Coincidentally at this time, a store of the Nyanza Oil Mills was broken into. Similarly, Messrs Karsandass Mulji and brothers' shop was broken into and bags of maize, trade goods and cash were stolen respectively. Suspicion was directed to some headmen and chiefs who the Asians believed had some political motives (KNA, PC/NZA/3/39/1, 1927).

Later, however, there was a rush by Indian traders to purchase shotguns for self-defence. The gun was a symbol of power and represented the brutal nature of colonialism. The Asians resorted to it in order to assert their dominance and superiority over the Africans. The members of the Indian Traders Association (I.T.A) were also compelled to report incidences of African harassment to Indian shopkeepers who took their goods and ran away without paying, beating and threatening the shopkeepers (DC/KSM/1/1/16, 15/6/1940). However, such incidences were not being organized by the Africans as a community but by individuals within the Yala area (Adjai, O.I., 2006).

Conflicts of interest between established Asian businesses and those of new African entrepreneurs also arose. This period also witnessed the expansion in African cash-crop production and the emergence of African small traders in the rural areas. Similarly by 1930s, a class of local African traders in Central and Western Kenya had emerged. Those in Nyanza were particularly opposed to both the magnitude of Asian trade in the reserves and the employment by Asians of African hawkers in trading centres there.

The Kavirondo Chamber of Commerce, an all-African economic pressure group representing the Luo and Luhya African traders, passed several resolutions seeking restrictions on the activities of Asian traders. The Chamber members even suggested separate trading centres for Asians and Africans and also condemned the Local African Council's unpopular practice of allocating plots to Indians in the newly established trading centres against the interest of African traders and designed to keep them in their former place as growers of *wimbi* (finger millet) and *mtama* (ordinary millet). The Council was therefore requested to cease inviting Indian traders to trading centres and trade in the prescribed areas be put into African hands (Memon, 1976:210).

Evidently, the level at which Asians and Africans interacted provided little potential for friendship or mutual respect between themselves. On the contrary, the context of interaction provided grounds for mistrust and conflict. This hostility became more visible after the World War (Atieno Odhiambo 1995). The sudden hostility between the Asian and the African traders could be attributed to the level of awareness that the latter group of traders was subjected to as a result of the colonial education and also the issue of returnee soldiers who also ventured into business.

In 1930, Kenya was hit by the worldwide depression which began in 1929. There was a drop in world commodity prices especially of agricultural produce that affected Kenya (Ngesa, 1996:79). After 1930, the great depression affected Kenya's international economic position forcing the colonial government officials to desperately search for any possible source of badly needed exports. Trade in most African areas of Kenya collapsed during the period and prices of primary commodities dropped.

Suddenly, African cash cropping appeared attractive in the minds of the colonial officials as a possible solution to their economic dilemma and they henceforth turned their attention to cotton production by Africans in Nyanza (Wolff, 1974:144). By turning attention to cotton production, Afro-Asian interaction was enhanced as the Asians started introducing cotton to some areas in Nyanza where the crop had not been grown. This therefore brought Asians and Africans into close contact in areas such as Ndere, Kendu Bay and Kisumu as the Asians bought cotton from Africans for export purposes.

Meanwhile by 1935, centralization of marketing for all African crops was crystallized in the Native Produce Marketing Ordinance of 1935. This Ordinance was also to control the quality and direction of African produce. Under this law, the government gave itself the right to limit traders in any African-produced commodities to individuals or firms chosen by it. The restrictions provided the means for further control of production and prices and thus provided the support for high priced European traders to continue in profitable capitalist business (Zwanenberg, 1975:212-213; Atieno Odhiambo, 1976:226).

Paradoxically, one of the objectives of this ordinance was to separate retail enterprises from trade in agricultural produce and to give African traders more scope in marketing. Many Asian shop owners who dealt in retailing and in produce marketing had to give up

139

one branch of their business, as trade licenses for the two activities were not issued to a single trader.

Unfortunately, the strict requirements for obtaining a trading licence effectively eliminated African participation in produce marketing (Furedi 1974:350). In Nyanza, this was facilitated by the Nyanza Trading Licensing Board. By this time, the process towards limiting competition and controlling prices and centralizing marketing was well under way for many crops and cotton was highly controlled through the Director of Agriculture (KNA, PC/NZA/1/12/115).

Moreover, the physical concentration of trade in the designated buying centres also worked to reinforce the tendency toward monopoly and this made African entry into commerce even more difficult (Kaplan, 1967:539). The government and white farmers portrayed African traders as agents of Indian business. Moreover, it was argued that they should be producers and not traders. This restrictive policy was, therefore, a strategy used by Europeans to fight both Indians and Africans in order to secure the postcolony. Such policies were to form the basis of nationalism which brought Asians and Africans together against the Europeans and enhanced Afro-Asian political relations.

Despite the fact that the Native Produce Marketing Ordinance of 1935 was in place, Asian traders got round the restrictive provisions of this ordinance by having different members of a family obtaining separate licences for retail and produce trade. The situation whereby Africans were dependent for a great part of their livelihood on the sale of produce to Asians was in itself bound to create a certain degree of suspicion. This suspicion was generalized by relatively few but well-known cases of business malpractices (like increasing prices of commodities and use of faulty weighing scales) committed by Asian traders (Furedi. Opcit 350).

By 1945, Oginga Odinga alongside other people formed the Bondo Thrift Association which was a fore runner of the Luo Thrift and Trading Corporation (LUTATCO). This association started off by collecting money from members earmarked for business. But also members in distress could borrow from this money. Later, the association began to think concretely about trade. The committee decided to consult some advocates and the Registrar of Societies with a view to soliciting their advice and support on how to launch a trading company. However, during this consultation, the association found itself snubbed and the Asians prevailed. Of the Asian advocates in Kisumu, Odinga had this to say:

> When I sought help in forming a company from Indian lawyers in Kisumu they advised a welfare society; companies would be beyond our knowledge and ability, they said. I went to kisumu to buy books on company law and settled down myself to draft our memorandum and articles of association. We were then ready to decide on a name. We called a meeting for that. Some said it should be called the Bondo Thrift and Trading Corporation. Others were in favour of calling it the Luo Corporation, others the Kenya Thrift and Trading Corporation, and still others the East African Thrift and Trading Corporation (Odinga, 1967:78)

It is, therefore, evident that trade rivalry was very rife in Nyanza. This rivalry depicted the African struggle to dismantle and challenge Asian domination in trade in Nyanza region.

4.3 Afro-Asian Relations and the Cotton Industry in the Interwar Period

Commercial cotton cultivation was introduced into Kenya's Nyanza Province by the British government. It was expected that cotton production there would produce similar results to the cotton industry in Uganda where 'cotton was King' and was produced for export (Shivji, 1976:46). However, it became clear that Kenya Africans had not enthusiastically-embraced cotton growing and that it would not become the major cash crop of Nyanza Province.

The British government attempted in a variety of ways to introduce cotton cash cropping but most of these attempts had little success, and African farmers generally received most of the blame. Indigenous people, it was argued, placed a high value on leisure time and their tastes were confined to traditions or ignorance largely to the goods they could provide for themselves (Fearn 1956; Reed 1975:53). This was the discourse about the Other which informed life in the postcolony

Ndeda (1991) states that despite some innovations in Luo agriculture during the interwar period, most parts of Luo land remained marginal to wage labour. The innovations included the acquisition of ploughs, water-powered flourmills, harrows and maize hulling machines by certain Africans. Insofar as they wanted to or were obliged to earn money income, the people of Central Nyanza found it more lucrative or congenial to hire out their services rather than exert themselves in cultivating unfamiliar and inedible crops

142

such as cotton. Most Luo peasants remained subsistence farmers and produced just enough to meet the immediate household needs (Ochieng' 1986: 11).

After failing to stimulate African interest in growing cotton, H.B Partington (the former District Commissioner for Central Nyanza) decided to utilize the small Asian enclaves as agricultural innovators. He argued that Asians were more western in both their economic and agricultural orientations. He also lost confidence in the ability of the Africans to adapt to cash cropping. He stated that:

> We are locating small colonies of agricultural *Swahilis* and Indians at different points where small areas of land are available. These people agreed to plant economic products. As they do so, they will be an object lesson for the different 'natives' near them and the influence will spread (KNA, PC/NZA Annual Report 1907/08: xxxii).

It should be noted that these Western forms of knowledge were met with some resistance from the Africans who had attached more commitment to their traditional values, which were under threat of being eroded. But we also see ambivalence at the centre of colonial encounters where Partington involved agricultural *Swahilis*, this is a community of Africans whom Partington initially did not have confidence in. From such colonial encounters there emerged, as Bhabha puts it, the question of the ambivalence of mimicry as a problem of colonial subjection (Buuck, 1997:125). Lack of interest on the side of Africans to plant cotton, therefore, depicted some kind of subversive resistance against the tyrannies of Western forms of domination

In a correspondence between the manager of Messrs Small and Company (Samia and Kendu ginning stations), and the PC Nyanza, the manager stated that, for some years after the inception of the company's business, the company was compelled to run at a loss. This was due to the insufficient production of cotton in the region. However, despite that loss, the company realized the importance of encouraging the African growers and bought cotton at reasonable prices in order to stimulate production and maintain at all time cordial relations with the African growers. The Asians paid African farmers promptly and issued seeds in time (KNA, PC\ NZA\2\12\1, 1928-38, Odera, O.I., 2006).

However, despite the seeming favourability, the Asian company simply needed a way of serving its capitalist interest. This was clear within the areas where they opened up ginneries, such as Kendu Bay where Messrs Small and Company initiated the development of infrastructure by applying for permission to the acting PC Nyanza to lay a trolley line for their ginnery at Kendu pier. This was to ease transportation of the products bought from African areas. The infrastructural expansion also created job opportunities for the Africans but even such were exploitative due to the low wages (KNA, PC/NZA/3/22/3 1931-42).

The administration's attempt to promote cotton production reached full intensity in the 1930s when it became one of the many policies designed to raise the colony's foreign exchange earnings in the depression years. Although the cotton crop had been introduced in Nyanza earlier, the 1930s saw a more systematic and intensified campaign to increase its production. Here too, the energies of the local administration were harnessed in

144

educating people about the growing of cotton and enforcing its cultivation (Kitching, 1980:74, Kanogo, 1989:121).

The government cotton planting campaign which centred at first on South Kavirondo spread to other districts. This campaign was intermeshed with the administration's zoning policy with the province being divided into three cotton production zones each with its own production targets and seed distribution system (Kitching, 1980:74). The government effort to encourage cotton production in Nyanza was, therefore, a precedent to the Afro - Asian interaction in this industry. This interaction would later characterize their relations as Asians went ahead to own cotton stores and ginneries in the areas zoned by the government. These cotton stores and ginneries served as centres of Afro-Asian interaction in the villages of Ndere, Kendu Bay and Kibos.

Apart from Siaya, Kisumu, and Homa Bay also grew cotton. Centres such as Yala, Ukwala, Asembo, Kendu Bay, Oyugis, Mbita, Maseno, Ahero, Miwani, Muhoroni and Chemelil in Kisumu were collecting centres for seed cotton. Ginneries were established at Lusumu near Mumias, Kisumu, and Asembo. But owing to the apathy of the 'natives' in two cases (Asembo and Kisumu) and the unsuitability of conditions at Mumias, three ginneries were closed (KNA, TR/18/59, 1973). The Asians later bought some of the ginneries and started engaging Africans in both cotton production and ginning. However, as has been argued above, this seeming apathy was a resistance to cotton growing introduced through the Indians. It was also a resistance to European economic imperialism.

The above cotton collection centres as well as the ginneries that were later opened by the Asians became sites where Afro-Asian relations and contestations took place. In these sites Asians paid Africans for the cotton delivered, while at the same time they employed Africans to guard these stores commonly referred to as *stoo pamba* (cotton store) on their behalf (Owiyo, O.I., 2007). Africans in such areas were thus compelled to sell their cotton to the Asians who owned capital. In essence, the kind of relations which emerged here was based on production and selling of cotton

Meanwhile, taking his always shifting position of neither being a colonizer nor the colonized, the Asian introduced cotton plantation in Kendu Bay through the first generation of Kassim Lakha family in the year 1930-31. However, before the Kendu Bay ginnery was erected, the cotton grown in Kendu Bay area was ginned at Samia (Samia Ginnery). Similarly, Tahidin, an Asian from Uganda who later owned the ginnery in Ke ndu Bay gave out 'free' cotton seedlings to African cotton growers. The 'free' seedlings were however, catered for when the Africans took their cotton to the ginnery (Ojijo, O.I., 2006). During this time, inadequate roads obscured traveling so the lake alone was the transport route and cotton was shipped by barges to Samia via Sio port. The ginnery at Kendu was built in 1933\34 (KNA, TP/5/29/, 1971-77).

The Kendu Bay ginnery served a wide geographical region since people came all the way from Homa Bay, Kosele and Kanyada so as to sell their cotton to the Indians who owned the ginnery. It could be said that Afro-Asian relations here were mutually beneficial. The

Asians employed some Africans in these ginneries where they worked as assistants to the Indian owners of the ginnery.

Basically, the Africans helped Asian employers in weighing of the cotton, tying up the cotton in bails, ginning process and accompanying the Asians to various Asian owned cotton stores and buying centres to collect cotton from the African producers (Mzee Malit, O.I., 2006).

At times, the Asians could leave Africans in charge of a certain collection centre after which the Asian would just come and collect cotton in bales. In such situations, relations based on opposite binarisms such as master-servant changed as the Africans in charge of such posts also played the role of a figure head. In Kendu Bay, the Asians bought land from the government but paid certain annual dues such as land rent. Therefore, the acquisition of land for the establishment of the ginnery received no resistance from the Africans. Africans were aware that Asians bought the land from the government.

Therefore the postcolony was full of masters and servants of different descriptions. These roles were temporal and fluid. The position of masters and servants kept changing as roles changed. For instance, when Europeans appeared on the scene they became masters, the rest servants. When the Europeans existed it was the Indian who was the servant. And in the absence of both the Europeans and Asians some Africans would become masters.

In the ginneries, the Asians trained the Africans in the new tasks, that is, how to gin cotton, operate the machines and how to weigh cotton. Asians too supervised Africans and taught them certain essential features of operations within the ginnery. In the ginneries, certain traits of the African workers were viewed as constant irritants to the Asians.

Asians felt that Africans required constant supervision and that if not supervised, their attention was easily distracted. Africans were also viewed by Asians as liable to damage tools and spoil raw materials (Sofer, 1954:73, Nyang'wara, O.I., 2007). Similarly, there were Asian traits which also irritated Africans in their relations with Asians within the ginning industry. The Africans complained that the Asians shouted at them saying for instance *bado maliza kazi, maliza. Maliza, veve(wewe) fanya nini* (You haven't finished your work, what are you doing?). To the Africans, Asians treated all of them as if they were unskilled labourers irrespective of age, education or occupational status and without regard to their personal qualities or values (Mzungu, O.I 2007).

In 1932, the Kassim Lakha family also introduced cotton planting at Ndere area, in Siaya District. Before the construction of the Ndere ginnery, cotton was always transported from Asembo to Sio port for ginning at Samia (Western province). The establishment of Ndere ginnery brought about land appropriation. In 1934, Mr Mehta Kalidas, of both Uganda Sugar Company Jinja, and Kenya Industries Limited searched for free land in Alego to open a ginnery.

148

Mehta's intention to acquire land in Alego aroused some tension and suspicion between him and the Africans in Alego. Given that there was no idle land available to be purchased, Mehta had to look for a site elsewhere as Africans in Alego were not willing to donate any land to him. After mounting a search for a willing seller for four months around the area without success, he chose what he considered favourable land and opened direct negotiations for the land with Chief Amoth Owira of Alego (Reed, 1975:88, Ogallo, O.I., 2006). Perhaps this is what caused some Africans in Alego to protest because their land was appropriated without replacement. Clearly, the Asian thrust into the Luo countryside of Ndere was facilitated by the chiefs.

Prior to 1935, the location of the ginnery was the most important prohibitive factor in growing of cotton in Alego. Cotton growers had to head load their harvest twenty miles to a place near Mumias. By this time, Mehta had been given a site in Rang'ala by the government. In 1936, however, with government acceptance, the Provincial Commissioner and the Deputy Director of Agriculture informed Mehta that in future, the proposed ginnery hitherto known as the Rang'ala ginnery should be referred to as the Ndere ginnery (KNA, AK/11/99 1936). Ndere ginnery was thus opened in 1936 (KNA, PC/NZA/1/3/11 1936).

The role of African chiefs in land alienation to Indians ensured that Africans embraced European agricultural knowledge by undertaking to use their land for commercial cotton production. This undertaking was retrogressive as it undermined the African traditional values. Africans substituted their traditional food crops by planting cotton, a cash crop which was initiated from the West, but which was never sustainable in the long run.

The administration's policy of zoning Nyanza into three-cotton production zones, created a site for contestation within this public space. To secure this 'public space,' various ginnery owners tried to lock out other competitors from their operating zones. The security of the public space could be exemplified in the activities of the Kibos Cotton Ginnery. In December 1936 Mr. R.E.G, Russel recommended to the Agricultural Officer of Nyanza that this ginnery should have exclusive buying licenses in respect to the buying posts in West Kano, East Kano, Kajulu, Kisumu, Seme, Sagam and South Terik.

All the ginning companies such as Rahim Jivraj and Company, Kibos Company, Hoima Cotton Company, Messrs Small and Company obtained protective rights in the respective areas which they operated such as Karachuonyo, Mumbo, Kabondo, Sega, and Hawinga among other areas (KNA, PC\NZA\2\12\58, 1934-46). Africans and Asians interacted in these buying posts because they were owned by Asians and were located right inside the rural villages (Owiyo, O.I., 2005). These protected buying zones ensured adequate supplies of cotton as a raw material for economic running of the ginneries around these zones (KNA, BV/6/628 1935-54). This zoning process, however, achieved the imperialistic objective of opening up these areas to the Western capitalist mode of production.

Whereas it is a fact that the Africans in Nyanza sold cotton to the Asians at the various cotton-buying posts, the manner in which these cotton-ginning companies acquired their exclusive protective zones, suggests that the terrain of contest was not equal. Communal land belonging to Africans was negotiated between the Asians and the African colonial chiefs sometimes without the involvement of the African owners and the office of the chief was used to ensure that the interest of the government prevailed. The Africans were marginalized in terms of the planning to zone their public spaces for ventures that did not seem directly beneficial to them.

In Mbembe's (2001) words, the postcolony was not made of one 'public space' but of several sub-spaces, each having its own logic yet liable to be entangled with other logics when operating in certain context. The Nyanza postcolonial sub-space was, therefore, contested and used as a site for cultivation of cotton and unfair land alienation.

Chief Amoth Owira of Alego was a darling of the British government but generally feared by his constituents. Within two months of Mehta's arrival in Ndere and through a variety of threats and promises, Amoth had convinced the farmers to give up some of their land for the ginnery. Other people were persuaded to exchange their land for a promise of an equal share in other sections of the location. Some people received no land compensation at all. Amoth promised that the ginnery would make it possible for everyone to make money by growing cotton and those who objected to giving up their land were sometimes personally caned by the chief (Odhiambo, O.I., 2007). The role of Chiefs as imperial functionaries was crucial in securing the postcolonial space.

151

Africans in all the cotton growing areas gained a new outlook of life and found the money obtained from the sale of cotton to the Asians at the Ndere ginnery of real help. This was indicated by the fact that some Africans made advanced payment of hut tax (KNA, AK\11\99 1935-53). Land alienation to Indians by African chiefs was retrogressive to the Africans as it could not solve African problems and address African realities in Nyanza Province. During the inter-war period, Africans and specifically in Nyanza Province experienced famine and the reality was that they needed to concentrate on planting food crops and not cotton which was a cash crop.

It should be noted from the foregoing discussion, that the chiefs and their allies were themselves a contradictory element in the colonial structure, very quickly becoming a source of internal conflict since they were the cutting edge of a process of class formation undermining both indigenous institutions and the legitimacy of colonial domination (Berman, 1990:66). The authority of the chief thus fused in the judicial, legislative, executive and administrative power of a single person. The administrative justice and the administrative coercion that were the sum and substance of his authority lay behind a regime of extra-economic coercion, a regime that breathed life into a whole range of compulsions: forced labour, forced crops, forced sales, forced contributions and forced removals (Mamdani, 1996:23).

Cotton growing in Alego moved along unsteadily. Around 1936, there were many complaints by the Africans about the chiefs and *milangos* (headmen) exploiting the

152

farmers. The farmers complained of not receiving proceeds from growing of the crop. Asian ginnery owners found out very early that it was to their advantage to provide chiefs with production presents. Africans complained of Asian exploitation especially at the buying centres. They were so organized as to be structured unfairly. Of greatest importance was the fact that the buyers were Asians and no Africans were licensed to purchase cotton from the growers.

Even if Asians had not constituted a despised minority, their sharp business practices would have caused at least negative comments. The Asians rarely issued receipts when making business transactions with Africans, and when they were, they simply contained the amount of money given to the farmer without indicating the balance and other vital information (Reed, 1975:85; Kenyatta, O.I., 2005).

The cotton buying posts were also sites of contestations in the sense that Africans could air their grievances and demonstrate over pricing of their products by Asians. There were demonstrations by the Africans at the buying centres against these vices by 1936. These demonstrations usually took the form of yelling and verbal threats towards the Asians at the buying centres.

Africans took their cotton to Indian stores such as Hawinga and Siro Apate. Here, separation of cotton seed from cotton wool was done by Africans working for Asians, and then, the cotton was taken to Kisumu (Odindo, O.I., 2005). However, the impetus for the disturbances was of course low prices and unfair treatment at these centres. Despite the fact that the farmers disliked the re-grading of their cotton, their major criticism focused on the price and modalities regarding payment.

First, farmers most of whom did not know how to read or write, were never told how many pounds of cotton they had and the cost of the cotton they sold. Usually, the paymasters' station was a scene of confusion (Reed, 1975:125). The disgruntled farmers vented their anger through 'curses', name-calling and threats to indicate their dissatisfaction. While there is no record of actual violence at buying centres, demonstrations would sometimes last several hours (Mzungu O.I., 2006). The postcolony was being run on language codes (signs) and systems of measurement which were mysterious and alien to Africans. This is the logic of every postcolonial space. It has its own owner who dominates the rest. Those dominated have to rise up and say no.

Evidently, the exchange rate was unequal. The African actions implied agitation for their rights which were being violated by the Asians. Such demonstrations, yelling, name calling and issuance of threats witnessed at the buying centres were decisive events for the future of Afro-Asian relations. These were also signs of protest against Asian activities. These malpractices by Asians generated anti-Asian opinion among Africans and changed their attitude towards Asians. This led to an unpleasant relationship between the Asians and Africans engaged in the cotton industry. A relationship fraught with antagonism and tension was, therefore taking shape. This found its expression through organizations such as the Kavirondo Chamber of Commerce which Africans used to agitate for their freedom.

Unlike the Ndere example, enthusiasm for cotton was not characteristic of the farmers' response. Ironically, during the early years of cotton introduction, there were no areas of total defiance and compliance. Reasons for this were that, one, low prices accounted for most resistance to cotton growing. Two, cotton was a non-edible agricultural product and this severely limited its acceptance. Three, the method of introducing cotton in Central Nyanza was, from the farmers' point of view cruel and contrary to traditional farming practices. Farmers also felt that they were being exploited in a variety of ways at buying centres (Reed, 1975:88). Therefore, the resistance of farmers mostly could be attributed to the African peasant economic view that scarcely meshed with the Western industrial thinking.

What is described above on Afro-Asian interaction, indicates a kind of unequal relations noted in the master- servant and seller/buyer relations. Africans were employed by Asians in the ginneries, and they also accompanied Asians during cotton buying days within the Asian owned cotton buying stores. However, these binaries were not permanent but depended on various situations. Africans working for the Asians were however paid low wages which were not commensurate with the amount of labour expended (Oketch, O.I., 2005).

Despite the rampant unequal relations marked by poor wages, some Asian buyers responded to African complaints. Musa Ramji, part –owner of the Kisumu Cooperative ginnery, toured several locations to explain the nature of cotton growing and in 1936 he attended a *baraza* (public rally) in West Kisumu to discuss prices for the next season. However, Ramji's efforts marked him as a lone ranger as it was not   duplicated by other buyers.

However, farmers frequently combined with the nationalists in organized protest (Reed, 1975:131). In 1938, Zablon Aduwo Nyandoje, the General Secretary of the Kavirondo Taxpayers Welfare Association, worked with African farmers from West Kisumu to prevent exploitation by Asians at Kisian market. C.G. Punjani, an Asian buyer, had the reputation of interfering with the weights and measures of the cotton bought by the farmer. Hence, before the sale of the cotton on this particular day, Aduo and Major Campbell, District Officer for West Kisumu weighed all the cotton.

After the sale, they compared payment receipts given to the Africans with their own figures and confronted Punjani (Reed, 1975:131, Mzungu O.I., 2007). It can be argued that the above incident shattered the colonial discourse that represented Africans as people 'without brains' and who could not even detect anomalies. They were also represented as people who should only serve as servants to the Asians. These were knowledge systems which the African postcolonial subjects were determined to dismantle. It is also evident that more informed Africans got better pay for their cotton as compared to the illiterate folks.

Around 1938/39, it became considerably difficult to get the Africans to plant cotton due to the low prices paid for 1937-38 crops. Consequently, a number of ginneries operated at a loss (KNA, PC\NZA3\1\353). This drop in production was not due to unfavourable seasonal conditions that were unconducive for the crop but was due to lack of interest by the African growers which was caused by the fact that cotton prices were low.

Similarly the drop could not be attributed to lack of instructors and knowledge as there were a number of African cotton instructors in the cotton growing areas paid by the Department of Agriculture and the Local Native Council (LNC). Messrs Rahim Jivraj and company Limited of Kibos also paid some of the cotton instructors. The role of such instructors was to help in the stimulation of cotton growing. At the same time, the question of ginners ceasing to bear the cost of contribution towards wages of native instructors had become most urgent and the Nyanza Province Cotton Association requested the government for its immediate consideration (KNA, PC/NZA/3/1/353, Annual Report, 1934-51).

Thus the lack of interest by the Africans to plant cotton depicted continued African resistance to Western capitalistic tendencies, founded on the principals of exploitation and championed through the Asian commercialization activities. The issue of cotton and Asian involvement in the Nyanza postcolonial space characterized the workings of colonial authority as well as the dynamics of resistance.

Even though cotton growing in Nyanza was a colonial policy, it was facilitated by the Asians and, therefore, it is the Asians who were in direct and frequent contact with Africans in the cotton industry. Afro-Asian interaction in this industry revolved around

157

the Asian ginneries, cotton buying and collection stores and also in their residential areas where they employed Africans as their assistants.

Afro-Asian engagement in the cotton industry did not limit their interactions in trade. The Indian trader played a very important function in the socio-economic life of Africans in Kisumu. The *duka* became a keystone in the country's entire system of distribution, selling goods to Africans and acted as a major outlet for the African agricultural producers (Kaplan, 1967:533).In their day-to-day activities Asian, racism caused more irritation among Africans. Furedi quoting Ngugi wa Thiong'o, portrays aspects of this uneasy relationship thus:

> The Indian traders were said to be very rich. They too employed some black 'boys' whom they treated as nothing. You could never like the Indians because their customs were funny in a bad way... the Indians were not liked and they abused women using dirty words they had learned in Swahili (Furedi, 1974:349).

In small townships, the practice of Indian traders dealing with Europeans before attending to Africans (and often at separate counters) was another irritation with Asians (Ibid).

One of the most important aspects of the Afro-Asian relations in Kenya before 1939 was the widespread socio-economic change which was precipitated by the extension of the cash based market economy. This process created the context within which Africans entered the market as sellers of both raw materials and cheap labour. This was a factor which made Africans to migrate from the reserves to look for jobs as migrant labourers (Olumwullah, 1986:143). The need to earn cash to pay taxes also accelerated this move. Most of the migrant labourers were men who were employed in Asian shops and homes.

Migrant labour, however, led to changes in relations between men, women and youngmen and elders. Absence of men from the villages meant that women now became more responsible for the reproduction of the day- to-day manning of the family.

Apart from cultivating land and performing other necessary domestic chores, women engaged in petty trade to maintain their families (Cliff, 1978:339, Cokumu, 2000:113). This explains why women were the majority as far as the delivery of cotton to Asians at the cotton buying posts was concerned. Women were also involved so much in the selling of foodstuff such as vegetables and potatoes to the Asians in their homesteads. On the other hand, some became domestic workers for the Asians in places like Kisumu where they had migrated to. There was a general feeling in the reserves that it was in places like Kisumu, Muhoroni and Songhor where money to meet all the tax demands and to buy items could be found (Owiyo, O.I., 2006).

The period 1939-45 witnessed resurgence in labour exploitation reminiscent of the earlier phase of primitive colonial accumulation. It was a period characterized by new legislation that gave the colonial governor power to order the administrative functionaries to produce quotas of workers for military, essential services and sometimes even private agriculture and industry. But perhaps, of the most importance in this period was the removal of manpower from peasant economies, economies which were at the same time meant to serve as major suppliers of foodstuff and other raw materials to the metropole (Olumwullah, 1986:283).

Such substantial removal of manpower and the expansion of production for the war effort produced an explosive combination whose observable ramifications were the severe food shortages of 1942-1943 in Nyanza (Zeleza, 1989:150). This situation forced Africans to enter into very determined competition with the Indians both in the purchase of produce and retail shop trade (PC/NZA/1/34/AR 1943, PC/NZA/1/40/ AR 1945). Zeleza (1989) quoting Harold Macmillan former British premier best summarized the colonial preoccupation at the outbreak of the war when he said that:

> The immediate task of the colonial government (was) the mobilization of all potential resources of the colonial empire, both men and materials for the purpose of war... we therefore needed to increase colonial production for war purposes on an immense scale (Zeleza, 1989:145).

As the colonial production was heightened, the Asian Manpower Committee enlisted Asian volunteers for various duties during the war. These Asians volunteered as mechanics, clerks, storekeepers, drivers, artisans, carpenters and motorcyclists. The African drivers and Indian artisans responded to the call for volunteers. During this time, Afro-Asian trade in Kisumu was virtually at a standstill but later recovered slowly

160

(PC/NZA/ 3/1/467, DC/KSM/1/22/1, 1939). It is, therefore evident that the war period had an impact on the Afro-Asian relations since their interaction was affected. However, the war situation also created a condition where Asians were to meet with Africans to exchange the scarce food produce and other essential items. Afro-Asian interaction was therefore increased.

4.4 Political Participation and Afro-Asian Relations In the Inter War and During the Second World War Period 1919-45.

The major challenge that faced Kenya during this period was the future of its tri-racial population, European, Indian and African. After the World War 1, the policy of the paramountcy of European interests was intensified by Major-General Sir Edward Northey, the new Governor. The Europeans defended their segregationist policies on the ground that neither the Indian nor any other section of the community- since they were not members of the ruling race-'have the same status or can claim the same right as British colonists in a British Colony such as Kenya (Ogot, 1968:270). The Indians opposed the colonial policies of residential and land segregation. It was this European-Indian struggle for the possession of Kenya that constituted the so called 'Indian question'. This led to the declaration of the Devonshire White Paper of 1923 which gave paramountcy to the African interest. This solution to the Indian question had wider imperial implications (Ibid, 1968:270).

For years, local European settlers, affirming a right to intrusive command, had advanced claims for election rather than nomination to the Legislative Council (Legco) and the

161

Asian followed suit. Despite continued protestations, Asians were not successful in acquiring either additional membership to Legco or any representation at all on the Municipal Council. Addressing the Nairobi Indian Association which would supply the nominations, the governor refused their admittance on the pretext that his government was not satisfied that the association was yet sufficiently organised to be generally representative of the Indian community. In 1919, the Asian members of the Legislative and Municipal Councils embarked upon boycott of these bodies (Seidenberg, 1996:131).

The interwar period also witnessed the emergence of modest attempts at 'radical' politics by African proto- elites from mission schools. While some of the mission graduates were co-opted into the establishment through their participation in the Local Native Councils, the more radical proto-elites articulated the people's grievances through a variety of political-cum-welfare associations, including the Kavirondo Tax Payers Association in Nyanza (Kanogo, 1989:113).

Both the African and Indian communities reacted sharply to these discriminatory and oppressive policies. To protect their interests, the Africans formed their first political organisation almost simultaneously in Nyanza and Nairobi. Young Kavirondo Association was founded in 1921 by the former students of Maseno School such as the Rev Ezekiel Apindi, Rev Simon Nyende, Reuben Omulo, Jonathan Okwiri, Mathayo Otieno, Benjamin Owuor and Joel Omino. This was a new crop of African leaders who had acquired Western education and culture. They were out to challenge the colonial practices (Ogot, 1968:269). One had to learn the language of the postcolony in order to challenge some of its dealings.

Berman, (1974:125) argues that the educated Africans who lived outside of tribal institutions and detached from the restraints of traditional controls was to the colonial administrator an unnatural being, no longer African but certainly not European, who challenged their conception of an orderly universe in which each individual had his proper place. These Africans were, therefore, a hybrid lot within the Nyanza postcolonial sub-space.

The colonial authorities tended to view them as detribalised malcontents and no attempt was made at this time to fit them into the political structure of the colony. On the other hand, the Asian leadership comprised people such as Mangal Dass, M.A Desai, Jeevanjee, Shams-ud-deen and Suleiman Virjee (Ogot, 1968: 269). Because of shared political grievances, the Asian leadership and the enlightened Africans sometimes coped well depending on the context of the situation and various interests.

In September 1923, Archdeacon Owen consented to become the official president of the Young Kavirondo Association. He immediately changed the association's name from Young Kavirondo Association (YKA) to Kavirondo Taxpayers Welfare Association (KTWA). This followed growing fears from the government quarters following the rapid increase in settler control of the political affairs of the country and the Thuku riots of

March 1922. All these combined to alert the government to the possibility of an impending revolt. Asked why the association had to change its name, its former Chairman Jonathan Okwiri gave this answer,

> This was done on the advice of the Archdeacon Owen who persuaded us to adopt this name to identify with our aims which were now beginning to take on a new turn- that of being law abiding, peaceful citizens who were willing to pay tax and to cooperate with the government in all its efforts to bring about social advancement and general welfare to the community (Okaro-Kojwang 1969:122).

On the above issue it can be said that Archdeacon Owen's role in the association was simply seductive, aimed at directing Africans to be law abiding, obedient and loyal. This position was to make Africans accept Western forms of knowledge. However, these forms of knowledge were later resisted by the radical Africans in the form of African nationalism.

Okaro-Kojwang (1969:125) affirms that a close watch was kept by authorities over potential African political agitators. Hence freedom to move from province to province, addressing meetings was virtually impossible. No political agitator could address political rallies outside his own tribal bounds without risking instant arrest and indefinite internment.

The government was sensitive to the psychological effects upon Africans after the World War 1 and would not allow anyone to tour the countryside arousing emotional reactions against established authority. Such hurdles according to Atieno-Odhiambo (1976:228) made the Kavirondo Tax Payers Association habitual petitioners as they engaged in such activities as dispatching memoranda to the colonial office in London and petitioning the Governor and the British House of Commons whenever government officials were approachable, thereby earning the name of *jo* memorandum (people of memorandum). All the same, they had laid the groundwork for struggle, for negotiation, for protest, for liberation and for true claim to their rightful space in the postcolony.

At this point, it should be noted that Afro-Asian relations in the political circles within Nyanza Province was minimal since each community struggled to air their grievances separately. The missionaries represented African interests, while Asians were agitating to get nomination to the Kisumu Township Committee. The Administration's recognition and concerns for the collective representation of Asian interest at least in Nyanza Province was evident by the appointment in December 1928 of two prominent Asians in the planning of the bazaar (Kingoriah, 1980). Mr Dhanwant Singh and Mr Augustino J. Menezes were appointed upon the recommendation of the Kisumu Town Planning Authority members to represent Asiatic community in the re-planning of the old bazaar (KNA, NZA/3/1/467, 1939).

On several occasions, the Asian business and political lobby in the province were at loggerheads with the colonial authorities. In 1931, non –cooperation was pursued by the Indian community in matters of representation in the Township Committee; they rejected requests to elect a member of their community to the committee (Annual Report 1931).

165

By 1933, after some years of abstention from active participation in council affairs, Mr N. J. Desai, a member of Kisumu Township Committee was nominated to the Council by His Excellency the Governor (KNA, NZA/1/28 Annual report 1933).

In 1938, Rehamtulla Kassim was elected to represent the Indian electoral area in Kisumu defeating Dhanwant Singh (KNA, PC/NZA/3/1/467, 1939). However, in areas such as Ndere, Yala and Kendu Bay, the Asians never engaged in politics as such, and were much more interested in trade. Therefore, their political relationship with the Africans was minimal because they could not interact on political matters (Ogallo, Faraji, K'abong O.I., 2006). But even in Kisumu where there was active politics, political relations were for the educated elite and not just ordinary Asians and Africans.

The 1930s had thus conclusively proved that Asians had no independent power base. Kept away from land through racial segregation, debarred from higher executive posts in the British colonial service and deprived of any sense of power or the ability to alter things, the Asians became politically dull, inward –looking but commercially aggressive and isolated community, sandwiched between the imperial Europeans and the Africans and identified more easily as a Patel, Sikh, a Shah, an Ismaili rather than a Kenyan, Tanzanian or a Ugandan (Tandon 1973:3).

This situation was also aggravated by the fact that, the administrative isolation of tribes and races meant in effect that there were limited chances of the members of various ethnic groups and races developing a national awareness. National awareness or nationalism even in the rudimentary form was slow in developing in Kenya. In this context, therefore, the protest movements and agitations that arose from 1920 to 1940 were basically tribally and racially based and with specific racial grievances to be addressed (Maloba, 1989:182).

4.5 Afro-Asian Social Relations During the Inter War and Second World War Period

4.5.1 Housing

Afro-Asian housing also formed the issue around which race relations revolved in Nyanza. The policy requiring Africans (except for domestic servants) to live in segregated areas was implemented through a variety of by-laws, including those which prohibited Africans from leaving those areas at night and those which required the local authorities to erect housing in African locations. It is true therefore that Africans who arrived in town in the period before the Second World War were segregated in terms of residence (Olumwullah, 1986:186).

During the interwar period, social developments continued to be carried out along racial lines. As early as 1919, Asians operated within the Indian bazaars and shops from where they carried out business, in towns, within the rural areas such as Ndere, Yala, and Kendu Bay. Mito, an oral informant who was asked whether Asians in rural areas visited people in their homesteads said that:

> The Asians never stayed inside *gweng*, (village) they preferred
> staying in the trading centres, therefore interaction with them
> in areas of residence was minimal unless one went to their

167

shops. Asians could also not visit Africans in their rural homesteads/houses or even attend a funeral of their employee(s) or friends in the village. They would always give financial or material support in such situations (Mito, O.I 2007).

It is evident that even though the Asians never liked staying with Africans, they were still able to support them in times of need for example during the loss of a loved one. Such gestures strengthened their relationship especially with the Africans whom the employed.

In the Town Planning Committee meeting of 2nd December 1936, it was recommended that Kisumu town be divided into two zones: Asiatic and African zones. However, this was objected to by the Acting commissioner for Local Government, Lands and Settlement who cited the White Paper of 1923 in which the policy of racial segregation in townships was definitely abandoned except in the few instances where the government was required by legal commitments to maintain occupation restrictions (KNA, PC/NZA/2/18/11, 1936). It is evident here that racism and the Town planning Committee were used by the colonialist to either include or exclude identities from specific areas.

The DC Kisumu responded to the Commissioner of Local Government, Lands, and Settlement, assuring him that the Kisumu Township Committee had been under no delusion with regard to the segregation of races. The terms "European residential area" had been used merely as a convenience to describe areas which were so used. The DC further stated that, the issue of non-segregation had been raised at a meeting of the Township Committee by Mr Dhanwant Singh and upon his motion it was decided to classify the areas in the township as follows: 'Milimani' – the portion used as European residential area to the south end of the town; 'Winam'- the portion including both the Bazaar and the Indian residential area North East of Milimani, "Manyatta" – the locality of the Arab village east of 'Winam'; 'Kibuye'- the locality of the Catholic mission swimming bath east of 'Manyatta', and 'Kaloleni'- the African residential Zone south of 'Kibuye'. The segregation committee comprised of the Asians, the DC and Medical officer of Health (KNA, PC/NZA/2/18/11, 1936, 1937).

Before 1939 two interacting ideas governed the African policy of urbanization with regard to African housing. First, all housing within the town had to conform to the building rules under municipal ordinances. Second, the African population was not, as had been earlier indicated, regarded as a permanent element in town as their accommodation remained largely unanswered in this period (Olumwullah, 1986:236).

The denial of elaborate African housing was a major factor in the control of African influx into the town. Therefore, most of the Africans who stayed in towns such as Kisumu resided in servant quarters provided by their Asian employers while others worked and went back to their homes which neighboured the town. These divisions were also marks of identity of varying degrees of superiority and inferiority on the postcolonial space of Nyanza.

There was an acute shortage of Asian housing in Kisumu and this was handled by the Kisumu housing Committee. Asians living in town and working for the government were housed in the Railway Asian quarters. These quarters were overcrowded and not enough to cater for the housing needs of the Asians. This made Asians acquire houses in areas that had so far been generally accepted as the European area. A program of building quarters for government Asian servants was also in progress to alleviate the problem (KNA, PC/NZA/3/41/3/1, 1928). Because of the shortage of housing, some Asians resided in the Indian bazaars from where they carried out trade.

It should be noted that the social status of the occupiers of the Indian Bazaar largely included poor class Indians whose interests dovetailed with those of Africans and who therefore had good reasons for promoting symbiotic relationship. Their social life involved people adjusting to and surmounting the tribulations of colonial urban life (Murunga 2007:10). It is no wonder then that the Bazaar housed many Indian traders and their families. In the bazaar, you could find tailors, barbers, blacksmiths, shoemakers and *dhobis* (*Dhobi* is an Indian word meaning washerman or washerwoman).

The word *dhobi* is in common use today among Africans to refer to people who wash and dry. Africans acquired the dhobi culture from the Indians. At the bazaar Africans supplied Asians with essential foodstuffs like vegetables, tomatoes, onions and millet while at the same time gaining the skills of making shoes from the Asian cobblers (Ajay, O.I., 2007, Owino, O.I 2007).This necessity was an important basis of Afro Asian relations in the bazaar residential area.

Zoning of residential areas according to race did not prevent Afro-Asian interactions. In the Asian households, Asian women prepared *chapatis, samosa* and *bhajias* (some variants of wheat baked bread and cakes) which they sold to both Asians and Africans. Some of their dishes were incorporated into the diets of Africans (Patricia, 1984; Seidenberg, 1996:102). At Jamnadas residence in Kisumu, African children would go to the compound to eat a certain fruit which was locally known as *jamna* coined from the name jamnadas. Henceforth they would say that they were going to *kajamna* (Jamnadas place) to eat that fruit. This name has stuck with the Africans up to date (Owiyo, O.I., 2006).

With the outbreak of the World War Two, conditions for Africans with regard to income and housing were little better than they had been a decade earlier. Indeed, between the two World Wars, policies involving expenditures on housing development in the entire colony were distinctly secondary to policies involving control over the African urban population (Olumwullah, 1986:215). The government policy on both Asian and African housing was therefore not conducive in promoting Afro-Asian relations. However because of necessity, the Asians found themselves relating with Africans by employing them as domestic workers, guards and housegirls.

In the meantime, because of the political, social and economic developments which characterized this period, Stitcher (1975:36) concludes that African consciousness of the larger social structure grew as demands for higher wages and better living conditions became linked for the first time, with demand for equality with Indian and European workers and for African equality with other races generally. Class consciousness became mixed with race consciousness, and labour protest became linked with African

171

nationalism. Some of the protests in the interwar and Second World War period would later form a common front within which Afro-Asian political alliance would be forged in towards independence as will be seen in the next chapter.

4.5.2 Education

The inter-war and Second World War period saw three phases of the development of education. Phase one, 1923-28, saw the rapid spread of 'bush' and catechiscal schools that were later to develop into elementary schools. Phase two, 1929-36 saw the emergence of Independent school movement and a new emphasis on upper primary school system. Phase three 1937-1944 saw a change, following the lifting of barriers that limited African education to below secondary school levels (Ogutu, 1981:146). However, all these developments fell short of improving Afro-Asian relations in schools as they only focused on African education which was under the missionaries.

The racial approach which we have noticed in the economic and political fields also applied to the provision of other social services. Education and even sports were organized on strict racial lines, with the Europeans always getting the best services; the Indians, the second best and the Africans having to do with whatever was left over. The education policy for Africans was first enunciated by the Colonial Secretary in a command paper in 1925, which said that:

> The first task of (African) education was to raise the standard alike of character and efficiency of the bulk of the people, but provision must also be made for the training of those who are required to fill posts in the administrative and technical services, as well as those as chiefs who will occupy positions of exceptional trusts and responsibility. The aim of Asian

education was 'to provide an eight years' course of primary education for all children of six years and over (As quoted in Ogot, 1968:276).

The racial attitudes of providing quality education were also reflected in the field of funding. Despite the fact that in sheer numbers school-age African children outnumbered Europeans at any given time during the colonial period, African education received very little funding. In 1925, for example, the colonial government spent Ksh 524,835.85 on European education which represented 33% of the national budget on education as compared to Ksh 424,279.47 on African education which represented 26.6% and Ksh 23,862.68 on Indian education which represented 15% with the remaining 25.4% going to administrative costs (Kisiangani, 2003:96).Despite the demographic superiority of the African enrolment, the colonial government spent very little money on the education of individual African pupils. Looking at the per capita expenditure for the education of the different races, Kisiang;ani (2003:96) notes that less money was comparatively invested in an African pupil (lumped together with Arabs) than either the European or Asian. This discrepancy in funding seems to have underscored the colonial government's belief in the inferiority of the black people (Ibid).

The emphasis in African education on producing clerks and other junior officials for the colonial administration was thus evident as early as this period. Colonial education, which was an extension of Western education, imposed on the African mind certain binaries including those of colonizer/colonized, primitive/civilized, European/other as well as religions/superstitions. These binaristic mapping of power relations gave the

173

impression that through colonialism, civilization and modernity would flow from the centre which was the West to the periphery which was Africa. This false notion had to be forced down to the oppressed African people with the result that colonial subjects surrendered their identity to the West. In this way, education seems to have been transformed into a critical instrument for destroying the African identity (Kisiang'ani, 2003:91). Institutionalized schooling in colonial East Africa prevented the mixing of boys and girls as well as grounding the segregation of the races (Seidenberg, 1996:106).

The above developments affected Afro-Asian relations in that both communities could not attend the same schools, therefore, interaction in schools was deliberately minimized. To show that Africans, Europeans and Indians were different, the platform of difference was used in setting up a postcolony which exploited the Africans and marginalized them. Indian education was chiefly centred at Kisumu with small struggle for existence in such places as Yala, Ndere, Luanda and Kendu Bay, among other areas. Each community, for instance, Arya Samaj and Ismailia communities had and managed their own school(s) (AR 1928/30).

Such schools as Arya Samaj Girls, Ismailia Girls and Siri Guru Singh Sabha up to 1938 continued to admit pupils on strictly racial lines (Annual Report 1938). As indicated earlier, in Kendu Bay the Indian School Kendu Bay (Ismailia) was at the *Sanatan* mosque where the Asians worshipped. Only Asian children attended this school and after standard four, they went to Kisumu for higher education (Ojijo,O.I., 2006). This also

174

applied to the Indian School Yala as well as in Ndere (KNA, PC/NZA/3/642, 1939). Therefore, Afro-Asian social relations in schools were minimal in this area of study.

As government schools were inadequate, emphasis was placed on communal schools, with sectarian groups resisting amalgamation with other groups and establishing parallel educational facilities for girls along sectarian lines. Although many groups had nursery schools, formal education at the primary and secondary levels was left to the large and well-organized groups such as the Arya Samaj (for Hindus), the Visa Oshwals (for Jains), the Singh Sabha (for Sikhs) and the Shia Ismailis (for Ismailis), who eventually established complete school systems.

With their constitution, administrative and judicial institutions, hospitals, schools welfare societies, insurance companies and banks, the Shia Ismailis were often described as a "state within a state" (Seidenberg 1996:106). Because of plural nature of the Asian community within itself, and because each Asian community organized their own schools, Afro Asian interactions in this area became minimal.

4.6 Summary and Conclusion

It was the objective of this chapter to interrogate Afro-Asian relations in the inter-war and the World War II periods. We have demonstrated that these periods witnessed the emergence of rival African traders who questioned the monopoly of Asians in the economic sphere. These were carried out through organised African organisations such as the Kavirondo Welfare Taxpayers Association and the Kavirondo Chambers of

175

Commerce. The Asians also encouraged the growing of cotton in Ndere, Kisumu and Kendu Bay areas by establishing ginneries in these areas.

Although the cultivation of cotton was an initiative of the colonial government of introducing capitalist mode of production into the rural economies of Nyanza through the Asians, their attempt to introduce this crop was met with some resistance, which was evidently viewed as a subversive resistance by Africans to western forms of knowledge and values. The office of Chief was widely used to marginalize Africans and ensured that the colonial government's objective of imperialism and capitalism were achieved.

The policy of separate development and racial segregation which was at its peak during the inter-war period ensured that each community developed its own schools. Such developments were not conducive for the development of Afro- Asian relations as their interaction was limited. However, because of necessity, some of these racial barriers were overcome.

It is, therefore, evident that strict opposite binarism could not completely work within the Nyanza postcolonial sub- space. This is because there were some positive values that Africans needed from Asians and vice versa. Politics was also pursued along racial lines thereby affecting Afro-Asian political relations in Ndere, Kendu Bay and Yala. In chapter five, we examine the Afro-Asian relations within the period 1945-1963, when the struggle for independence was heightened

176

CHAPTER FIVE

5.0 THE AFRO-ASIAN RELATIONS IN LUO NYANZA IN THE PERIOD 1945-1963

5.1 Introduction

In Chapter Four we discussed Afro- Asian relations in the inter war and during the World War 11 period and argued that this period witnessed the emergence of rival African traders who questioned the monopoly of Asians in the economic sphere. We concluded that despite the racial segregation in the social places strict opposite binarism could not completely work within the Nyanza postcolonial sub space since there were values which the two communities borrowed from each other. The current chapter analyses Afro-Asian relations in Luo Nyanza from 1945-1963.The year 1945 did not simply mark the end of the World War 11; it also signalled the beginning of a new era for both the imperial metropolitan powers and the colonial world. Social and political struggles were intensifying.

The old colonial framework could no longer contain the political crisis in the colonies as African nationalism was on the rise. The years 1945- 1960s saw a rapid expansion of the agricultural sector. There was growth of secondary industries and the percentage of those in the African paid labour force rose (Ongile, 1988:3). The post-war political and economic activities were therefore to shape Afro-Asian relations in a remarkable way.

This chapter explores the impact of the independence struggle on Afro-Asian relations. It also analyses Afro -Asian relations in the cotton industry and how government involvement shaped these relations. During this time, Asians started moving towards Kisumu town away from the interior rural parts of Nyanza. Consequently, the effect of this movement in regard to the Afro-Asian relations in Kisumu is also investigated.

5.2 Afro-Asian Economic Interactions in the Period 1945-1963

The British Empire virtually disintegrated between 1945 and the late 1960s (Barley 1989:218). Through concerted international and local pressure in favour of African development, the period witnessed the reversal of colonial policies. It has been argued that in this period of Kenya's history, there was a disposition towards reforms because the political and economic strife of the colony would jeopardize the status quo of Kenya's Europeans (King'oriah 1980: 237).

As a result, the period witnessed developments at the national level, which included the enactment of the Swynnerton Plan of 1953-55 to look into land and population problems in East Africa. The East Africa Royal Commission recommended the operation of a market economy for East Africa without any racial or tribal restrictions. The effects of the commission's recommendations in towns was that it sanctioned the existing land use system but that future distribution of land would depend on the economic ability of all racial groups (King'oriah 1980:240).

There was an impressive economic growth in Nyanza province after World War II which reached its peak around 1950-1952 due to increased exports in agricultural goods. During this time, various communities made significant headways in the acquisition of land. The acquisition of land was mainly for housing developments but also in commerce, industry and education in Nyanza and more specifically in Kisumu. In the late forties, the spiritual leader of the Khoja community- the Aga Khan told his people to identify themselves with African aspirations because to him the Indians were like Africans (Farson, 1949:131). This pronouncement by the Aga Khan, which favoured acculturation, contrasted with that of other Indian communities who could not see themselves being equated to Africans (Larimore 1969:61).

In the post-war period, as the returning World War II veterans (*Jokeya*-Luo nickname for carrier corps) sought to invest their war time savings in business such as in shops, tea rooms and water mills, they found themselves placed in direct competition against the Asian traders whose primary life of accumulation had been based on collection of produce. These soldiers also came against the trading pattern that had developed over the last four decades. Such men as *Ogonji* (Govindji Karsandas Karia) had built their rural wealth by being the grain produce and cotton buyers of Ndere, Luanda, and Nambale in the inter-war years (Atieno Odhiambo, 1995).

Second, there was the racial strain with regard to the Asians. The Asians were receiving preferential treatment (being agents of colonialism), for they had the monopoly of the wholesale and retail trade. African traders were, therefore, seen to function at the mercy

179

of the Asians, since they had no capital to rival the Asians. It was against this background of frustration on the African because of the unequal economic relation which had flourished since the establishment of the economy that one must see the motive force behind the rise and emergence of African initiative in the field of trade after World War II (Ibid. 1995).

Asians in areas such as Ndere, Yala and Kendu Bay were not comfortable with Africans being given licences to do the same business in these areas where they enjoyed business monopoly. This aroused some bitterness among Africans who felt that Asians were colluding with government officers to deny them trade licences on the same category of business that Asians were also engaged in (Owino, O.I., 2007).

Several organizations such as the Kenya African Union, Central Nyanza Chamber of Commerce, the Ramogi African Welfare Association (RAWA), the Nyanza Soldiers Association, the Luo Union, together with numerous clan and sub-clan welfare organizations were formed to air African grievances and challenge the dominance of Asian traders in the rural areas. Even the defunct *Piny Owacho* (a local political organization) organization was revived (Ogot, 1999:46). These organizations represented voices of negotiation, protest and compromise on the African postcolony. They were initial avenues through which Africans wanted to take over the political and economic power of the postcolony.

At this time, one of the most prominent African commercial outfit was the Luo Thrift and Trading Company. Jaramogi Oginga Odinga was outstanding in directing the affairs of the organization. Under the motto of *Kinda e teko, Riwruok e teko* (In struggle and persistence lies unity and strength), Odinga mobilized the traders, teachers, chiefs plus other locals into the premier African enterprise of Western Kenya during this period, known as Luo Thrift and Trading Corporation. This Corporation sought to create an economic kingdom as well as a national identity for the Luo African rural folk (Atieno Odhiambo, 1995). This development seemed to be a rebellion against the Asian monopoly and the wider colonial structures and institutions. As a result, Africans began to engage in business activities that posed a real threat to Asian and European commercial activities.

The Asian stranglehold on wholesale buying and the inability of the African traders to obtain their goods in wholesale or to buy on credit, remained a significant feature of the postwar era. It was exacerbated in 1948 by the general shortage of imported trade goods and by the tendency for Asian competitors to be supplied much more readily with what little there was. Both these handicaps generated resentment among African retail traders (Kitching, 1980:180, Ogada, O.I., 2006).

The widespread resentment against Asian traders was intensified around the middle of 1948 by what was felt by Africans to be a number of particularly serious malpractices. There was a common view among Africans that Asian traders deliberately hoarded certain commodities and only sold them on the 'black market' for high prices (Furedi,

1974:351). Similarly, Afro-Asian trade rivalry was also witnessed in the distribution of maize for the Maize and Produce Control Board. In some cases where Africans were reliant on Asian mechanics to repair their vehicles used in the distribution, repairs were badly done or not done at all (Fearn, 1961:190, Owiyo, O.I., 2006). It is, therefore, evident that Asians used some forms of knowledge to undermine and dominate Africans in business.

While Africans tried to compete with Asians in produce distribution, Asian wholesalers responded to the African threat to their dominance by offering lower prices to African traders than could be obtained from the Collective Group Buyers Organization, and when such ventures had collapsed, the Asians returned to their status quo (Kitching 1980:186). Such were the Asian malpractices that Africans resented and which led to tension between the two communities.

But even though the Luo Thrift Trading Corporation Limited was a rival and counter corporation to the Asians' dominance in trade in the Nyanza area, the directors of the company still sought some help from the Asians. The Ramogi Press, whose proprietors were members of the Luo Thrift, was relocated from Nairobi to Kisumu in the year 1949. The leaders found it necessary to construct premises for the company to avoid rental increases that would have militated against its progress. This led to the construction of a new building named the 'AFRIKA HOUSE' owned by the Luo Thrift Corporation.

During the opening ceremony of this house in July 1956, the managing director of the corporation, Oginga Odinga applauded the Asians who supplied materials for the construction of the house. These included M\s Shamji Harji and Bro limited, M\s E.A Hardwares Limited, M\s Narshi Laxman Bros, M\s Surat Furniture Mart, M\s Dean Brothers and M\s Teja Singh and Sons, (all Asians) who had been assisting considerably (KNA,PC\NZA\3\1\404, 1955-57). This support by Asians depicted the ambivalent nature of subjects within the postcolony.

The Luo Thrift Company also built Ramogi House which they leased to an Asian for a period of two years and operated as a cosmopolitan hotel under the business name 'Imperial Hotel' suggesting imperial and colonial aspirations through the Asians (KNA,PC\NZA\4\4\47, 1950). Names such as Afrika House, Ramogi House suggest the aspirations of Africans to maintain their identity and traditional value systems which vastly differed from the Western values.

The period under review also witnessed a concerted effort by the Asian traders to acquire licenses from the Nyanza Liqour Licensing Board in Kisumu to sell liquor to 'natives' in the various trading centres. For instance, Mr V.N Badiani the proprietor of the Nyanza Trading Company who operated a shop on Odera Street in Kisumu, applied for a license in Kisumu from the Liquor Licensing Board, on the basis of the fact that he already had this grocery shop on plot 65 (DC\KSM\1/19\302, 305).

Beyond Kisumu, Asians also operated some of the liquor stores and shops or businesses under local names such as Asembo Trading Stores based in Asembo Bay owned by Premilav Patel. However, the naming of business enterprises using local names by Asians would suggest that Asians wanted to give Africans a false sense of ownership. And this is the confusing nature of a postcolony.

Nikanor Aduda Owuor, an African liquor merchant from Ndere rivalled Vallabhdas Govindji who operated Lucky Trading Stores and who had also applied for a licence to sell non-spirituous liquor in the area. In a letter to the chairman of the Liquor Licensing Board, Aduda Owuor complained that he had already been licensed to sell beer at Ndere and given that Ndere was such a small place, it was going to be uneconomical to issue two licences for the same trade. For this reason, he lodged an objection against Govindji's application and suggested its consideration at the next meeting of the Liquor Licensing Court (DC/KSM/1/19/280, 1952-53).

The basic argument here is that, competition enhanced the ability of the Asian and African communities to learn how to bargain within the market place as well as shape their relationships. This kind of contestations and competition disintegrated the walls of Asian domination. But on the other hand, Nikanor Aduda represented, as Aschcroft would say, subdued African voices which had been recovered in the postcolonial sub-space of Nyanza (Ashcroft, 1989:178).

5.3 Afro-Asian Relations, the Government and the Cotton Industry in Nyanza

After the World War II, there was a boom in demand for agricultural produce. But also, the rate of migration from the reserves to town was also higher in subsequent years during and after World War II. This was due to the modernization of European agriculture and the establishment of secondary industries in the colony.

The World War II period created conditions favourable to these developments (Olumwullah, 1986:157). The proprietors of the cotton ginning industries urged both the PC and the Provincial Agrarian Development Officer that it was necessary to boost cotton production especially in the Central Kavirondo cotton belt (i.e Alego, North Ugenya, South Ugenya, Asembo area and Manyala). By 1947, through the instructions of the Senior Agricultural Officer, the Kenya Industries supplied cotton seed to Africans for planting in Seme (Kombewa) area (KNA, PC\NZA\2\12\133).

After the War, the government again took a keen interest in the growing of cotton which led to the establishment of two bodies, the Nyanza Province Cotton Committee and the Cotton Lint and Seed Marketing Board (CLSMB) which came into existence in 1948 and 1955, respectively (PC/NZA/2/12/133). The Nyanza Cotton Committee set up in 1948 to report on the redundant ginneries recommended that Ndere ginnery be closed because of lack of cotton and serious soil erosion.

185

Similarly, it recommended the closure of South Kavirondo and Kibos ginneries because of their small sizes (KNA, PC/NZA/2/12/133). However, the director of Ndere ginnery objected to its closure arguing that cotton was grown in Alego area only because of the existence of the ginnery (KNA, AK/11/91 1941-1952). The decline of cotton production therefore had a great impact on the Afro-Asian interaction since their frequency of meeting and interaction at the cotton buying stores reduced (Mbudi, O.I., 2006).

These two cotton committees comprised both Asian and African members and were charged with the general development of cotton production in Nyanza. Their function also included domestic marketing and export processing and distribution of cotton (KNA, PC/NZA/3/2/83 1951-9, KNA, AK/11/151, 1957-60, KNA, PC/4/4/72 AR 1959). The new colonial arrangements would later affect Afro-Asian interactions. This is because Africans were the main growers while Asians bought the produce from the Africans.

Despite the fact that the relationship between Asians and Africans in trade seemed cordial to some extent, there were instances when Africans felt exploited by the Asians within the cotton industry. S.K Winter, the District Agricultural Officer, Central Kavirondo, wrote to the Executive Officer of Nyanza Cotton Committee over cotton buying and stated that although the organization of cotton buying was the most important operation of cotton cultivation, the growers had raised two vital concerns, that is, control of cheating in weights at buying centres of buying agents and inconvenient locations of the buying stores.

186

It was necessary for the buying stores to be conveniently placed in easily accessible places. The District Agricultural Officer further stated that although the Locational Advisory Council (LAC), which tried to control this cheating, posted certain African elders to every buying store, the LAC , the Agricultural Development Committee or the government did not pay these elders. This left them unaccountable and consequently, the growers argued that Indians bribed African elders thereby authorizing and encouraging cheating. These elders were therefore considered more dangerous to the trade. Perhaps, if these elders had been remunerated by the Locational Advisory Committee, they could have served their purpose well (KNA, AK\11\151, 1957-60). So corruption was also a feature of the postcolony.

It is evident that African elders charged with the responsibility of controlling this vice were a mimicry of the Asians since they encouraged this exploitative vice. Thus African elders acquired some corrupt values from Asians. Such malpractices were however detested by Africans at the various cotton buying centres. For instance, in 1960, Mr Howard Luck the Provincial Inspector of Weights and Measures for Nyanza found weighing instruments belonging to the Kenya Industries (Asian ginning factory) which had been tampered with in Kisumu and Ndere respectively (AK/11/151, 1957-60). From the above observation, it may be argued that the losers in this kind of relationship were the African growers while the Asians got huge profits. These were some of the causes of Afro-Asian conflict in the Nyanza region.

Towards independence, the Cotton Lint and Seed Marketing Board considered the possibility of using its funds to extend loans to cooperative societies to purchase cotton-buying stores from Asian ginners and for investment into cotton ginneries. This move was to create, open and increase participation of African growers in the cotton industry. This led to the formation of cooperatives such as Rachuonyo, Siaya and Victoria Cotton Cooperative Unions. This probably marked the beginning of change of ownership in the cotton industry which later affected Afro- Asian relations (KNA, BV/14/203, 1963-4).

Asians started to consider selling these ginneries to Africans as they prepared to leave the rural areas of Ndere, Yala and Kendu Bay and the entire country in general due to political uncertainty during this time. This had some consequences. One, the Afro –Asian interaction in the ginning factories was threatened, and second, Asians started relocating from rural areas to town centres like Kisumu.

The encouragement of African cooperatives by the government adversely affected Asian interest in the cotton industry. This was also accelerated by political awareness of Africans demonstrated through their vehement demand for participation in the processing of cotton. All these developments alongside Africanization program led to the Asian withdrawal from the cotton industry thereby affecting Afro-Asian interaction in Nyanza Province.

Two significant issues, namely, the marketing of the African produce and the role of the Asians in the distribution of the same remained very crucial to Afro-Asian relations.

Correspondence between the DC Central Nyanza Mr. T.A Watts and Chief Amoth of Siaya, Alego location, on the marketing policy, indicated that an efficient marketing system was essential for the disposal of the crops grown in the district given that the marketing system in the location was not very good. According to the DC, one contributory factor was the lack of encouragement from the Chief to the African traders to participate in the marketing of produce (KNA,AE/3/1961,1960   KNA, DC/KSM/1/3/48 1951).

Consequently, Indian traders especially at Ndere market took control of most of the trade. Perhaps this explains why in March 1960, Mr Owalla Owino, the president of Central Nyanza Chamber of Commerce requested the Ministry of Commerce and Trade to establish a common market and free trade. He also requested the same ministry to provide any expert advice to assist African traders. Generally, the African business community in Nyanza felt that they were not obtaining a reasonable share of the potential trade in the marketing of agricultural produce (KNA, AE/3/961, 1960   KNA, DC/KSM/1/3/48 1951). This was therefore a protest by African representatives and a call for an equal opportunity as far as marketing of agricultural produce was concerned in Nyanza postcolonial space.

It is therefore evident that Afro-Asian relations were characterized by a lot of competition for economic space within the Nyanza postcolonial sub-space. Such competitions and contestations formed the basis of African nationalism. But also we see the imperial and capitalist agenda in the institutions created by the colonial government to control and market African produce. According to Zwanenberg (1975:223), colonial institutions such as the Cotton Lint and Seed Marketing Board ensured security and efficiency of the colonial government. Money from such institutions formed part of the much needed revenue for the protectorate government. Government support of African cooperative unions therefore affected Afro-Asian relations that marked ensuing change of ownership of the cotton ginning in the rural areas.

5.4 Afro –Asian Interaction and Political Participation in Nyanza 1945-63.

The demand for independence by Africans must be seen in the light of the need for democratic rule. Alien rule was hated, but above that there was the desire to participate in the government process, to influence decisions and policies, and to have a local government in the hands of the locals who would be accountable to the citizens for their actions.

Arbitrary rule, which was characteristic of colonial rule, was loathed because it was essentially an exercise of power without consultation or restraint. At the heart of colonial rule was the premise that the state and the subjects did not have identical aims, and since the state 'knew better', it discharged its responsibility of forceful guidance while the subjects were to follow meekly and gratefully (Maloba, 1995: 16). Politically, colonialism was a dictatorship. It was imposed by violence and maintained by violence, and anything between the oppressors and the oppressed according to Fanon (1967:65) could only be solved by force. Socially, it was racist and it economically linked Africa tightly to the world capitalist system dominated by Europe.

Guided by the World War II years when the barriers to social change began slowly to erode away, the politics of a new national identity gradually replaced airtight ethnic allegiances. Against a background of hard colonial intransigence to change, by 1945, the African political agenda had altered. The Kenya African nationalist movement was taking shape as Asians, pulled along by the tide in India as well as Africa, began to envision a new future.

New strategies were being developed that would lead in the direction of the militant protests of the 1950s and 60s (Seidenberg, 1996). The tendency for the colonial system to arrange people on racial lines began to collapse when Asians joined hands with Africans to fight Europeans. Racial discrimination was thus a European discourse aimed at marginalizing non-Europeans. So on the postcolony relations are not also permanent. They are fluid. In the past Asians supported Europeans but now they seem to support Africans thus showing the chaotic nature of the postcolony.

Atieno-Odhiambo's (1981:87-8) distinction of five groups among the Asian community at this point is very important in comprehending the role of Asians in politics and their relations with Africans both nationally and locally in Nyanza Province. The largest group, for him, was made of petty traders, the *dukawallahs,* who kept aloof from politics. The second group comprising clerks, employees of the railway and harbour organization and the banks was the most politically minded while the third class made of artisans often supported the second.

The fourth and fifth classes dominated the leadership roles and comprised lawyers and professional politicians, respectively. Atieno Odhiambo argues that the "low standard of commercial integrity" of its large class of petty traders trumped the rapport that the more politically inclined Asians had with Africans. The political agitation was kept up by lawyers and professional politicians for example, D.B, Kholi, I.E Nathoo, while the petty traders like Ghulam Ali, Mohamed Hassan who formed the majority in Yala, Ndere and Kendu Bay remained apathetic.

During 1945 to the time of political independence in Kenya, the Asian political class was embittered by a series of regulations which marked the beginning of strict control of Asian immigration into the colony. As a result, Asians began to form an alliance with the African elites. They hoped that the two communities, if united, would be more effective in combating common grievances against colonial rule and European supremacy. By 1946, Asian aims were to converge with the growing African political forces, thereby opening the door to joint Afro–Asian agitation for increased representation on the legislative council, universal suffrage, and the removal of the colour bar from all aspects of colonial life (Seidenberg, 1996:150).

Again alliances kept switching on the postcolonial terrain as interests converge or conflict between the various players. In late 1947, a bill was finally raised for debate in the Legislative Council, and a few months later, the Immigration (control) Ordinance, 1948 requiring the closure of the colony to future Indian immigration became law (Makhan,

192

1969:7). This was probably to reduce the number of Asian dissenting voices within the postcolony. Those in favour of restricting a further influx of Indians alleged that food scarcities, a housing shortage due to an Indian population explosion and an influx of unemployed Asian artisans necessitated new controls (Seidenberg 1996: 142).

To some extent, national politics influenced local politics in Nyanza. However, at the local level, Afro-Asian political interaction was a matter of class interaction and relations between the African and Asian educated and political elites. These class relations went beyond opposite binarism created by the colonial racial system and structure.

At the national level, the period opened with racial tensions between settler Europeans, Asians and Africans. Asian political activities were conditioned by the consolidation of the new African nationalist interests including the development of the Kenya African Union. But more important was the fact that the Asian press, centred around the Colonial Printing Works, became the Asians' official news agency as well as a focus of African political expression. Indeed, the *Colonial Times* probably played a bigger part than any other newspaper in championing the cause of African independence (Seidenberg 1996:151-153).

Mbembe (2001:31) postulates that beginning with the high age of colonialism, 'power and authority' were founded on illiberal grounds that systematically shunned decent notions of right. In the colony, the dominated "had no rights against the state. He/she was bound to the power structure like a slave to the master". The colonial government restricted African political activities to district level. This restriction, however, laid a better foundation for Afro-Asian political alliance.

The government encouraged the Africans to air their political demands through the local institutions (Ogot, 1995:52). The idea of restricting African political activities to the district level was designed to ensure that the colonized acted within the colonial political structures which denied them the right of equal participation and representation. The Afro-Asian political alliance and activities were therefore a subversive resistance to colonialism and a means of achieving political freedom.

A number of African vernacular newspapers began to emerge, many of them printed by the Asian owned presses and backed by Indian finance. For instance, Pranlal Sheth a close ally of Oginga Odinga contributed immensely in the *Ramogi* Press's Kiswahili publications after moving to Kisumu from Nairobi where he worked as Odinga's right hand man. Described by Kenya's first Vice-President Jaramogi Oginga Odinga as 'the fire which burns behind the scenes that cooks the food for the people to eat', Sheth wrote first for the *Chronicle* and then *Ramogi,* a weekly edited by the late Achieng Oneko.

With Odinga, Sheth wrote several influential articles on African development, helping to formulate policy regarding the future of Kenya. He also urged Asians to support Africans in their struggle for land and freedom (Rattansi, 2004:21, Seidenberg, 1996:166). So as identities and postcolony changes, the tools of bargain and struggle also changed on the postcolony. In this case the press became an important instrument of liberation struggle.

In Nyanza, there was unease about the political situation, regarding the difficult road to independence. The DC Central Nyanza reported that the clan system of the Africans and particularly of the Luo ethnic group remained as strong as ever and many of the then administrative problems arose out of inter-clan jealousies and disputes (KNA, PC/NZA/4/4/119 AR 1954).

Because of the clan jealousies where *milango* (Headman) was chosen through lineage system, the British government had to resort to a system where the headmen could be chosen territorially (Ogot, 1999:44). The colonial administrators were appointed and not elected and therefore owed their allegiance to foreign centres of power represented in the colonies by governors. This colonial arrangement denied local people, both Asians and Africans, a chance to engage in elective politics. Another feature of the postcolony in its formal status was lack of democracy. Leaders were handpicked not because of competence but because of support of the colonial system.

In May 1949, the African labour movement was made more effective as a political pressure group when Makhan Singh consolidated Kenya's various trade unions under one umbrella organization- the East African Trade Union Congress (EATUC). This created a new and a potential avenue for the representation of African labour interests hitherto limited to local level organizations (Makhan, 1969:126). At the beginning of the 1950s, political positions hardened, with the white settlers talking of partition, which was followed by the Declaration of the State of Emergency from 1952-60 (Burgman, 1990).

195

In 1954, the Kenya government decided to increase the number of nominated Africans in the legislative council, and in May and June of that year, elections and nominations for the council were held. Since Africans were still regarded as unprepared for direct elections, selections for nomination by the governor were made by an Electoral College system. The Provincial Advisory Nomination College then voted by secret ballot in order to submit a list of names to the Governor. As a result of the 1954 elections in Central Nyanza, F.W Odede was nominated to represent the district (Ogot 1999:48). The colonial government allowed limited African political activities throughout the country by 1955.

There was permission to form district based organizations in which Africans were to learn the complexities of government before aspiring for national politics. The political reforms by the administration in 1955 were aimed at engaging African political energies at the local level. These reforms naturally pointed to a slow growth of African nationalism, controlled tightly by the administration. It was in this spirit that the Lyttelton Constitution of 1954, which was meant to regulate and control African political consciousness and growth, was proposed (Maloba, 1989:191). These political reforms would later affect Afro-Asian political relations within the postcolonial space of Nyanza.

In the meantime, Afro-Asian political relations started to take a new dimension at the national level, which of course, affected relations at the local level in Nyanza. The twenty fourth open session of the Kenya Indian Congress held in Nakuru in 1956 marked a turning point in Asian-African relations. In his second presidential address N.S Mangat, echoed the concerns of the majority present, jittery over the country's precipitous slide towards independence. Invoking the familiar Swahili saying, *asante ya punda ni mateke* (the appreciation of a donkey is a kick). Mangat executed a complete U- turn in official Congress policy- advising the Asians to unite with the settlers. He stated:

> We have often flattered ourselves by claiming that we have supported African aspirations. We started doing this probably before the Africans knew what their aspirations were. Whether that is so or not the fact remains that today there are undercurrents in Africa going by the various names of nationalism, Africanism or tribalism. Good luck to any African tribe which is sociologically evolving itself into a nation. But to aid and abet those who are trying to reduce the Europeans to the same level as the Africans is to court our own disaster. It would be a tragedy, for us of all people, if the British lion in Kenya dies of ass's Kick (Mangat, 1956:11 Mangat, N.S The Presidential Address delivered at the 24th Open session, Kenya Indian Congress, Nakuru 4, 5, 6 Aug).

Reversing in a few minutes the Asian political achievements of the last fifty years, he concluded: 'the time has come when we should declare an end to our fifty years feud with European community and bury the hatchet. Again, the chaotic political terrain on the postcolony does not follow well-defined straight forward lines. Here again there is a switch of loyalty to join the 'enemy' camp and abandon Africans. Mangat's declaration changed Afro-Asian political relations at the national level. This influenced Afro-Asian socio-political relations at the local level

In 1958, the African District Councils began to operate in the rural areas. Presentations were made for the election of members of the municipal board of Kisumu in place of the then arrangement by which they were nominated by the government (the governor).

While negotiating for their own interest in the Nyanza postcolonial space, the Asian and African members of the municipal board declared that, their communities preferred elections and wanted the European members to respect the wishes of their community. The Indian Association representatives met the Minister for Local Government, Health and Town Planning Mr Havelock over this issue, before the minister met representatives of other African and European communities (KNA, PC/NZA/4/6/2 ,1951-59 26/5/1958).

During this time, the Asian community had become increasingly fearful for its future, finding itself between a rock and a hard place as anti-Asian feelings spread among Europeans and Africans alike. On the one hand, Asians were accused of fence-sitting by the Europeans who hoped that the Asians would have thrown their support behind them. So Asians had different identities to the Europeans and to the Asians, identities which made their acceptability untenable. On the other hand, Africans began excluding them from their own organizations. Additional problems to be confronted by Asians included a new spate of attacks by Africans. Although the State of Emergency had ended officially in November 1959, sporadic attacks against Asians particularly *dukawallahs* in the rural areas of Ndere in Nyanza were reported in the press, thus reviving tension between African and Asian traders (*East African Standard* 21, Dec 1969).

By 1960, Kisumu had changed from the status of a municipal board to a municipal council (KNA, HT/17/3 Annual Report 1960-65). Henceforth, Asian involvements were felt in the activities of the council. This is exemplified by the participation of Mr M.F Shah, Mr M.P Ondiek (Mayor of Kisumu) and the DC in the activities of the Allocations of Plots (African location) Committee. Their business was to approve African applications for plots within the town for business and residential purposes. Mr. M.F Shah even chaired some sessions of the committee meetings (KNA, DC/KSM/1/30/ 53 1959). Thus a compromise to work together between Asians and Africans together was emerging.

In August 1960, a leading organ of political agitation- Kenya African National Union (KANU), announced that its membership would be "Monoracial." Later, Tom Mboya, the Secretary General of KANU remarked at a congress meeting in October that the resolutions, statements and ideas of support from the Indians in Kenya did not mean much to Africans who questioned "just what these people have done and what they intend to do to assist in the struggle for independence" (Seidenberg 1996:172).

Like Mangat for Asians in Nakuru, Mboya was also pouring scorn on Asians on behalf of Africans. The chaotic plural postcolony was manifest as positions kept on changing. Such statements caused concern to Asians in the interior parts of Nyanza especially, Ndere, Yala and Asembo and some of them started to relocate to Kisumu fearing that, at Independence, Africans would rise against Indians because of the spite Asians had shown towards them. Asians also feared attacks from Africans since the colonial system which gave them protection was also on the verge of relinquishing power to Africans (Muganda, O.I., 2006).

Asian anxiety was further exacerbated by events which took place in the Congo. In June 1960, after the Belgian Government abruptly withdrew its presence, a complete breakdown of law and order occurred. War broke out among various ethnic factions and many people were killed, including Asians (Bennet & Rosberg, 1961:200). Asians were therefore very uncertain about their security in Kenya and feared that the political situation could get out of control.

It should be noted that despite the involvement of some categories of Asians in politics in the towns, the Asian *dukawallas* and traders in Kendu Bay, Yala and Ndere never engaged in local politics in those areas. However, whatever happened at the national level affected their relationship with the Africans at the local level thereby causing racial tension and suspicion between the two communities. This is what characterized the postcolonial relations of power as independence approached. This 'independence' was actually the Africanization of colonialism. Africans as Mbembe (2001:103) puts it, sought to institutionalize themselves and to achieve legitimation and domination.

Maseno (O.I., 2007), however, states that in Yala, Indians were just busy with their businesses selling merchandise to the locals. His remark is also supported by A. Asif, an Asian whose father owned a plot and a hardware at Yala trading centre. There were no situations when Asians mobilized Africans politically or when Africans mobilized Asians politically to either participate in a political rally or otherwise.

At the grassroot level especially in Yala, Ndere and Kendu Bay, Afro-Asian political activities were missing thus affecting their political relations with Africans. This could be attributed to the fact that most Indians who were in these areas were mostly traders and *dukawallas* (Maseno, O.I., 2005, Malit, O.I 2006). In Kisumu, given the existence of a class of professional politicians and lawyers, the agitation was lively but each racial group concerned itself with the improvement of the lot of their group at the municipal council.

The year 1961 was an active one for Nyanza and Kisumu in particular and the main political event was the general election in February. This led to the election of leaders such as Oginga Odinga, F. W Odede and Argwings Kodhek who were elected to represent Central Nyanza District while I.E Nathoo and D.B Kholi represented the Kisumu municipality (KNA, HT/17/3, AR 1961 Central Nyanza District). Before the end of the year, I. Nathoo left for Britain. Six months after Nathoo's departure, an election was called and Amir Jamal contested and won on a KANU ticket (*Daily Nation*, 2/2/1990). Jamal says that,

> With the blessings of the former Vice President Oginga Odinga and the late Tom Mboya who at times used to address my campaign rallies, I waded through the swampy challenges into parliament. I'm still grateful for the confidence the locals had in me (Daily Nation, 2/2/1990 p18).

Jamal's win could be said to have come from a combined effort of the former Vice President and Tom Mboya thereby showing how much support Asian politicians needed from African politicians. Jamal had to shed off the Asian racial tag and wear an African tag in order to identify with Africans and their aspirations. Racial binaries therefore had little role to play.

By 1962, the Municipal Council of Kisumu continued to reflect on its dealings during the year that atmosphere of inter-racial harmony, which was experienced in the preceding year. And in July of the same year, councilors Ondiek and Bashir Ud –Deen (an Asian) were re-elected as Mayor and Deputy Mayor respectively for a second term of office. In October, the council obtained added dignity by the elevation of councilors Ondiek, Bashir Ud – Deen, and M.F Shah to an aldermanic bench (members of the council). This event produced pleasurable reactions from councilors of all races (KNA, HT/17/3 AR Central Nyanza District 1962).

With the above developments, it is evident that political relations were between a certain class of people and not ordinary Africans and Asians. Suffice it, therefore, to say that Afro-Asian economic and political relations went beyond opposite binaries and class interests superseded racial interests in the Afro-Asian relations. Petty Asian *dukawallahs* interacted at the same level with the African villagers while the Asian political elite interacted with African political elites.

Locally, 1962 was the year of preparation for constitutional change for the administration of regions and towns to fit the concept of regionalism agreed up at Lancaster House. The basic issue at the Lancaster House was the structure of government which independent Kenya should assume. Both the Kenya African National Union (KANU) and the Kenya African Democratic Union (KADU) were basically agreed on the creation of a democratic, capitalist society (Ochieng', 1989:204).

In the same year, after a common voting roll had been introduced to Kenya, the Indian Congress decided, with some disagreement, to withdraw from participating in all public political actions. Any assertion of united Indian interest was judged to be unwise at the time. The motive behind this move was basically fear and uncertainty of their future in Kenya. Thus, Indians in Kenya, who had acted in the political field as a partly corporate community since the end of World War One voluntarily decided that it would be sensible for them to cease acting as a social group and become merely a category of the population (Morris 1968:145, Anyumba 1995).

The Asian decision meant that they would not participate in Kenyan local politics as a social group/community but as individuals. During the 1962 Lancaster House conference, Amir Jamal, an Asian who was to become the first Kisumu Member of Parliament in independent Kenya participated alongside other Africans (Daily Nation, 2/2/1990). As independence approached, politics within KANU began to polarize. One wing consisted of Oginga Odinga, Bildad Kaggia, Achieng Oneko, J.D Kali and Pio Gama Pinto and their political associates. These were the radicals. The other wing of KANU consisted of conservatives led by Jomo Kenyatta, Tom Mboya and James Gichuru (Ochieng, 1989:206).

By 1963, the general elections were the highlight of the political year. In Nyanza Province, election results for the districts showed that D.O Makasembo went for the senate. In the House of representative was John Odero Soi for Ugenya, Luke Obok for Alego, Tom Okello Odongo for Kisumu Rural, Amir Jamal an Asian for Kisumu Town and Okuto Bala for Nyando. In the regional assembly, were Omondi Opudo for Kisumu Town and Elisha Wagude for Kisumu Rural (HT/17/3 1963 AR Central Nyanza District 1963). Jamal Amir had just been re-elected Member of Parliament for Kisumu Town. For a second time, three powerful Africans including Walter Fanuel Odede had fallen yet again to this man in the 1963 General elections (*Daily Nation* 2/2/1990). This means that the interests of the voters on the postcolonial space went beyond racist concerns.

According to Owiyo (O.I., 2006), many Africans wondered how a *muindi* (Indian) who knew very little Dholuo could beat Luos in their own home. Jamal had a daunting task of convincing majority blacks to vote for him. This is because his opponents, at every political rally emphasized the point that blacks must be led by fellow black people.

However, Jamal's argument during his campaigns was different. He questioned whether the racial issue should strike a valley between the minority Asians and blacks. To him, the two could live together in harmony. He pleaded with the African voters by telling them that, "My dear brothers, my own father came here young and innocent. I was born here. My colour, my race does not make me different. We are all brothers. I love you all. I love Kisumu. I know no other home (*Daily Nation*, 2/2/1990)".

During his campaigns in Kisumu, he used both Kiswahili and *Dholuo*. Even though he knew little *Dholuo*, he frequently used Kiswahili and sometimes English. Were Olodhe was his interpreter in situations where he could not articulate issues properly in Dholuo (*Daily Nation*, 2/2/1990). Jamal was, therefore, able to use captivating words to lure African votes thereby confirming that language is power because words construct reality (Ashcroft, 1989:89).

In the run up to independence, and taking the policy of+6 exclusionary African organizations as a warning that there would be no place for them in an African dominated state, many skeptical Asians decided to get out of Kenya to Britain. A massive transfer of capital out of the colony occurred – not to India or Pakistan but to London, mostly remitted by Asians (Seidenberg, 1996).

According to Berman (1990:91), both the Europeans and the Asians had personal and organizational links with individuals and groups in Britain, while the representatives of metropolitan mercantile capital in the colony were linked to their head offices and to the chambers of commerce and other business associations in the metropole, which pressed their respective views directly in parliament and the colonial office and served as alternative channels of information. This was the action taken by Asians with the emergence of a new political dispensation towards African independence.

It is important to note that European colonialism was merely Africanized after independence with all colonial institutions and values remaining intact but secured by black. This meant that Afro-Asian relation which was in most cases capitalistic was not going to be based on a purely colonial racial structure within the Nyanza postcolonial subspace. These developments affected their social lives with Africans in Ndere, Yala and Kendu Bay.

5.5 The Afro-Asian Social Interaction 1945-1963

5.5.1 Education

Between 1945 and 1963, Kenya was a society stratified by race. Social status was still largely determined by skin colour and racial group identification. Europeans stood at the apex of this structure as a privileged class. Below the whites in the colonial social hierarchy came the Asians and the Arabs. The African majority occupied the bottom ranks of the social ladder. As in most such class systems, segregation by race was a part of the Kenyan social system. The result of legal mandates and colonial social practice, schools, hospitals, clubs and various restaurants and hotels reserved admittance to selected racially determined clientele (Maxon, 1995:110).

The racially stratified social structure was particularly evident in the areas of occupation, income and education. Educational inequality formed an obvious and important indicator of the racial structure. Colonial education in Kenya was not only characterized by segregated schools, but also, as in other parts of the world where racial segregation was practiced, inherently unequal.

African children had fewer educational opportunities than either Europeans or Asians. But as discussed elsewhere in this work, the Asian caste system also played a role towards segregating Africans from their schools. As indicated elsewhere in this work, the colonial state spent much more per pupil on the latter than on Africans. This meant that, on the whole, the educational facilities provided for Europeans and Asian children were far superior to those available to Africans (Rothchild, 1973:54, Maxon, 1995:111).

Asians in Kendu Bay had a separate school for their children. However, an African teacher was employed to teach them arithmetic. This was probably to prepare them for the capitalist lifestyle that the community was used to. No African child attended this school at all. This school was just a single corrugated iron structure which stood within the mosque compound (Faraji, O.I., 2006). Asian children were never allowed to play with African children and after school Asian children went back to their houses. This exclusive tendency could be viewed as an attempt by Asians to prevent their children from acquiring some African cultural values which they felt were not good to their children. This act formed the basis of Afro-Asian prejudices and stereotypes which characterized Afro-Asian relations. These prejudices, authored by the by West were passed on from one generation to another, given that Asian children were raised with knowledge that they were not supposed to mix with Africans.

In Ndere, the Asian community used a small plot (100x 50m) to construct a simple Indian Nursery school which catered for the education of their children. This school was situated within the compound of the current Oseno Komolo Primary School (Ondiallo, O.I., 2006, Mbeya, O.I., 2006). The Indian community was prepared to put up a suitable school building and had applied for the survey of a plot for the Indian public school site at Ndere trading centre (KNA, PC/NZA/3/14/241, 1956-8, 4/10/58).

In Yala also, racial segregation was evident in the Afro-Asian relations. The school which the Asians built was purely for Asian children where they were taught in their own mother tongue. This school is currently the Yala Township Primary School (Odwa, O.I., 2006, Ravalia, O.I., 2006).

Owing to the difficulty of obtaining schools offering upper primary education for their children in rural areas, a large number of Asians migrated from rural Nyanza to Kisumu in the 1950s. Some of the areas affected by the Asian migration included Ndere, Yala, Kendu Bay, Kibigori and Kisii. The Government Asian Schools Committee, therefore, recommended that Asian students be allowed to stay in Kisumu where municipal camps were available. Some children also moved in Kisumu to stay with their relatives so as to attend school.

However, some families also moved with their children and stayed in rented houses and shops in Kisumu so that their children could attend school (Ochieng', O.I., 2005). Kisumu also possessed boarding facilities and since the Lohana community kept admissions open for other communities at the boarding facility, the committee had no objection to allowing such children to join the primary school (KNA, DC/KSM/1/10/10, 1931-56). The point here is that racial prejudices characterized the education system and did a lot of damage to Afro-Asian relations in school. Similarly, the plurality of the Asian community also ensured that each community whether Arya Samaj, Khoja, Ismailia among others pursued their own education interests. This not only made interaction among the various Asian communities difficult but also made accessibility to these schools by Africans impossible.

The movement of Asians from the rural areas to Kisumu to seek education marked the period of the development of Asian hostels. By 1958, the Aga Khan community seriously considered the issue of hostel accommodation for Asian children from remote areas of Nyanza Province because the Aga Khan Mixed Primary School only catered for the education interests of Aga Khan (Ismailia) community (AR 1958). The issue of separate and segregated school system was sustained into the independence era before the African government came up with the policy of integration in public schools (Omollo, O.I., 2005).

Before then, the confinement of Asian children to their respective community boarding facilities affected their interaction with African children. The Indian segregation policy in schools was reinforced by the official colonial policy of separate development among races in which even Indians never attended European schools. Segregation meant the races lived in perpetual suspicion of each other thereby posing no threat to Europeans colonialism. The same principle applied to housing

In general, the Indian community developed its own communal schools with the increasing help of the government. Nevertheless, whatever was taught in the African schools was determined by the missionaries and the government. Culturally, colonialism operated from the racist principle that barbarism pervaded Africa and there was no culture to be salvaged.

Missionaries in their evangelical duties championed this outlook and in some cases succeeded in replacing them with the Western European culture. This racial school system was, therefore, meant to serve a purpose of cultural imperialism. Even though colonialism laid the foundation of racial antagonism between Indians and Africans, it can also be argued that the caste prejudices among Indians also contributed to Asians' general unwillingness to mix with the African population who were viewed as belonging to the lowest caste.

5.5.2 Housing

By 1947, the position regarding housing of the African labourers in Kisumu was not satisfactory (KNA, CS/8/11/134 1939-54, KNA, DC/KSM/1/30/53, 1957). The crisis of housing in areas like Ndere, Yala and Kibos was not very acute given the nature of the centres in which they worked and resided. In Ndere for instance, the Asians acquired land and built a ginnery as well as shops within the trading centre.

While some of them continued to stay within the ginnery area others stayed in the backyard of shops within the trading center. These shops were about six in number and each Asian trader exclusively stayed with their families. Such shops were in the neighbourhood of African village homes, hence there was no mixing up of accommodation. Their point of interaction was in the shop when Africans came to buy items like clothes, blankets and soap (Ondiallo, O.I., 2006).

Suffice it to say that within the shopping centre Asians had servants quarters where their African domestic workers could stay. The latter were the only people housed by Asians (Mbeya, O.I., 2006). Asians also built some houses opposite the Ndere ginnery where they stayed. These houses bore the Asian architectural designs quite different from that of the local but which Africans never copied. These designs ensured that all family members stayed in the same house, which was against African traditional values. Perhaps this could be the reason why the Africans failed to copy the Asian housing designs.

With this kind of interaction, the colour bar introduced by the colonial government also affected Afro-Asian relations. Asians had a stake in colour bar (*kala ba*) and dished it out on Africans with impunity. With colour bar came arrogance, experienced most acutely by 'houseboys' (*boyi*) who were *shenzi* in English and *suthru* in Hindi, dog in daily parlance. However as indicated earlier, African workers appeared to resent the use of the term 'boy' and similar words which were derogatory to their status and dignity. The insults practised by Asians against the Africans, all seamed on the individual a collective memory. The frustration of semi-professionals in the work place aroused hate and hostility between the Asians and the Africans (Atieno Odhiambo 1995).

By 1951, the Kenya government report described the appalling condition of Asian overcrowding in some of the smaller towns. The East Africa Royal Commission of 1955 notes that, conditions of life for the poorer Asians and the majority of Africans in the towns had been deteriorating over a considerable period. It also notes that the acute shortage of living space and employment opportunities were not only due to the increased population, but were the result of restrictive policies (Delf, 1963:47). These restrictive policies dealt a major blow to the Afro-Asian interaction in residential areas.

The Kisumu Asian Housing Committee catered for the interests of the Asians who were posted to Kisumu to work for the government. The Asian Housing Committee was a purely ad hoc instruments appointed by the PC to assist him in the allocation of houses. Similarly, the Kisumu European Housing Committee was established to help Europeans access good housing (KNA, PC/NZA/2/16/60, 1946-51 10/2/1947). In 1956, the Kisumu Ismailia Housing Society Limited put up sixteen flats for Asians namely, the Aga Khan flats near the new Goan school. The directors of this committee were the Patel Samaj family, whose name was given to the famous Patel flats in Kisumu (KNA, PC/NZA/3/1/404, Olingo, O.I., 2006). Later, some Africans within the same economic class started staying in these flats

Apart from the formal housing schemes that the government came up with to solve the problem of housing in Kisumu, Asian *dukawallas* who were actually not government employees decided to reside in the trading centres where they operated their businesses. According to Obudho (1976), most of the commercial land in Kisumu was in the hands of non-Africans. Because the Asians had the money, most of them rented business premises which they also used as residential places within the town centre. This was the

212

characteristic of the Kisumu Indian bazaar as well as other shopping centres where they operated from.

Chatur (O.I., 2005), states that Asians had to stay near the government institutions such as police stations where they were assured of protection. Areas like Kaloleni and Manyatta, which were peri –urban areas, were by then surrounded by thick bush and were not conducive for residential purposes. But segregation policies did not permit Africans to stay with the Asians within their houses except if the Africans were *jopidi* (baby sitters*)*. Any other person could not be allowed to enter these premises, not even the immediate neighbours. This made the African neighbours to develop a negative attitude towards the Asians (Sidera, O.I., 2005).

As pointed out earlier, the policy requiring Africans to live in segregated areas was implemented through a variety of by-laws, including those which prohibited Africans from leaving those areas at night and those which pledged the local authorities to erect housing in African locations (Olumwullah, 1986:186). The Municipal Board of Kisumu succeeded in alleviating the shortage of African housing when in 1958, sixteen new tenant purchase houses were completed through the Kisumu African Tenant Purchase Scheme.

Under this scheme, plots were availed to Africans in Kaloleni, Kibuye and near the Jubilee market (KNA, HT/17/16 AR Central Nyanza 1955-9 KNA, PC/NZA/4/4/105 AR 1958, KNA, /DC/KSM/1/30/53 1957). The plots near the jubilee market attracted Asians, and this influenced their interaction with Africans since these plots were also for commercial purposes. Asians constructed shops where they sold items to Africans. At the same time, a few Africans also operated shops within the same area. This move by the colonial government was to permanently restrict and confine Africans to designated residential areas thus furthering the colonial racial policy of segregation.

Between 1961 and 1962, the Municipal Council of Kisumu started considering the ways of alleviating the Asian housing problem by negotiating for a site suitable for economy standard Asian housing. This came in handy after the Commissioner of Lands had served a quit notice to a number of families living in temporary wartime dwellings. It was thought that a number of the Asian families would be able to move into the councils' Asian Tenant Purchase houses, which were to be completed in the near future. The council treasurer further proposed that twenty houses similar to those constructed under the existing African Tenant Purchase scheme should be built and made available on rental terms (KNA, NHC/1/152, 1961).

It is clear that housing development was directed along racial lines by the colonial government and this influenced Afro-Asian relations because it reduced interaction only to areas of economic exchange like the trading centres. Africans were given land in the peri-urban areas of Kaloleni, Shaurimoyo and Kibuye. Asians did not move to these areas but concentrated in getting houses within the Central Business District in Kisumu.

However, it is true as Mamdani (1996) observes that in societies organized around thick markers of identity, like race, the presence of these markers and the political, social and economic differentiation and discrimination that they support provide forms of familiarity and security for negotiating and consummating various forms of human interactions. These were some of the reflections on late colonialism in Africa and which were replicated in Nyanza Province.

Gripped with the fear of insecurity which engulfed the entire region towards independence in 1963, there was movement of Asians from the rural areas of Ndere, Yala and Kendu Bay to Kisumu. Some also left Kisumu for Britain. However as Siddiqi (2004: 6) puts it, Africans who were genuinely upset by such developments were the poor, many of whom were employed in Asian businesses and homes. Not only would they be losing their jobs but many had also formed close bonds with their employers.

Occasionally, an Asian baby/child would not mind his mother going missing for a few days but would be inconsolable if the *Ayah* failed to turn up to work. These *ayahs* especially were so much attached to the Asian children (Tieni, O.I., 2007) Because of the close nature of working relationship between Asians and their loyal African servants, Asians left some of their houses to these people.

5.6 Summary and Conclusion

It was the objective of this chapter to examine Afro-Asian relations in Nyanza from 1945- 1963. We have demonstrated that there was a heightened trade rivalry between

Asians and Africans as the Africans started questioning authoritatively forms of western knowledge through organized welfare and political associations. The move by Africans to form these organizations was aimed at dismantling Asian domination in trade. These relations were also characterized by malpractices that brought about tension and suspicion between the two communities.

The government involvement in the cotton industry during this period slowly marked the beginning in the change of ownership in the cotton industry from Asians to Africans as Africans started organizing themselves into cooperative societies in order to buy the ginneries. It should be noted, therefore, that areas where cotton was grown and ginnery established such as Alego, Ndere and Kendu Bay were areas of economic contestations as Africans resisted the planting of this crop.

We have concluded that socially, colonialism was racist. Racial segregation was witnessed in the housing and education sectors. However, domestic servants in the dynamics of Afro-Asian relations were a vital link in the whole scheme of things. Their hard work and total dedication contributed to the idyllic lifestyles of Asian women, who sometimes helped them during crisis.

But more important, African servants were also the link that Asians had to African culture. Asians also helped in championing the African cause by financing African press like *Ramogi*. In spite of the colonial racial policies, Africans of Kisumu elected Jamal Amin as the first Asian Member of Parliament for Kisumu in the post independent

Kenya. Jamal Amin had, therefore, acquired some African values which made him to easily identify with both Asians and Africans. In the next chapter, we examine Afro-Asian relations during Kenyatta era from 1963-1978.

CHAPTER SIX

6.0 THE AFRO–ASIAN RELATIONS DURING THE KENYATTA AND MOI ERAS 1963-2002

6.1 Introduction

In Chapter five we discussed Afro-Asian relations in Nyanza Province from 1945-1963 and argued that Africans started questioning some forms of western knowledge through organized welfare and political organizations. We concluded that opposite binarism sometimes could not work in the Nyanza postcolony since there were Asian and African cultures and values that were borrowed by the two communities from each other. In this chapter we propose to discusses Afro-Asian socio-political and economic relations during the Kenyatta era and Moi era between 1963-1978 and 1978-2002 respectively.

It examines issues such as Africanization, citizenship, Asian political participation, Moi-Asian nexus and how these issues influenced Afro-Asian relations within the postcolonial space of Nyanza. This is because soon after independence, an anti-Asian hysteria swept the land as Africans reached out to claim their rightful place in the society and the middle level Asians became the target of their attention. During this transition period from formal colonialism to Independence, nothing changed much in terms of structures. The chapter demonstrates that there were significant social and economic changes in the Kenyatta and Moi eras which had a strong impact on Afro- Asian relations.

6.2 Afro-Asian Relations and the Africanization Process in the Kenyatta era

The achievement of political independence in 1963 resulted in many changes. Besides bringing vital political decisions under the control of the indigenous Africans, independence also enabled some leaders to make important economic decisions that enhanced the economic standing of the local bourgeoisie. 'Africanization' in particular, was one of the most emotive political slogans in the tumult before independence and Kenyatta's promise to the people.

Before independence, large scale agriculture, industry and commerce were dominated by non-Kenyans. Europeans controlled agriculture and industry while commerce and trade was dominated by Asians. After independence, one of the most urgent and pressing problems was to break foreigners' dominance of the Kenyan economy and transfer it to black Kenyans. This objective was tackled through the mechanism of legislation and licensing (Ochieng', 1995:85).

The government of Jomo Kenyatta introduced various indigenization policies and programmes. Among these were quit notices served to non-citizen Asians in the distributive trade that enabled Africans to acquire their shops in the main shopping areas in the urban areas (Finance, May 13, 1997:7). In addition to such direct measures, the government introduced statutory institutions to encourage and support African participation in the economy such as the Industrial and Commercial Development Corporation (ICDC), Kenya National Trading Company (KNTC), Industrial

Development Bank (IDB) Kenya Industrial Estate (KIE), Development Finance Company of Kenya (DFCK) as well as commercial banks with deliberate bias towards financing African businesses and individuals (Ochieng, 1995:86, Finance, May 13, 1997:7).

These institutions were created in order to incorporate the Kenyan businessmen such as small retail traders and transporters, within the capitalist mode of production, a process which had already been introduced during colonialism. Africans were simply replacing whites as new capitalists. This was basically a colonial legacy in the post-independent Kenya. All these developments were part of the Africanization programme. The postcolony in its post independence dispensation was now practicing racism and segregation in reverse.

Independence did not mark the beginning of a postcolony but it constituted a mere transition from the dominant phase of colonialism to the hegemonic phase of colonialism (JanMohammed,1985). The politics of Africanization was simultaneously unifying and fragmenting. Mamdani (1996:20) argues that its first moment involved the dismantling of racially inherited privilege. The effect was to unify the victims of colonial racism. The second moment turned around the question of redistribution and divided the same majority, both Asians and Africans, along racial lines that reflected the actual process of redistribution: ethnic and regional.

With the 'end' of colonialism and the departure of the British, the former political

relationships were reversed and decision-making was in the 'hands' of Africans for the

first time (Latimore 1964:6). However, some decisions had to be made in consultation

with the former colonial masters thus introducing the issue of neo-colonialism into the

system of the newly formed African government. Because of the Asian dominance in

commerce and trade, a lot of ideological labour had gone into the creation of fixed image

of the East African Asian subject and more so Asians in the Nyanza area of study. Within

the Western knowledge regimes, Asians and Africans had been allocated certain social

identities and constructions. Much of the early colonial complaints about the 'Asian

menace,' for instance, established a trend in which the nuances of Asian identities would

be flattened out to create an image of the Asian as a uniformly rapacious and duplicitous

character.

Standard notions of the cultural distinctiveness of the Asian were created and consistently

applied in a manner that had had serious consequences (Ojwang' 2005:5). These colonial

representations of Indians and Africans took root in both communities and continued to

order present day constructions of Indians and African identities (Rampersad, 2007:33).

Bharati has summarized both Asian and African stereotypes thus:

> Africans viewed Asians as sneaky, mistrustful; they stick to
> each other and do not mix with others, they are arrogant, they
> cheat in business...they are clannish, they monopolize trade
> within their fold, they are not trustworthy in business nor in
> social matters. The Asians on their part accused Africans of
> being lazy, inefficient, irresponsible, dirty, awkward,
> primitive and incapable of doing hard work on acquiring
> skills. These stereotypes gradually developed and came to be
> regarded as universal characteristic of both Asians and
> Africans (Bharati 1972:170).

221

These negative stereotypes, based on very limited experience, soon gained widespread acceptance and were a hindrance to the establishment of better relations between the two communities. In Kisumu, such stereotypes constructed an Asian as thrifty and prone to exploiting others. Africans viewed Asians as people who had come to grab their resources and who needed to be repatriated to India. Asians, on the other hand, viewed Africans as 'thieves' (Ramadhan, O.I., 2006, Chatur O.I., 2006).

Within the scheme of stereotypical representation, Asian subjects were always well-known even before they were actually encountered, but in the event that they were finally encountered, they were routinely slotted into roles that had already been scripted for them. Ojwang', (2005:4) argues that, for the European colonial purveyors of negative myths about the Asians, such interpellations were mostly a way of perpetuating the existent political arrangements which favoured white settlers.

For Africans working for Asian employers within the modern capitalist economies, stereotypical descriptions of Asians provided a potent tool for expressing their own class aspirations. Through constant repetition, this particular image acquired a currency that persisted to date. In an important sense, the reduction of Asian identity to a small, knowable quantity could be construed as an attempt to make sense of an excruciatingly complicated social universe. Indeed, stereotyping was in a sense a precondition for understanding- an abstraction meant to reduce the complexity of a particular reality to a codified one that provides for predictability and consistency (Ojwang' 2005).

This stereotype has its root in the relationship of Africans to Indian petty traders since it was with this group of traders that Africans had the most contact. The general opinion towards Asians as a whole was based on that experience. Therefore, Asian government officials and artisans among others also became part of the Asian stereotype (Furedi, 1974:351).

Without the reduction of a seemingly chaotic reality to an undifferentiated one, meaning and judgement was continually deferred, thus frustrating the quest for a final knowledge of the subject. Yet, as Homi Bhabha has pointed out, stereotyping depended on a kind of mis-cognition for it 'must always be in *excess* of what could be empirically proved or otherwise logically construed' (Bhabha,1994:66). For Bhabha, 'the stereotype was not a simplification but a false representation of a given reality'. It is a simplification because it is an arrested, fixated form of representation that, in denying the play of difference (that the negation of the other permits), constitutes a problem for the representation of the subject in significations of psychic and social relations (Bhabha 1994:66, 75).

The corollary of stereotypical mode of representation is, for Bhabha, the hybridities of colonial and postcolonial condition (Zeleza, 1997). The stereotypical mode of representation thus formed part of forms of knowledge authored and authorized by the West. It is, therefore, important that the literature by the colonized people should articulate their identity so that they could possibly reclaim their past in the face of that past's inevitable otherness (Iye, 1998).

So Africanization seemed to had borrowed from the pot of stereotypes. The process was to be tackled through the mechanism of legislation and licensing. The Kenya National Trading Corporation, which had been formed in 1965 to handle domestic import-export trade, was also used extensively in the period after 1967 to penetrate the wholesale and retail sectors which had formerly been the exclusive preserve of non-Africans. The first legislation to this effect was the Trade Licencing Act of 1967. This act came into effect on 8th January 1968. However, the exercise went into full swing in March of the same year. This act excluded non-citizens from trading in rural and non-urban areas and specified a list of goods which were to be restricted to citizen traders only. These included most basic consumer goods, such as maize, rice, sugar, textiles, soap and cement (KNA, HT/17/22 Annual Report 1968, Ochieng', 1995:85).

One of the major amendments incorporated in the Trade Licensing Amendment Bill and the Citizenship Act of 1969 required that all partners of business would henceforth have to be Kenya citizens before their firms were registered as citizen firms. According to the then Minister for Commerce and Industry, Mr Mwai Kibaki, this amendment was aimed at plugging various loopholes and removing administrative difficulties experienced during the one year that the act had been in operation.

More than 50 % shareholdings by local people in companies would remain as a requisite for firms to be classified as citizen undertakings. It had been experienced, Kibaki said, that provision for allowing a partnership concern to deal in scheduled goods by merely having citizens as some members had been abused, and membership would in future have to be wholly African (*Daily Nation* 10th October 1969). With the Africanization process in place, many Africans entered into business, but the sector became an active site for Afro-Asian contestation.

Africanization, therefore, caused fear among the Asians and some of the Asians started closing down their businesses. This interfered with Afro-Asian economic and social relations in areas such as Ndere, Yala and Kendu Bay since Africans who were employed by Asians as househelps and shop assistants left their jobs. Similarly, Asians doing business in these areas also had to leave these areas thus affecting their economic and social relations.

During this time, Asians were given the option either to acquire Kenya citizenship or leave. Some took Kenyan citizenship while others refused and left the country. However, some of the Asians who acquired Kenyan citizenship found it difficult to operate business in some areas in Nyanza. Since the notion of citizenship overlapped that of nationality, the colonized (Asians) were not simply consigned to the fringes of the nation, but were virtually strangers in their own 'home' (see Mbembe, 2001:35).

The issue of citizenship at this point needs to be looked at critically within the postcolonial thinking. Citizenship was a construction of the African government and given meaning in a particular social or economic context. In the context of Kenyan Africanization, non-citizens were taken to be the Asians and Europeans while citizens were the Africans. Therefore, citizenship in the post-independent Kenyan state was based on colour/ race which was a colonial legacy. The division between the citizen and the subject, the non-native and the native was characteristic of all colonial situations (Mamdani, 1996:48).

Evidently, in the post-independence situation, this showed the ambivalence of power and whoever holds it since it clearly suggested the Africanization of European colonialism. The issue of citizenship thus strained Afro-Asian relations in the rural areas as most Asians started to withdraw from these areas (Mandhavia, O.I., 2006). The Kenya National Trading Corporation thus functioned as an institution of the government to entrench Western capitalism in the rural areas. This was neo-colonialism being propagated by Africans, a confirmation that structures of the African government did not change much as compared to the structures of the colonial government.

The Asian community was affected by the government's policies, implemented nationwide, of putting Africans in the economic saddle (Larimore, 1969). The general and popular view was that the government was waging an economic war against Asians in order to enable Africans to take over businesses of non-citizens. As a result, there was a second mini 'exodus' of the members of Asian community, which was caused by the Citizenship Act of 1969 when most members of the community left for Britain and many former government clerks returned to India. The earlier exodus had been caused by the uncertainty of the impending African government. The final exodus climaxed with the Trade Licencing Act 1969 (Khosla, 1993). Evidently, the Asian community reacted negatively towards Africanization; some sold their businesses at exorbitant rates and others destroyed fittings in their business premises (*East Africa Standard* 17th August, 1978, Jagpal, O.I., 2006).

Main streets in Kenya's big towns were also to be limited to citizen traders from the beginning of 1970. The minister for commerce and industry Mr Mwai Kibaki had announced a significant increase of urban trading areas earmarked for 'citizens only' in a Kenya gazette notice. Non-citizens required special permission to trade outside General Business Areas and had been warned that they would only be allowed to remain in areas reserved for citizens if fewer citizens could be found to operate businesses (*East Africa Standard* 10/10/69).

In Nyanza and specifically Kisumu, the boundary of areas set aside for 'citizens only' were Accra Street, Otieno Oyoo Street, Joshi Avenue, Achieng' Oneko Street and new station road. Others included Kibuye Estate, Mosque Estate, Makasembo, Shaurimoyo, Ondiek, Kaloleni, Lumumba, Nyalenda, Omino Crescent and Pembe Tatu estates surrounded by the Nairobi road, Street, Sailors Close, Karachi Road and Kakamega Road (*East Africa Standard* October 10, 1969).

With this development, it became so difficult for Asians including those who had acquired Kenyan citizenship to own houses in places like Nyalenda, Shaurimoyo and Manyatta because they feared staying in the midst of Africans (Aguya, O.I., 2005). But this could have also been due to the fact that some of them felt that they would not be accepted within the African society.

227

In the mid-70s, for instance in Kisumu, there were complaints regarding some Africans who secretly resold business premises to Asians. The overall image of Asians was so negative that Kisumu was referred to as the 'Bombay of Kenya' on account of the Indian hold on commerce (*East Africa Standard* August, 13 and17 1978). In local terms, this reference was considered demeaning.

The public space in Nyanza seemed pluralistic and included both citizens and non-citizens. These were political constructs within the postcolony which gave both Asians and Africans certain identities of inclusion and exclusion. Nyanza as a sub-space within the Kenyan postcolony, was made up of a series of corporate institutions and political machineries. In this situation, the space in Nyanza was a particularly revealing, and rather dramatic stage on which were played out the wider problems of subjection and its corollary, discipline (Mbembe 2001, 103). In this case, Asians appeared to be the subject. But at the same time, there was evidence of a mimicry of the colonial style of rule by Africans. The 'Citizens only area' was thus a space and stage where economic negotiations and contestations were fulfilled.

The government policy affected the relationship between the two communities. Asians developed fear, and felt that Africans were about to start taking their property by force. Asians also started laying off some African workers who they had employed as shop assistants. Interaction was also reduced, since Asians started to buy essential items which could sustain them for more days.

However, they maintained limited contact with their African suppliers of foodstuff. (Apiyo, O.I., 2005). But at the same time, a kind of social stratification based on economic wealth rather than race was emerging. Asian professionals and wealthy businessmen started identifying with some wealthy African businessmen, local government leaders such as the District Officers, District Commissioners, Mayors, and the police bosses of the town by organizing visits to their offices.

The main objective of this was to get protection from these officials and also ensure that their interests were catered for as a community (Olingo, O.I., 2006). These developments involved all the Asians including the *dukawallahs* who formed a certain class of Asians (Mayoor, O.I., 2006). This was an evidence of the way spaces were negotiated for within the plural and chaotic space within the Nyanza postcolony.

In a meeting of the Kenya National Chambers of Commerce, Kisumu branch, the Acting Nyanza Provincial Trade Development Officer disclosed that thirty one non- citizens had been served with notices by January 1970 to wind up their businesses within four months (*East African Standard, December 11 and 12, 1969*). This notice also applied to the Asians in the rural areas of Ndere, Yala and Kendu Bay. He also expressed his great concern that only a few African businessmen were members of the Chamber of Commerce and urged African traders who had not become members to join the Kenya National Chambers of Commerce and Industry through which they could channel their problems. He also advised African traders who took over businesses previously run by non-citizens to try to maintain the sale of goods sold by previous owners of these shops.

The commissioner noted that no specified goods would be handled by any expatriates in future and strongly warned some of the African traders who took up businesses and later handed them over to foreigners to run them. This, he said, was hindering the progress of other African traders. He also made it clear that no license would be issued to any non-citizen (*East Africa Standard* December 11 and 12 1969). This notice followed a nationwide notice where the Ministry of Commerce and Industry had told approximately 1000 Asian tradesmen that their licenses would not be renewed (*Daily Nation,* January 9, 1970).

A significant consequence of these political and economic changes after independence was the reduction in size of the Asian community. It was caused by their emigration to Britain. The emigrants could not remain in a Kenya ruled by the African majority and one in which Africanization policy seemed to promise a loss of employment and/or business opportunities and economic status. Such feelings were particularly manifested in the way the immigrant communities responded to the issue of Kenya citizenship (Maxon, 1995:112).

However, it can be argued that Asians acquired some identity(ies) by virtue of their contact with the Europeans and Africans which allowed them to move and settle in Britain rather than go back to India. The main cause of the Asian exodus after independence was the uncertainty felt by their businessmen on the issue of Africanization of commerce and also partly due to the threats, fear and criminal activities from Africans in Ndere and Yala centres (Olingo, O.I., 2006).

In Ndere, the notice marked the beginning of the withdrawal of Asians from the trading centre. However, this withdrawal was received with mixed reactions from both communities. Because there was good relationship between Asians and Africans in this area, especially in economic terms, the Africans found the Asian withdrawal unacceptable since it led to the shortage of goods previously sold in the Asian shops. They were forced to purchase goods from the nearby town of Siaya or Kisumu which were very far and costly (Ondiallo, O.I., 2006).

Some Asians who lived in Ndere, for instance Jamnadass, gave out their shops to some of their local friends. Others sold these shops at very low prices. Musa Mbeya, Ooko Kasira, and Ouma Kamwalo were some of the beneficiaries of such kind of gesture from the Asians. Indians left them with so many items, shops, and other households. Chief Amoth Owira also got many items from the Asians who left Ndere (Mzungu, O.I., 2006, Ondiallo O.I., 2007). Some of these Indian shops in Ndere are currently rented out to new tenants.

After independence, the general opinion of the Asians towards the new government was negative. Their main fear was that Africans would retaliate and mistreat them and indeed later, the African thugs started raiding them. They therefore decided to leave Ndere so as to be secure and save their wealth. Theft was now common in Ndere and this made the Asians to fear and be suspicious of Africans. This fear was also increased by the fact that the colonial administration which offered the Asians adequate security was not in control. This, therefore affected their relations with Africans immensely (Wambia, O.I., 2006).

Unlike Ndere, the Africans in Kendu Bay welcomed Asian withdrawal and one African Faraji says that 'People felt good'. In Kendu Bay, Asians feared attacks from Africans despite the lack of evidence of organised attack on them. According to Malit (O.I., 2006), some of the Asian *dukawallahs* were very moody. In their shops, Africans were not allowed to make item price enquiries more than once as this could lead to their being thrown out of the shop summarily. However, most of these Asians had already established great networks both in Nyanza and beyond Kenya during this time and moved out of Kendu Bay to various towns (Orenda, O.I., 2006).

Asians loathed the Africanization policy because it destabilized their businesses (Kassam, O.I., 2006). Individual traders like Habib Okore (Asian) went back to Uganda where he operated a bakery and a dairy farm. But still in Uganda, he employed a lot of *Jokarachuonyo* (People from Karachuonyo, South Nyanza or Kendu Bay) who went there owing to the good relations he previously had with them. Tahidin, the owner of Kendu ginnery sold it to Rachuonyo Cooperative Union and relocated permanently to Kisumu.

In Kendu Bay, very few Asians remained and this was due to reasons such as being married to African ladies. For example, Abdul Kassam (Khoja) married a local lady hence he became an in-law to the Luo of the area. Faraji says that *en orwa* (he is our in-law). Marriage was thus a tool of compromise and negotiation on the postcolony.

Due to his marriage to a local African woman, he was forced by the locals (as a condition for marriage) to change his religion from Hindu to Islam since the woman he married was a Muslim and Kendu generally was predominated by Luo Muslims. This depicted constant negotiations and change of identities by Asians.

Muslim Asians were more social with Africans than those who practised Hinduism. For instance, Mohammud Khan, Ogola Malikhan, Pheroze Khan who were Muslims, attended and prayed together with the locals in their mosque. This is because the Islamic faith preaches the brotherhood of all adherents (Faraji, O.I., 2006). The Muslim Indians who left Kendu Bay gave their houses to the Muslim community so that the money accrued from rent could be used to help in the mosque. However, some of the plots which they owned were sold back to the locals and especially those Africans who worked for them.

The situation in both Ndere and Kendu Bay was also replicated in other parts of Nyanza. In Yala, the departure of Asians was celebrated by the Africans but shortly after, they began regretting when they could not get goods stocked by the Asians in their shops. Africans who were employed in their shops as tailors and shop attendants however felt bad because of loss of jobs and other gifts which they were used to receiving from the Asians. Most of the Yala Asians moved to Kisumu, while others went back to India. A. Asif, son to one of the earlier Yala Asians called Kaka, however continues to operate in Yala in a plot which his late father bought during the colonial times (Kabong' O.I., 2006).

Within the cotton sector, the owners of Ndere Ginnery sold the ginnery to the Siaya Cotton Cooperative Union in 1973, thereby shifting ownership from Asians to Africans. Through its director, A.A Kassim Lakha, the Kenya Industries wrote to the general manager of the Cotton Lint and Seed Marketing Board in November 1973, informing him of the sale of their ginnery (Ndere) to Siaya Cotton Cooperative Union limited. Kendu ginnery was also handed over to Rachuonyo Cooperative Union, after Asians started withdrawing from these areas.

By January 1974, final talks for the hand over of Ndere cotton ginnery between the Kenya Industries and Siaya Cotton Cooperative Union were held and the committee members were pleased with the useful advice Mr. Kassim had given on the running of the ginnery (KNA, TP/4/17, 1973-82). The sale of these ginneries meant that Asians had to relocate and venture into other businesses. The impact of this change of ownership on the Africans was that they had to cope with delays in payment during cotton delivery to the cooperative unions which subsequently led to their withdrawal from growing cotton. This resulted in the collapse of the ginneries and the end of good Afro-Asian interaction in Ndere (Omoro, O.I., 2006).

By 1975, another Asian industrial undertaking, the Kisumu Cotton Mills (KICOMI) came into the scene as a textile industry (*Weekly Review, 21/1/1983*). Contrary to the ginning factories in Ndere, Yala and Kendu Bay, this was a more advanced industry where Asians were manufacturing ready-made clothes, bed sheets, and curtains for both local and international markets. The Asian owners employed a number of African workers whom they trained on how to operate weaving machines. This was done under the supervision of the Asians.

However, there were complaints over low wages paid to African workers as compared to their Asian counterparts in the same company (Bodo, O.I., 2006). The establishment of this industry was to form the basis of conflict between African second-hand traders and the KICOMI products later in the Moi era. KICOMI survived Africanization because it was a joint venture between the Kenya government and the Asians.

6.3 Afro-Asian Political Relations in the Kenyatta Era

After Kenya's political 'independence', it was clear to Kenyan leaders that nation building was critically dependent upon the development of sympathetic political and economic institutions, for, in the immediate preceding years, the people of Kenya had hoped that the attainment of 'independence' would mark a transition from the realm of necessity to that of building a democratic socialist state strongly committed to Pan-African ideals and world peace (Ochieng, 1995:91).

Asian political activities in Kenya declined as independence drew near. On 1 June 1963, Kenyatta was able to bring his party to an electoral victory and become Kenya's first Prime Minister. In November of the same year, Freedom Party members apparently felt that there was no longer any justification for continuing as a separate organization. As a result of this, the Kenya Freedom Party (KFP), formed by far sighted Asian leaders such as Pio Gama Pinto, K.P Shah, I.T Inamdar, and S.K Anjarwalla who resolved to align themselves with the African nationalist leadership, was officially dissolved with the express intention that its members join KANU (Zarina, 2006:14). Asians therefore were fast in seizing opportunities to remain relevant on the postcolony. It was a struggle not to be overlooked. The dissolution of the KFP was perhaps a logical conclusion to the organization's consistent policy of political alignment with African prospectus. Yet, it also represented the end of a strong Asian voice in determining Kenya's future (Seidenberg, 1996:174).

By announcing that his government would build a democratic African socialist state, Jomo Kenyatta's idea was that the benefits of economic and social development would be distributed equitably, that differential treatment based on tribe, race, belief or class would be abandoned and that every national, whether black, white or brown would be given an equal opportunity to improve his lot (Ochieng, 1995:92).

The year 1964 was one of the most important years in the history of Kenya. It was the first year of independence and the end of it saw the birth of Kenya as a republic under a revised constitution. In the enthusiasm generated by Independence, the Nyanza Regional

Assembly members added their support to the abolition of the Regional constitution. Generally, the whole of Nyanza had been KANU's stronghold, which advocated for the introduction of a unitary government as opposed to KADU, which had strongly advocated for the introduction of a regional constitution. Therefore, most people in Nyanza very heartily welcomed the new changes in the government machinery (KNA, HT/17/5, 1964).

Some of the political developments at the national level affected and shaped what was happening at the local level as far as Afro-Asian political relations in Nyanza Province were concerned. By 1965, Pio Gama Pinto's critical attitude and closeness to Odinga brought him into conflict with powerful elements within the ruling party. On 24th February 1965, Pinto was shot dead in the driveway of his home (Zarina, 2004:22). This occurrence sent a shocking wave to the Asians whose fear increased in urban centres and rural areas like Ndere, Yala and Kendu Bay where they lived. This affected Afro-Asian political relations in these areas as Pinto's death was perceived by Asians as racially and politically motivated (Mbudi, O.I., 2007).

By 1966, the radicals led by Oginga Odinga, Bildad Kaggia and Achieng' Oneko broke away from KANU and formed the Kenya People's Union (KPU). However, the most important point to note here is that some Asians who were close associates of Oginga Odinga such as Pranlel Sheth who resided in Kisumu were deported to India. No reasons were given for the action against these individuals, except for a statement put out by the official Kenya News Agency that:

The six Asians deported had shown themselves by act and speech to be disloyal towards Kenya, joining it with a warning that those who chose to take up Kenya citizenship must identify themselves with the country in all its aspects and not engage in 'subversive activities against the state or any other activities. The newspaper also printed a summary of a broadcast the previous day in which the official Voice of Kenya declared that the entire Asian community in Kenya today 'stands indicted by the activities of some of its members (Rattansi, 2004:24).

Intimidation was a feature of the postcolony in its formal disposition. It is still the practice of the postcolony in its informal dispensation. Africans were simply replicating what whites did. Thus the struggle by Odinga, Kaggia and Pinto was still the struggle for decolonization against an informal postcolony still operating under British colonial rules.

In August 1966, president Kenyatta himself took up the theme when addressing the KANU branch at Nyali Beach Hotel in Mombasa, by sternly urging the 'immigrant communities' to either identify themselves with the aspirations of the people of Kenya, or pack up and leave (Ibid., 25). These statements were not favourable in harnessing Afro-Asian relations as they showed the ambivalent nature of the state towards Asians after

Independence. In fact, it heightened tension and suspicion which already existed in the run-up towards independence.

These statements destabilized Asians already living in the rural areas of Nyanza leading to the withdrawal of many more from these places. Even though the Asians viewed these statements as racist diatribes, they also demonstrated that with the onset of independence, nothing much had changed in terms of the government structure. It is only the leadership which changed. As Fanon (1967:27) says, decolonization is quite simply the replacing of a certain 'species' of men by another 'species' of men.

On Madaraka Day 1967, President Kenyatta gave a stern warning to non-Africans who abused Africans and the government because of their wealth as quoted by Theroux:

> But I have got information that some Europeans and Asians in Kenya have not realized that this country is independent and go on abusing..' He attacked some Asian shopkeepers who because of wealth showed no respect to the ordinary Africans saying *Uhuru* was nothing. Some of these people have not even realized that there is now an about turn. This is a final warning to them and unless they change their ways, they should not blame the government for any measure that they may take to deal with their nonsense (Theroux, 1969:4).

Such warnings laid the foundation upon which Afro-Asian hostilities were laid during the Kenyatta era.

By 1967, the Asians who were in politics as members of the Kisumu council were Abdul E. Dahya who was the deputy mayor, M.F Shah, and Y.J. Farjallah (KNA,DC/KSM/17/40, 1964, KNA, HT/17/19, 1967). When the 1969 elections came,

239

Jamal Amir never defended his parliamentary seat which fell to the first female mayor, Mrs Grace Onyango (Daily Nation, 2/2/1990). Abdul Dahya did not quit politics but was not successful in his quest to secure a civic seat in the subsequent elections. Despite some racist anti-Asian rhetorics by a section of Kenyan African politicians, physical molestation was, however, rare (Chege, 2004:17).

6.4 Social Participation and Afro-Asian Relations in Nyanza in the Kenyatta era 1964-1978

6.4.1 Housing

A part from Africanization, another change that affected the non-African and African communities alike was the scrapping of segregation at Independence. No longer would schools, hospitals, or residential areas be reserved exclusively for whites or Asians. Segregationist regulations relating to public facilities were also dropped, and the government pressured formerly exclusive clubs to revise membership requirements to allow affiliation from all racial groups. Along with these measures, the government sought also a change in non –African attitudes towards the majority of the population. On many occasions, President Kenyatta, attacked the colonial idea of African inferiority and warned non-Africans (Asians and European) against *Ubwana* or a bossy mentality (Maxon, 1995:115). It is out of this racial segregation that Ashcroft (1989:6) questioned why post colonial societies should continue to engage with the colonial imperial experience.

Generally, Asians chose to be confined within their business premises which they used as commercial and residential quarters. The scrapping of racial segregation in residential areas was not felt much in the rural areas of Ndere, Yala and Kendu Bay because as Asians had massively withdrawn from these areas, they sold off their shops to Africans which hitherto served as their residences. Towards the end of Kenyatta rule, such structures had been occupied by Africans who bought them from the Asians (Rosaline O.I., 2006).

Similarly, in Yala town, Asians relocated to Kisumu and sold their premises to the Africans. It could thus be stated that real integration was never achieved within the housing sector. Integration would mean Africans renting and staying with Asians within the same compound or *landhies* and sharing other housing facilities together. Asians might have probably wished to integrate with Africans in Yala and Ndere but the government policies forced them out.

Housing shortage in Kisumu persisted into the post independence period. Initially, most Asians were concentrated in the town centre where they conducted business and also resided. Typically, former residential spaces in the upper floors of these structures were converted into small office spaces (Anyumba, 1995). Afro-Asian interaction within the residential areas even after independence was not common as such. The Africans who neighboured them complained of inaccessibility to their houses and isolationism. But also Africans were not able to pay high rents for some houses within the town centre.

Because of their favorable economic status, the majority of Asians bought houses in the high class Milimani area while others occupied houses belonging to the East African Railways and Harbours at the lower railway quarters near the current Kisumu railway station (Bodo, O.I., 2005). Thus, although the Asians and Africans lived in the same towns and localities, initially segregation militated against their interaction, but later, it is their wealth that gave them a higher class and therefore, an edge above the Africans.

Given the Asians' financial status they were able to buy and own houses in Kisumu town. This also made it possible for the Asians to stay in estates and houses without shifting from one house to another thereby limiting their interaction with the locals in residential areas. Whenever they moved to another house, they ensured a fellow Asian occupied the vacant one (Ramadhan, O.I., 2006). Therefore, economic status played a greater role in defining Afro-Asian social relations in Nyanza during the Kenyatta era.

6.4.2 Education

Another focus of government policy and development planning after independence was education. The government took the initiative to foster social change and promote development through education. Kenyatta's government was committed to removing inequalities inherited from the colonial period. These were outlined in the Sessional Paper No. 10 of 1965 on African Socialism and its Application to Planning in Kenya, which argued that the state had an obligation to ensure equal opportunities to all citizens, and to eliminate all forms of exploitation and discrimination. The state too must provide needed social services such as education, medical care and social security (Maxon, 1995:126).

Within one week of independence, the government appointed the Kenya Education Commission, under the chairmanship of Professor S.H. Ominde to survey the country's existing educational resources and advise the government on future strategy. The commission endorsed integration, with a single curriculum but different fee structures, for Kenya's racially divided school system among other recommendations (Ministry of Education, 1967).

The policy of integration in schools almost bore fruits in Ndere as some of the Asians took their children to Oseno Komolo Primary School in the early periods of independence. These Asian children were taught together with the African children. In the lower classes, African children related well with their Asian counterparts as they went about their classwork and shared items such as pencils and textbooks. Asian children who attended such schools as Oseno Komolo Primary belonged to low/middle class Asians who could not afford to take their children to better Asian schools in Kisumu (Odhiambo, O.I., 2006).

In Kendu Bay, the Asian school was closed in 1965 but the *Sanatan* was retained until about 1970 when the majority of the Ismaili Asian except Hassam Jamal's family left Kendu Bay. Hence, there was no integration in education in Kendu Bay. Later, this house was transferred to an African and is currently used as a residential house by an African family. In the 1970s, the government took the Yala Indian School (the current Yala Township Primary School) which was an Asian academy before then. At this school, African children learned with a few Asian children before the Asians completely withdrew from the Yala trading centre. The medium of instruction was English in these schools (Ongudu, O.I., 2006), the language of the coloniser.

The relocation of the Asians from rural areas of Ndere, Yala and Kendu Bay to Kisumu was an obvious indication of a crisis within the education sector in the Area. However, most important is the fact that apart from the government schools which were inherited from the colonial system, Asians had their own schools managed by various Asian communities. Communities such as Arya Samaj, Ismailia and Sikh owned the Arya group of schools, Aga Khan Primary School and Siri Guru Singh Sabha schools, respectively.

In these schools, Asians employed African teachers to teach their children. The Asians' relations with the African teachers depended on the performance of the children and this either enhanced it or diminished the relationship. When their children performed well, Asians rewarded the teachers and sometimes a teacher would be allowed to give extra tuition to the Asian children in their houses (Tieni, O.I., 2007).

Attached to the issue of schooling was the responsibility of the African maid, employed by the Asian, to escort the Asian children to school and to pick them after the classes. This responsibility came with a lot of trust from the Asian employer on the employee (Rajiv, O.I., 2005). Africans who had worked for Asians for a long time earned high degree of trust from these Asians and they could entrust such workers with their cars, money and children (Odhiambo, O.I., 2007, Patel, O.I., 2007).

Owing to the provisions of the Sessional Paper No. 10 of 1965, many Asian schools opened up their doors to Africans. The Asian government school, later Kisumu Boys started admitting Africans. In the 1970s, Africans who attended this school were usually bright students. In class, they intermingled with their Asian counterparts and helped each other to solve complex problems in any subject. Some Asians also brought Asian food to their African friends in school (Obeid, O.I., 2006). Towards the end of the Kenyatta era, Asians who had acquired Kenyan citizenship started building schools for commercial purposes.

In these schools, they employed Africans as teachers, secretaries and general workers. For instance DHT Secondary School, Siri Guru Singh Sabha Secondary School currently New Kisumu High School and Muslim Secondary School are some of the schools which were started by Asians in Kisumu and which admit both Asians and Africans. A number of Asians work in these schools as teachers imparting knowledge to both Asian and African students. Asians liked in-door games such as table tennis, scrabble and other games such as hockey, lawn tennis and swimming and, therefore, interaction with Africans in such schools also revolved around these sports (Orengo, O.I., 2005, Chatur, O.I., 2005).

It is important to note that Asians who were born in Kenya came to terms with the realities of their identity and citizenship. This group of Asians, therefore, embraced all the opportunities available to fight for economic and social space within the postcolony of Nyanza, thereby conveniently earning them a working relationship with the Africans.

Some prominent Asians also sat on various education boards in Kisumu District, for instance Abdul Dahya was a member of the Kisumu District Education Board while Mr. K.D. Parker served as secondary schools inspector in the late 1970s in Nyanza. Therefore, unlike in politics Afro-Asian relations in education and housing in Ndere, Yala and Kisumu were mutually beneficial. This is because schools such as Yala Township, New Kisumu High School and Kisumu Boys High School among others were the initiatives of the Asian communities wherever they were, but later, the schools opened their doors to Africans.

But more important, almost all the Asian schools in Yala and Ndere were later to be owned by Africans under the new political dispensation. Integration in schools was therefore partly achieved during the Kenyatta era. Allowing Africans to learn alongside Asian children marked another phase of dismantling the legacy of colonial racial structures and barriers which characterised Afro-Asian relations before independence.

6.5 Moi-Asian Nexus and Afro-Asian Economic Relations in Nyanza Province in the Moi era 1978-2002

President Daniel Arap Moi ascended to power after the death of President Kenyatta in 1978. The period following Moi's accession to power was full of anxieties and

246

apprehensions on the one hand and high hopes on the other. President Moi came up with the philosophy of nyayoism. *Nyayo* is a Kiswahili word meaning 'footsteps'. He announced that he would follow in Kenyatta's footsteps. In other words, he told Kenyans not to expect any major administrative shift for he was determined to continue with Kenyatta's policies. There would definitely be social, economic, and political reforms, but he assured Kenyans that these would be carried out without any discontinuity. *Nyayo* thus became a national motto, symbolizing continuity, love, peace and stability (Ogot, 1995:192).

The Moi administration allowed Kenyan Asians to be at the leading edge of the economy (Himbara, 1994). Some Kenyan Asians did spectacularly well with government favours and partnerships with well placed politicians close to Moi. Asian wealth was visible and it aroused growing popular resentment because the wealth of some Asians was suspected to have been acquired dubiously through cooperation with some functionaries of the Moi regime. A variety of factors drew many Kenyan Asians close to the regime. Their historical sense of political vulnerability and their general absence of political allies led many of them to believe that they must support whatever regime that was in power for reasons of protection and advance (Holmquist, 2002:10)

During the Moi era, Asians continued to extend their domination not only in the retail and distributive sectors, but also in practically every aspect of the economy (Finance, May 1997:7). Their investment thrived in manufacturing and the service sector (hotels, banks, wholesale trade and construction). This was driven by local demand originating from the cash crop boom from African smallholdings in the 1960s to the 1980s (Chege, 2004:17).

In the 1980s, especially in Kisumu, Asians engaged in wholesale trade were involved in cases of hoarding of essential commodities such as sugar, flour, cooking oil and other commodities. This was always common especially a few months before the national budget. This was done in anticipation of an increase in the prices of such commodities so as to capitalise on price increases (Siderra, O.I., 2005).

Although hoarding of goods was a feature of the Asian trade practices, it was also a reflection of Moi's failing economic policies which undermined production and distribution of essential commodities. Such malpractices increased hostility between the Asians and Africans to an extent that, whenever a riot erupted in the towns, Asian shops suffered great loss as a result of looting by Africans. This, was for, instance evidenced in Kisumu during the 1982 attempted coup when Asian shops were the main targets of looting (Odongo, O.I., 2006, *The Weekly Review* 26, 1982:11). Riots and looting targeting Asian shops were a protest to the exploitative tendencies that were practised by Asians. But they also depicted African resistance to Asian domination in trade which continued to flourish during the Moi era.

Such hatred and hostility prompted the Asian community to organise for a delegation to meet the president. In 1982, a delegation drawn from all Asians in Kenya's major towns made a courtesy call on President Moi. Aware of the unease which had developed among

248

the Asian community, the President assured the delegation that his government appreciated that the Asians, along with other investors had played a critical role in the country's economy and assured them that Kenya was committed to the constitutional safeguards which protected private property as well as the ideals of a plural society in which there was no discrimination of any kind.

Moi reminded them that the government was doing everything to encourage investment and business confidence in the country (*The Weekly Review*, August 1983). The statement by the Head of State reassured Asians of the security of their investment. It also laid the foundation for the Moi-Asian nexus as Asians started to identify strongly with the President and the ruling party, KANU.

During the 1978-2002, many Asians were no longer living in Ndere, Kendu Bay and Yala. In Kendu Bay, the only Indian doing business there apart from Kassam Abdul, did not stay there but commuted from Oyugis where he resided (Ochoko, O.I 2006).

The Asian community reasserted themselves by investing in Nyanza and moreso in Kisumu in areas such as construction, real estate and outlets including supermarkets, banks, hotels, housing and the manufacturing sector. Nearly all the local entrepreneurs within the town belonged to the Asian community (Olima, 1993, Anyumba, 1995). Apart from textiles, metal works, engineering, weaving, spinning and soap making which were of Asian interest among the first large-scale manufacturing to be established in Nyanza Province, many more Asian industrial interests continued to emerge.

These companies could be classified according to the products that they produced for instance flour, bread, concrete pipes, soft drinks, mattresses, matches, soap, fishnets, sweets, shipbuilding, general engineering, fish filleting and freezing (Opondo, 1989:51). These Asian manufacturing companies supported a majority of Africans who could not get jobs in the civil service. Indeed these industrial ventures represented the Asians' contribution towards the economy of Nyanza Province.

Afro-Asian relations in the Moi era were unique in the sense that many Africans had acquired education and professional skills compared to the colonial and Kenyatta periods when most of them were employed as domestic servants and unskilled labourers. This educational background made Africans to be employed in Asian firms as professionals such as doctors, engineers, mechanics, teachers and accountants among others. Afro-Asian relations within these categories of people were, therefore, different from the Afro-Asian relations that existed between the Asian *dukawallahs* and the local Africans in the village. This is because the Asians recognised the professionalism of the people they employed.

In most cases, relations between African professionals and their Asian employers in places such as Jalaram Hospital, United Millers Company and Kisumu Senior Academy, Southern Credit Bank among others in Kisumu, were often more or less equal since African professionals knew their rights and would always negotiate for pay commensurate to the services offered (Odhiambo, O.I., 2006).

As the Indian investment continued to thrive in the manufacturing and the service sector in the 1980s, there were some misunderstandings which characterised Afro –Asian relations. Africans could not understand Asians and their many divisions like, Sikh, Khoja, Ismailia and Lohana. Asians also could not understand Africans in their many ethnic identities (Chege, 2004:17). For instance, Africans in Nyanza believed that Ismailias were social and easy to work with compared to other groups of Asians. The complexity of the Asian community influenced their relations with Africans in that, they were choosy as regards employment of Africans as they tended to employ Africans from particular ethnic backgrounds. This diversity, therefore, helped in strengthening relations and development of Afro-Asian trust.

In 1987, tension and suspicion between Asians and Africans in Kisumu went up. This tension arose over the issue of entry into Simba Club (Sikh Union). This was a 'members only' club owned by Asians, but was used as a checkpoint during the 1987 Safari Rally competitions. As the rallying cars started arriving at this checkpoint, the management of the club decided to allow Asians only into the club to watch the rallying cars while African entry was restricted (Olingo, O.I., 2006). This was evidently an act of discrimination and a clear show of racial prejudice which offended the Africans.

The result of this was the revival of conflict between Africans and Asians. It also brought into focus the question of Asian citizenship in the minds of Africans in Kisumu. This scenario of strained relations was filled with emotional undercurrents that made the area

251

volatile as indicated in the statement of Maseno to the effect that " there is tension which can explode if ignited" (Maseno O.I., 2006). The move by Asians to restrict Africans from entering Simba club was proof that they still harboured some colonial racial prejudices.

By 1988, there was competition between the Africans who were selling second-hand clothes (*mitumba*) and the Indian cloth manufacturers who felt that this business was a threat to the textile industry (Kisumu Cotton Mills - KICOMI). The *mitumba* business within the postcolony symbolized the nature of unequal economic life of the postcolony. Therefore, there is a struggle among different categories of people which makes this chaotic space to be negotiated through all means.

Through political connections, Asians prevailed upon the government to ban the sale of second-hand clothes in Kisumu and in the entire country (*The Weekly Review,* 1987). This did not auger well with the local business people and caused some tension between those Asians who engaged in the textile industry and the African businessmen and women as well as the general African consumers in Kisumu who relied so much on second-hand clothes which they considered cheap as compared to the KICOMI products (Owiyo, O.I., 2006).

In the 1990s in Kisumu, the number of supermarkets and other businesses owned by Asians increased remarkably and these included Ebrahims, Yatin, Sai and Ukwala supermarkets. Some of these supermarkets emerged from what was initially the wholesale trade which Asians upgraded and expanded to supermarket status. Other businesses which Asians engaged in were social pubs like *Monami*, Club *Kiboko* and Tivoli Cinema (Ravalia, O.I., 2006).

But it is also at these business avenues that one could clearly see the glaring economic differences between Asians and Africans. In many ways these economic disparities were a critical feature of the postcolonial space. In these places, close Afro-Asian relations emerged to an extent that Asians would entrust some Africans with their business money. They could give such Africans money belonging to the business to take to the bank without any security escort.

When asked about the safety of their money in the hands of Africans an Asian oral informant remarked that '*yeye pana weza kupotea, tumefanya kazi miaka mingi* (we have worked with him for many years and he cannot get lost).These close individual relations were developed after a long time of working together (Mbudi, O.I., 2006). Such relations made some Africans not to look for jobs elsewhere even if the pay at the Asian firms was 'low'. It is also important to note that these businesses could not thrive on Asian clientele alone. The business depended on the purchasing power of Africans. In the end, interaction was inevitable.

Afro-Asian relations, therefore, depended on the trust and what one had in common with the other. If there was nothing in common to share, then one could not freely relate or interact with Asians and vice versa. These interactions were mostly at the level of business since the Asians rarely invited Africans to their houses unless one was employed as a domestic worker (Odhiambo, O.I., 2006).

Despite these problems, Africans commended the Asians in that they opened up job opportunities in Kisumu. Without them, the business sector in Kisumu would not have thrived (Odhiambo, O.I, 2006). In most cases, they brought their fellow Asians from India and established businesses for them. Africans helped such Asian newcomers by teaching them Kiswahili and other local languages.

At the same time, Africans were also well entrenched as shopkeepers in various trading centres within Kisumu town such as Kondele, Nyalenda, Manyatta, Arina among other places. However, most of the African shopkeepers bought their supplies in bulk from the Indian wholesalers (Owiyo, O.I., 2006). But also there were situations when Asians entered into business relationship with Africans at a higher level. For instance in 1991, there was a joint business venture in Kisumu between Asian and African personalities like J. Nyaseme, Mr J. Shah, the late Bishop H.Okullu and the late Hon H. Omino who jointly run the Victoria Finance and Lake Credit Finance (*The Weekly Review,* 8/3/1991). This partnership therefore gave these organisations an ownership identity that was neither Asian nor African. Such kind of business relationships ensured growth of the business sector in Kisumu as well as enhancing Afro-Asian relations.

With their diversity in businesses, such as hardware, construction and engineering and general shops, Asians met the demands of Africans by either employing them or providing essential services to the people around the town. Asians like Teja Singh made clothes for both Asians and Africans. Others like Lal sold tea leaves to the Africans from his grocery in town.

During Christmas holidays, Asians would normally call their regular African customers to receive some presents as a token from their shops. These were in the form of bundles of wheat or maize flour, calendars, sugar and so on (Nyamondo, O.I., 2006). This gesture was to ensure that the Asians maintained their African customers.

Apart from business and trade, many Asians were actively involved in various programmes that supported local African communities. The Asian community funded some well – known programmes in the province through the provision of public health and other social services. For instance, the Asian community donated wheelchairs to the physically disabled people drawn from Kisumu District and its environs (Omondi, O.I., 2006). Similarly, on many occasions, Asians have been donating food to less fortunate Africans who always sit or stand by the entrances of the Asian temples in Kisumu.

However, some Africans within the town have viewed these Asians as dishonest people. They felt that the Asians only engaged in charitable activities to gain publicity and favours from the government (Ayiemba, O.I., 2005). As Bindra (2005) argues, the Asian community needs to get involved in systematically building the productive capacity of the poor in the region by doing something sustainable and methodological, that is, by going far beyond the food handouts and donations at childrens' homes.

These gestures could be construed to mean Asian determination to seek acceptance and inclusion within the African community after a very negative relationship and attitude that developed between the two communities during the colonial period. This also showed Asian determination and attempt to dismantle their own cultural beliefs which excluded them from Africans whom they viewed as inferior and could not socially relate with as a community. Whether they dismantled their cultural beliefs or not this move made them to make sense and profit on the chaotic postcolony.

But even with their charitable donations, it was always characteristic of Asians in Kisumu region and elsewhere to leave the country for India and Britain as political elections approached and to come back when elections were over due to fear of violence. This means they knew that they were aliens in the political subspace of the postcolony. This was witnessed in 1992 and in the run up to 1997 general elections. Harassment of Kenyan Asians by Africans in public rallies as Africans advocated for constitutional reforms raised the level of Asians' anxiety in the run up to the 1997 elections.

During this time, some Kenyan politicians like Kenneth Matiba renewed the anti-Asian discourse and called for their expulsion from Kenya. In Kisumu for instance, residents threatened Asians to either support Raila Odinga's presidency in 1997 or leave the town (Omollo, O.I., 2006). This situation made some Asians to move closer to the Moi regime which, in turn, upset some Africans. There was a sense of relief among the Kenyan Asian community after the election, but much of that feeling was eroded as the reality of economic difficulties sunk in (Holmquist, 2002:30).

Local African leaders in Kisumu such as Dennis Akumu, former trade unionist, supported anti-Asian sentiments by claiming that Asians had exploited Africans for far too long and should thus be expelled from towns such as Kisumu where they dominated trade and commerce (*The Weekly Review* May 24, 1996:17/18). Most of the Africans working for Asians bought this idea and were just waiting for the moment when they would be told that Asians were leaving so that they could takeover their businesses (Owino, O.I., 2007). It is from such tensions both psychic and political that a strategy of subversion emerged (Bhabha, 1994:89).

Seemingly, such sentiments affected Afro-Asian relations in the sense that Asians developed fear which further isolated them from the Africans. As Bindra (2005:2) argues, 'the more we are resented, the more we isolate ourselves, the more we isolate ourselves the more we are resented'. A section of the local African populace called for the Asians to go back to India as they were dominating in business and also paying Africans low wages (Kadogo, O.I., 2006).

As resentment grew, Asians continued to isolate themselves from the African community into the 'islands of safety and comfort'. This 'island mentality' according to Bindra (2005:6), was the community's greatest mistake. This was because it affected their relations with Africans since they could not interact freely in social places. He further states that:

> We live among ourselves, surround ourselves with things South Asian, and follow our own rituals and practices to the exclusion of outsiders. Our contact with the African majority around our 'island' is formulaic: They are our customers, employees and suppliers, they are policemen, bureaucrats and regulators who get in the way of our business and demand bribes, they are beneficiaries of our occasional largesse; and they are the unfathomable masses surrounding us with their impenetrable stares and the whiff of latent violence (Bindra, 2005:6).

Such was the kind of ambivalent relations that characterised Afro-Asian interaction in Kisumu.

It should be noted that the Asian community, being a conglomeration of many diverse communities, languages, religions and customs is not a monolithic community with a cohesive leadership (Zarina, 2004:42). The internal character of the Kenyan Asian community was such that the many religious divisions meant that there was no dominant leader or authoritative institution that could speak for everyone.

However, towards the end of 1990s, the leaders of some of the plural Asian communities were quite close to some top government officials and some Asians were believed to have prospered fabulously by these relationships. In turn, they were expected to act as cheerleaders for government in their communities (Holmquist 2002:32).

Such kind of political relationship affected Afro-Asian relations at the local level in terms of business. For instance, the Hindocha and Somaia families appeared to have had powerful business connections with top officials in the government, a connection which they used to cover up several underhand economic deals (*The Weekly Review*, 13 1996:17). Because of their closeness to the Moi regime, they were able to manipulate the provincial labour and police offices in order to safeguard and protect their business interests. This was basically through bribery. On the contrary, middle-class Asians never wanted anything involving them with the Police or the Labour office.

In case of any disagreement between the Asian employer and their African employees, the Asian would rather clear with the employee by paying them their dues before dismissing them. This was because Asians feared police and court cases involving them with their African employees (Ramadhan, O.I., 2006). Their fear was not only because there was no justice in the post independent African institutions, but also they did not want to appear before African judicial, labour and prosecution officers. This was an antithesis of whatever happened during the colonial times when the Asians were racially superior to Africans.

Through such political connections, Asians who employed Africans could sometimes hire and fire them without giving any notice or without giving any benefits. In case of an accident or even death   in places of work, most Africans employed by the Asians complained of lack of compensation (Ochieng, O.I., 2007). Asians also changed names of their business enterprises and reopened others on a different name to avoid paying benefits and government taxes in case they realised that their business was becoming insolvent. African businessmen who dealt with them complained of corrupt means of doing business.

Milton Owino, an oral informant who worked as a technician with Copy Cat Business Enterprise (owned by Asians) in Kisumu in the late 1990s and who is now a businessman involved in the selling of Electronic Transfer Register (ETR) machines remarked that 'They do not always buy from Africans but sell to them, in such business transactions; they would always want to undercut Africans' (Owino, O.I., 2006). Because of their political and business connections, Asians could evict small-scale African businessmen who operated right in front of their shops.

Such kind of dubious means of doing business affected Afro-Asian relations in that Africans viewed Asians as corrupt and dishonest people. This was an image which Asians could not shake off with ease (Bindra, 2005:6). However, some Asians also gave African hawkers goods to sell and get commission while returning unsold items and the proceeds to the Asians. However, this only happened in the context where there was trust between Africans and Asians.

It is evident that Afro-Asian relations were characterised by upheavals, sometimes good or bad. The Asian fear was rejuvenated again towards the turn of the century around the year 2000 when the country was approaching elections in the year 2002. This fear came as a result of economic stagnation, doubts as to the governments' protective capacity and fears that the Moi regime was losing its grip on power and because of chronic corruption and their feelings that they must participate in it or face unfortunate consequences (Holmquist, 2002, Bodo, O.I., 2005). Many of them read the political signs and with the help of Shakeel Shabir, the former Kisumu mayor, they voted for the National Rainbow Coalition (NARC) government which was popular in Nyanza Province. However, there was no Asian candidate both at the parliamentary and civic level.

At a professional level, Afro-Asian relations were always good as Asians, especially doctors, had a lot of African customers. Asian doctors would even visit their African clients and treat them in the village and estates. Some of the doctors such as Somaia, Patel and Shabir often offered treatment to their regular and long time African friends on credit. Africans liked them because of their professionalism and general good interaction with their customers (Olingo, O.I., 2006). Doctor Shabir gained a lot of respect from Africans due to his effective medical practice to the extent that some of the children that were delivered in his hospital (*Ka dakta Sabir*) were named after him (Owiyo, O.I., 2006).

Within the medical circles, Asian doctors were able to dismantle the racial barrier in order to discharge their duties to Africans. But also, Africans willingly sought medical attention from Asian doctors, some of whom became family doctors for certain African families. These doctors were neither for Asians nor Africans but served the two communities indiscriminately. Therefore, even though Africans and Asians were racially different, there were some values (medical) which Africans sought from Asian doctors. This enhanced their relationship with Africans especially those Africans who had Asian doctors as their family doctors. But also doctor Shabir managed to train some African women whom he employed in his clinic as midwives. A good example was a lady (deceased) popularly known as Mama Leah who later owned the Nyawita Maternity and Nursing Home in Kisumu after working for doctor Shabir for several years.

Afro-Asians' interaction and relations continued to be manifested in the medical circles as Asians initiated medical facilities in Kisumu town where both Asians and Africans continued to be treated. They created their own medical spaces with services and values which reflected their aspirations. They established the Aga khan Hospital, Guru Nanak Hospital and Jalaram Hospital. In these hospitals, even though some were high-cost and could only be afforded by a certain class of Africans, racism was not practised and Asian or African doctors did not discriminateagainst patients across the racial divide.

However, Asians did not frequent public hospitals such as the New Nyanza General Hospital or Kisumu District Hospital. Facilities in Asian hospitals must have made favourable financial provisions for them. In a way, we can say that most of them

262

preferred exclusive lifestyle and maintained their colonial mentality of being superior to Africans and their institutions.

6.6 Afro –Asian Social Interaction in the Moi Era

In the Moi era, Afro-Asian social interaction continued to take the usual isolationist tendency by the Asians. They stayed in the same segregated housing zones they had occupied before, namely their shops cum residential houses within the town centre. Others stayed in Milimani, Kibuye and Patel flats. They maintained minimal interaction with their African neighbours. Those who stayed in Patel flats, continued to secure their own flats while Africans also stayed in separate flats. In such areas, social interaction was always minimal. They rarely invited Africans to their houses because they shared nothing in common unless one was assigned some duties by them. Africans also rarely invited Asians into their houses or homes.

In schools, the government policy of integration, was achieved in various schools especially in the late 1970s and in the 1980s (*Finance Magazine*, May 1997:13). However; some Asians took their children to schools which offered the British Curriculum at secondary school level.

There was, therefore, an element of class as far as Afro-Asian relations in schools was concerned. Very affluent Asians took their children to high cost Asian schools such as Kisumu Senior Academy and Kisumu Junior Academy. Some Africans of the same class also took their children to these schools where the British curriculum formed the core part of the syllabus. Colonial legacies, therefore formed a fundamental component of the postcolonial discourse that informed the Nyanza postcolonial sub-space while on the other hand, there were Asian and African children who attended public primary and secondary schools such as the M.M Shah primary, Arya primary, Kisumu Girls and Kisumu Boys High schools.

It should be noted that all these schools were formally Asian owned schools but were later taken over by the government. The curriculum was based on the 8-4-4 system of education. It is, therefore, clear that some Asians and Africans continued to suffer from neo-colonialism while the other 'middle class' identified themselves with the social aspirations of the independent African state. The most important point here is that most of the teachers in these Asian schools were African.

Relations in the school set-up were twofold. First, it was between African and Asian children themselves and second between African teachers and Asian pupils. This latter relation went beyond the school compound to Asian houses in the estates such as Milimani, Tom Mboya and Patel flats where these African teachers conducted private tuition services on a daily basis to the Asian children (Ochieng', O.I., 2007). The idea was for Asian children to excel in school so that they could continue to dominate the affairs of the postcolony

Full integration in schools was not achieved even in the Moi era. Bindra (2005:6) states that by 1990s, wealthy Asian families started taking their children out of the public education system and were busy building academies that were exclusively Asian. Such schools were Kisumu International School, Jalaram Academy and Mahavir School. However, some African children of the same economic class later found their way into these high-cost Asian schools (Maseno, O.I 2006). Therefore, relations in such schools were determined by economic class. This was the characteristic of Afro-Asian relations that kept on shifting depending on economic interest and class by 2002.

Afro-Asian social relations in both public and private schools owned by Asians mostly revolved around academics and sports. Asian students identified so much with bright African students. This was probably because of what they gained from each other in terms of classwork. Relations were also skewed in the direction of sports. Games such as table tennis and hockey were areas which enhanced Afro-Asian relations in schools. For instance at Kisumu Boys, the hockey team was a mixture of both Asians and Africans. Sometimes during hockey practices, instructions were given in vernacular (Dholuo) to the players. Owino Matheus a former student and hockey player at Kisumu Boys says that terms such as *chwad gino, kode* (hit that thing in reference to the hockey cork and with him respectively) were simple communications which were understood by Asians and African hockey players (Owino, O.I., 2007). Games like table tennis enhanced close relations since it involved only two people. As such, Asian and African students engaged in the sport would organise their own time table to go and practise (Odhiambo, O.I., 2006).

6.7 Summary and Conclusion

It was the objective of this chapter to examine Afro-Asian relations during the Kenyatta era and Moi era from 1963-1978 and 1978-2002, respectively. We have demonstrated that this era was characterised by the Africanization policy and a massive expansion of educational facilities which went beyond racial segregation which the government was keen on eradicating.

Organisations such as the KNTC, ICDC, IDB, KIE and DFCK were used to encourage and support African participation in the economy and to entrench African capitalism in the Kenyatta era. Due to Africanization policy and increased theft and attacks on the Asians by Africans during the Kenyatta era, many Asians withdrew from Ndere and Yala areas. The end result was loss of jobs by Africans in the ginneries and Asian shops.

Socially, in both Kenyatta and the Moi era, the process of Afro-Asian social integration was encouraged in schools and residential places. However, this was not fully achieved as anticipated. This, therefore, raises the question of redefining the term integration and its various aspects. It has been demonstrated that the Moi-Asian nexus that developed in the Moi era allowed Asians to be at cutting the edge of the economy. This nexus was also attributed to their historical sense of vulnerability which forced them to support the regime in power.

The chapter concludes that political developments such as the killing of Pio Gama Pinto, deportation of Pranlel Sheth to India among other Asians and the stern warning from

President Jomo Kenyatta instilled fear among the Asians. But this not withstanding, many Asians who had developed good relationship with Africans gave out their property to their African friends and workers as they withdrew from Yala and Kendu Bay areas of Nyanza.

Similarly, the Moi-Asian nexus affected Afro-Asian political relations since Asians were viewed by the locals as supporters of a political leadership which had oppressed the people of Nyanza. This was evident by the way Asians were threatened by Africans in Nyanza when general elections approached. Asians were threatened with eviction from kisumu town if they did not vote for the dominant political party in the area thus forcing Asians to compromise their democratic rights. In chapter seven, we summarise the main findings of this research project. Besides, we draw a number of conclusions.

CHAPTER SEVEN

7.0 SUMMARY AND CONCLUSIONS

This study set out to investigate race relations between Asians and African communities of Kenya's Nyanza Province. The objectives of the study were to examine the roots of Asian presence and settlement in Nyanza Province of Kenya, to examine the role played by Asians in the socio-economic and political activities in Kisumu, Ndere, Kendu Bay and Yala areas of Nyanza with an aim of looking at whether these relations were beneficial or conflictual.

It also examined the outcomes and extent of Afro-Asian integration in Kisumu, Ndere, Kendu Bay and Yala. Besides, study addressed the following questions: What were the roots of Asian presence in Kenya's Nyanza region? What are the historical causes of suspicion, tension and conflict between Asians and Africans in Kisumu, Ndere, Kendu Bay and Yala areas of Nyanza? How have the Afro-Asian relations manifested themselves in the social, cultural, political and economic spaces of Kisumu, Ndere, Kendu Bay and Yala areas of Nyanza? What were the outcomes and extent of Afro-Asian integration in Kisumu, Ndere, Kendu Bay and Yala? The literature reviewed in this work established that some studies had been undertaken on the Asian question. However, several gaps including the one on the Afro-Asian relations in Nyanza were identified as possible avenues for scholarly research.

This study is important because it deviates from the nationalistic analysis of interracial relations by embracing localized investigations in the realm of area studies. It also contributes to the scarce literature on Asian activities in Nyanza Province which have so far, not received serious scholarly attention. Methodologically, the study employed a question guideline and oral interviews to harness primary data. Secondary data was also obtained from local libraries.

In this study, Nyanza is treated as a postcolonial sub-space, which is grappling with imperial hegemony and legacy. The subject of race relations assumes even greater significance in such plural sub-spaces as the Nyanza region in which the population is divided not merely on the basis of race, but also by language, culture, value system and religion. In such societies, unless a common consensus exists or a sense of nationhood is developed, divisive tendencies may intensify an atmosphere of suspicion, hate, and violence (Bhatt, 1976).

Loomba (1998) argues that it is now helpful to think of post colonialism not just as coming literally after colonialism and signifying its demise, but more flexibly, as the contestation of colonial domination and the legacies of colonialism. Racial relations between Asians and Africans in Nyanza region were studied as one of the colonial legacies within a mixed plural society characterized by people of complex identities, opposing values and interests. The postcolonial theory brings questions of subjectivity to the fore. It illustrates the complexities of the postcolonial identity, particularly at a time of intense globalization. The thrust of postcolonial thinking is to recognize the existence of the otherness and dismantle formulations, which inform discourses on the otherness (Kisiang'ani, 2003).

In Chapter Two, the study examines the roots of modern Asian origin and settlement in Kenya and specifically in Nyanza. The study has demonstrated that the Asian contact with Africans started way back in the first century. Historical references such as the *Periplus of the Erythrean Sea, Nuzhat-al Mustag* (The pleasure of travelling) and the Writings of Marco Polo attest to the fact that Asians were in contact with Africans much earlier before the construction of the Kenya-Uganda Railway. However, the study has demonstrated that the first formal Asian settlement in Kenya and specifically in Nyanza came with the construction of the Kenya-Uganda Railway where they came as indentured labourers. It has been established that Kibos Indian Settlement Scheme was the first authorized settlement scheme in the colony to come up in 1903 out of contestations for public space within Nyanza province. The second Asian settlement scheme was established in Nyando area of Nyanza.

The chapter concluded that by settling Asians in the lowlands, the colonial government laid the foundation upon which Afro-Asian relations and interaction were to be built. Although, Africans imitated farming techniques introduced by Asians, there were cases of invasion on their farms by Africans which symbolized resistance by dispossessed Africans against some forms of knowledge authored and authorized by the West. Colonial institutions such as Lands Department, Public Works Department, Temporary Occupation Licences and Trading License Ordinance ensured that the Asians penetrated, exploited, and settled in the interior parts of Nyanza as traders thus entrenching capitalism and imperialism.

Chapter Three explores Afro-Asian interaction from 1900-1919 and characterizes the colonial government's space creation for interaction. It has been noted that this is the period when trading centres and towns such as Kisumu, Ndere, Yala and Kendu Bay emerged thus setting the stage for Afro-Asian economic interactions in the area. It has also been demonstrated that Asians played a major role in the establishment of these towns and trading centres as they inter-racially engaged in business from the early times. These trading centres thus became active sites where Afro-Asian economic interaction took place. By selling exotic wares such as clothes, corrugated iron sheets, *kitenge*, biscuits, flour and cereals, Asians were able to change the cultural lifestyle of the Africans. Their dressing and eating habits also changed.

The chapter concludes that in the early colonial period, Afro-Asian relations were cordial in some areas of Nyanza to an extent that Asians were given local names thereby indicating linguistic hybridity which characterized Afro-Asian relations in Nyanza Province. However, the use of such names as *kadogo, mrefu, boyi and yaya* by Asians and which aimed at fixing rigid class categories between Asians and Africans were contested by Africans. Social and political relations during this time followed a racial pattern.

In Chapter Four, the study focuses on the Afro-Asian social, political and economic relations in the inter-war years and during the Second World War 1919-1945. This period witnessed the emergence of rivalry between African and Asian traders with the former questioning the monopoly of the latter in the economic sphere. In addition, the chapter has pointed out that organisations such as the Kavirondo Welfare Taxpayers Association and the Kavirondo Chamber of Commerce were some of the organisations which questioned Asian monopoloy.

There was also a shift in Asian economic activity from small-scale businesses such as shopkeepers and artisans to large-scale businesses and also into the cotton industry. However, in some places like Yala, incidences of crime targeted at the Asian merchants strained Afro-Asian relations. Such activities increased hatred, suspicion and conflict of interest between the two communities. Conflict between Asians and African farmers frequently arose over returns from the sale of cotton to the Asians and also on how Africans were handled at the cotton buying centres by the Asians.

It was demonstrated that although the cultivation of cotton was an initiative of the colonial government of introducing the capitalist mode of production into the rural economies of Nyanza through Asians, their attempt to introduce this crop was met by some resistance. This was evidently viewed as subversive resistance by Africans to Western forms of knowledge and values. It is evident in the chapter that the office of the chief was widely used to marginalize Africans and to ensure that the colonial government's objective of imperialism and capitalism was achieved. This was evident by the administrative encouragement of the spread of Indian traders into African areas through the support of these chiefs in places like Ndere and Yala.

The chapter concludes that the policy of separate development and racial segregation ensured that each community developed its own schools. Because of necessity, some of these racial barriers were overcome. This suggested that strict opposite binarism could not work within the Nyanza postcolony.

In Chapter Five, the study explored Afro-Asian relations from 1945-1963. It has been argued in this chapter that there was a heightened trade rivalry between Asians and Africans which continued to flourish during this period. But more importantly, African elites and returnee soldiers from the World War II started questioning some forms of dominance through organized welfare and political associations. It has been demonstrated that Afro-Asian economic relation was also characterized by malpractices which brought about tension and suspicion between the two communities especially in the cotton industry. Areas where cotton was grown and ginneries established such as Alego, Ndere , Yala and Kendu Bay thus became areas of economic contestations.

Fundamentally, the chapter argues that the government involvement in the cotton industry in the Nyanza region marked the beginning of change of ownership in the industry from Asians to Africans as Africans started organizing themselves into cooperative societies. On the other hand, the dynamics of Afro-Asian social relations was experienced in situations where African women working for Asians taught them local languages including *Kiswahili* and *Dholuo* while the Asian women taught African women whom they employed how to cook foods such as *chapati* and *samosa*. The chapter concludes that the Asians helped in championing the African cause by financing the African press like *Ramogi* . In spite of the racial colonial policies, the people of Kisumu went ahead and elected Jamal Amin as their Member of Parliament. This period witnessed some form of Afro-Asian political integration in Nyanza Province.

Chapter Six examined Afro-Asian social, political and economic relations during Kenyatta and Moi eras between 1963- 1978 and 1978-2002 respectively. The chapter argues that nothing much changed in terms of structures as European colonialism was Africanized making Kenyatta the first black governor (East Africa Standard, 14/12/ 2008). Kenyatta era brought in several social and economic changes which had a great impact on Afro-Asian relations. This was characterised by the Africanization policy and a massive expansion of educational facilities that went beyond racial segregation which the government was keen on eradicating. This policy together with thefts and attacks on Asians by Africans later forced the Asians out of Ndere, Yala and Kendu Bay areas leading to many African losing jobs. But viewed from a different point of view, this policy was to help the government in entrenching capitalism which was a neo-colonial means of administering the colony.

The Moi-Asian nexus affected Afro-Asian relations in Nyanza because Asians took advantage of this position to dominate Africans especially in the textile industry. Africans' effort to sell *mitumba* clothes and the Asian campaign to have these clothes banned were therefore a testimony of how the chaotic space within the postcolony was negotiated. It also depicted how economic life within the postcolony was unequal. A new aspect of Afro-Asian relationship emerged. The relationship was characterized by skilled African labourers and professionals working for the Asians in their firms.

The Chapter concludes that political developments during the Kenyatta era such as the killing of Pio Gama Pinto, deportation of Pranlel Sheth and the stern warning by President Kenyatta to Asian community in his regime instilled fear among Asians thereby affecting their relationship with Africans in Nyanza. This is because Asian participation in the local politics in Nyanza was determined by whatever was happening at the national level.

The connection between Moi and Asians provided an avenue where Asians were viewed as pro- KANU in Nyanza, an area which was an opposition zone and anti- KANU government. This made the Asian community in Nyanza to be vulnerable to attacks and intimidations whenever general elections approached thereby affecting Afro-Asian relations in the Nyanza postcolony. Even though Asians were involved in some charitable activities by donating foodstuff and wheelchairs to the less fortunate Africans, Afro-Asian social integration in schools and residential areas was minimal and not fully achieved in the two eras.

The study had set out to address the following premises: That forced immigration played a remarkable role in the emergence of interracial relations between Africans and Asians in Kisumu, Ndere, Kendu Bay and Yala areas of Nyanza, that government policies were the main causes of suspicion, tension and conflict between Asians and Africans in

Kisumu, Ndere, Kendu Bay and Yala areas of Nyanza, that the contest between Africans and Asians manifested itself in the social, political and economic space and lastly, that racial integration and harmony have been achieved between Africans and Asians in Kisumu, Ndere, Kendu Bay and Yala areas of Nyanza.

This study has achieved its objective by establishing that the roots of Asian presence and settlement in Nyanza goes back to the first century and came with the formal settlement of these people in Kibos and Nyando areas in 1903 as a result of contestations over the issue of the white highlands. This disapproves the premise that forced immigration played a remarkable role in the emergence of Afro-Asian relations in Kisumu, Ndere, Kendu Bay and Yala. Similarly, the study has traced the historical causes of Afro-Asian tension, suspicion and conflict to colonial policies of racial segregation which partly confirms one of the research premises of this study.

Apart from the colonial policies of racial segregation, economic exploitation, malpractices and domination, Africanization policy, anti-Asian sentiments by African leaders as well as the Moi-Asian nexus emerged as some of the main causes of Afro-Asian suspicion, conflict and tension within the Nyanza postcolony. This confirms the research premise of the study which stated that the contest between Africans and Asians manifested itself in the social, political and economic space. Morever, Asians played a role in running the economic and political activities in Nyanza. This was achieved through establishing shops, ginneries and manufacturing industries in Kisumu, Ndere, Yala and Kendu Bay where Africans were employed. Politically, their role was witnessed

276

in the way they allied with Africans to champion for their cause towards independence by financing African press like *Ramogi*. Although Afro-Asian relations revolved around social, economic and political spheres, these spheres also remained as major sites where Afro-Asian contestations took place.

It was difficult for this study to analyse the outcomes of the Afro-Asian integration in Kisumu, Ndere, Kendu Bay and Yala since the definition of integration was problematic and it raised many questions. The study therefore concludes that full Afro-Asian integration was not achieved in the Nyanza postcolony thereby disapproving the last research hypothesis that Afro-Asian integration and harmony have been achieved in the Nyanza postcolony.

In conclusion, therefore, the problem of race relations in Nyanza was deeply embedded in the historical development of the country. The rivalry, animosity and antagonisms between African and Asian communities had their origin in the colonial period and especially in the institutional structures imposed by the British. These institutional patterns gave rise to certain attitudes and beliefs, which were conducive to a state of conflict and interracial hostility. The racial structure, capitalism and imperialism were the main causes of these animosities.

Therefore, as Africans continue to radically rethink and reformulate forms of knowledge and social institutions authored and authorised by the West, the study recommends that Asians should also rethink and re-examine their caste system with a view to dismantling it particularly within the context of Nyanza and Kenya in general as a space where opposite binaries based on colonial racial structure has failed.

By embracing such radical moves, issues such as full integration in all aspects of Afro-Asian relations discussed above will easily be achieved. As a result, issues of suspicion, tension and hatred will be avoided. This is because the genesis of all these tension and hatred in areas where they were experienced in the Nyanza postcolony was unequal relations. The study therefore recommends that there should be a way in which resources should be equitably distributed. Further, the study recommends that both Asians and Africans should be involved in joint socio-economic and political endeavours so as to realize full integration within the Nyanza region.

Further research also needs to be carried out on the role of each Asian community in Nyanza province and in other parts of the country in order to compare and see how such roles have shaped their relations with Africans in those areas. Further research should also be done on the Asian religion and culture with a view to examining how religion and culture have affected Afro-Asian relations in the country. Finally, the study recommends the development of a viable theoretical model to study the Afro-Asian relation in Africa.

BIBLIOGRAPHY

Oral Sources

Adhiambo Christine, O.I 30/12/2005
Adhiambo Rosaline, O.I 22/4/2006
Adjai Omollo, O.I 7/1/2006
Aguya John, O.I 28/12/2005
Ajay Gosh, O.I 28/12/ 2006
Ajay Gosh, O.I 30/12/2006
Akinyi Beatrice, O.I 10/1/2006
Apiyo Philis, O.I 30/12/ 2005
Ayiemba Hezron (R.I.P), O.I 22/11/2005
Bodo Charles, O.I 25/12/2005
Chatur Farouk, 5/4/2006
Chatur Mobin, O.I 27/11/2005
Chatur Mohammed, O.I 22/11/2005
Devji jamal, O.I 22/ 7/2006
Faraj Ojijo, O.I, 29/12/2006,4/1/2007
George King, O.I 17/11/2005
Jagpal Singh, O.I 20/8/ 2006
Kabong Jeckonia, O.I 10/10/2006
Kabong' Owino O.I 2005
Kadogo Alex, O.I 2/2/2006
Kassam Aziz, O.I 30/3/ 2006
Kenyatta Mattews, O.I 16/11/ 2005
Malit Mboya, O.I 29/12/ 2006
Malit Nasser, O.I 11/12/ 2005
Malit Richard, O.I, 29/12/2006
Mandhavia Gopal, O.I 10/4/ 2006
Maseno Obeid, O.I 20/11/2005
Maseno Obeid, O.I., 14/1/2007
Mayoor Mulji, O.I 23/4/2006
Mbeya Richard, O.I 12/4/2006
Mboya Tom, O.I 12/10/2006
Mbudi Erick, O.I, 28/11/2005
Mito Dickson A, O.I 4/12007
Muganda Benard, O.I 12/4/2006
Mzungu Isaih, O.I 3/1 2007
Nyamondo Bob, O.I 28/5/2006
Obeid Olingo, O.I 30/12/2006
Ochich Alice, O.I 29/11/2005
Ochieng Felix, O.I 2/1/ 2006
Ochieng James, O.I 12/12/2005

Ochoko David, O.I 12/1/2006
Odawa John, O.I 10/11/ 2005
Odera Peter, O.I 10/10/2006
Odhiambo George, O.I 30/12/2006
Odhiambo Martin, O.I 2/2/2006
Odhiambo Monica, O.I 10/1/2006
Odhiambo Stephen, O.I 2007
Odhiambo, O.I 2006
Odindo John, O.I 15/11/2005
Odingo ,O.I 2005
Odongo Chrisopher, O.I 23/5/2006
Odwa Richard, O.I 10/10/2006
Ogada James, O.I 20/1/2006
Ogallo Galgalo, O.I, 22/1/2006
Okech Agengo, O.I 4/4 2006
Okech Julius, O.I 2/11/ 2005
Olingo Joseph, O.I, 30/12/2006
Omar Faraj O.I, 4/1/2007
Omedo John, O.I, 20/7/ 2006
Omollo George, O.I 9/11/2005
Omoro Rogins, O.I 15/11/2005
Ondiallo John, O.I, 31/12/2006, 3/1/ 2007
Ongudu John, O.I 12/1/2006
Orenda Eleazar, O.I 30/3/2006
Orenda Joshua, O.I 29/12/2006
Orengo Joseph, O.I 22/11/2005
Otula Akoko, O.I 3/3/2006
Owino Milton, O.I 1/1/2007
Owiyo Joab, O.I 17/11/2005, 20/1/2006
Patel Jayesh, O.I 2007
Rajiv Raja, O.I 22/11/2005
Ramadhan Shaban O.I 29/12/2006
Ravalia Jayant, O.I 3/4/2006
Rawat Singh, O.I 9/10/2005
Shah Ajay O.I, 25/11/ 2005
Shah Sennan, O.I 30/12/2006
Siderra Henry, O.I 23/11/2005
Siderra Joel, O.I 10/11/ 2005
Tieni Susan, O.I 5/1/2007
Tieni Susana, O.I 30/12/2006
Wambia David, O.I 23/4/ 2006
Wasonga Peter, O.I 1/11 2005

Archival Data

KPAR   Kisumu Province Annual Report   1907, 1908, 1909

AR   Nyanza Province Annual Report 1910-1962
M.C.K AR   Muniicpal Council of Kisumu Annual Report
KNA, PC/NZA/1/2 Nyanza Provincial Annual Report1906/07
KNA, PC/NZA/1/3 Nyanza Provincial Annual Report 1907/08
KNA, PC/NZA/1/4 Nyanza Provincial Annual Report 1909
KNA, PC/NZA/1/5Nyanza Provincial Annual Report 1910
KNA, PC/NZA/1/7 Nyanza Annual Report 1912
KNA, PC/NZA/1/8 Nyanza Province Annual Report 1913
KNA, PC/NZA/1/2 Nyanza Province Annual Report 1910/14
KNA, PC/NZA/1/10 Nyanza Proviince Annual Report 1916
KNA, PC/NZA/1/12 Nyanza Province Annual Report 1917
KNA, PC/NZA/1/13 Nyanza Province Annual Report 1917/18
KNA, PC/NZA/1/16/Nyanza Province Annual Report 1920-21
PC/NZA/1/18/ Annual Report Nyanza Province 1923
PC/NZA/1/20 Nyanza Provincial AnnualReport1925
KNA, PC/NZA/1/27 Nyanza Province Annual Report 1927
KNA, PC/NZA/1/23 Annual Report 1928
PC/NZA/ 1/23 / Nyanza Province Annual Report1928/29
PC/NZA/1/30 Nyanza Province Annual Report 1930
PC/NZA/1/26 Nyanza Province Annual Report 1931
KNA, PC/NZA/1/28 Nyanza Province Annual Report 1933
PC/NZA/1/31/ Annual Report Nyanza Province 1936
KNA, PC/NZA/1/33 Annual Report 1939
PC/NZA/1/34 Annual Report 1940
PC/NZA/1/34 Annual Report 1943
PC/NZA/1/40 Nyanza Province Annual Report 1945
KNA, PC/NZA/1/12/115 Traders Licensing Ordinance1933-45
KNA, PC/NZA/2/12/133 Crop Production Specific Crops –Cotton
KNA, PC/NZA/2/12/1 Cotton Ginneries 1928-38
KNA PC/NZA/2/12/58 Kendu Ginnery Lease 1934-46
KNA, PC/NZA/2/12/68 Cotton Buying Shares 1937
KNA, PC/NZA/2/16/60 Station, and Site 1946-51
PC/NZA/2/17/13 Cooperative Societies 1942-47
KNA, PC/NZA/2/18/11 Municpal Board and Township Committee 1936
PC/NZA/3/1/264 Central Nyanza 1951-53
KNA, PC/NZA/3/1/353 Nyanza Province Kenya Cotton Association
KNAPC/NZA/3/1/404 Invitations 1955-57
KNA, PC/NZA/3/1/467 Monthly Intellignce Report Kisumu-Lndiani 1939
KNA, PC/NZA/3/2/80 Cotton 1951-52
KNA, PC/NZA/3/2/83 Cotton 1951-9
KNA, PC/NZA/3/3/20 Sim Sim 1914
PC/NZA/3/6/42 Organisation and Establishment of Schools 1938
PC/NZA/3/6/45 Asian Schools 1952-53
KNA, PC/NZA/3/14/241 Land Alienation 1956-8
KNA, PC/NZA/3/14/314 Nyanza Trading Centre and Fishing Stations 1931-51
KNA/PC/NZA/3/14/315 Trade Centres 1931-1944

KNA, PC/NZA/3/14/319 Nyanza Trading Centres and Fishing Stations 1933-1951
PC/NZA/3/14/322 Trading Centres 1937-51
KNA, PC/NZA/3/15/142 Native Liqour 1931
KNA, PC/NZA/3/15/145 Crime Report, and Invesstigation 1943
KNA, PC/NZA/3/22/1/11-12 Kibos Indian Settlement 1908/10
KNA, PC/NZA/3/22/1/2-13 Kibos Indian Settlement Gulam Mohamed 1910-12
KNA, PC/NZA/3/22/3 Port, and Shipping Service 1931-42
KNA, PC/NZA/3/39/1 Police Distribution, and Reduction 1927
KNA, PC/NZA/3/41/3/1 Building Kisumu District 1928
KNA, PC/NZA/3/42/3 Roads, and Bridges Kisumu District 1927
KNA, PC/NZA/4/4/47 Central Nyanza Political and Social Reports 1956
KNA, PC/NZA/4/4/72 Annual Report Central Nyanza District 1959
KNA, PC/NZA/4/4/119 Nyanza Province Annual Report 1954
KNA, PC/NZA/4/4/111 Annual Report Central Nyanza 1961
KNA, PC/NZA/4/4/105 Annual Report Central Nyanza 1958
KNA, PC/NZA/4/6/2 Municpalities, and District Councils1951-59
KNADC/KSM/1/1/16 Monthly Intelligence Report 1940
KNA, DC/KSM/1/3/48 Crop Production
KNA, DC/KSM/1/10/10 Indian Education 1931-56
KNA, PC/NZA/1/12/116 Traders Licensing 1933-45
KNA, DC/KSM/1/17/40 Reservist Annual Report 1964
KNADC/KSM/1/19/280 Nyanza Liqour Licensing Court 1952-
KNA, DC/KSM/1/19/302-305 Nyanza Trading Company
KNA, DC/KSM/1/32/12 Trade and Customs Fish 1943
KNA, DC/KSM/1/30/53 African Housing in Township 1957
KNA, DC/KSM/1/30/53 African Housing in Township and Trading Centres Vasey
Report
KNA, DC/KSM/1/36/48 Central Kavirondo Annual Report 1948
KNA, AE/3/961 African Chamber of Commerce 1960
AK/2/17 Annual Report Central Kavirondo1934-51
KNA, AK/4/11/Development Policy Central Nyanza 1949-52
KNA, AK/11/91Messrs Small and Company Ginners and Posts Nyanza 1941-1952
KNA, AK/11/99 Cotton Ginnery Applications for New Ginneries Ndere Ginnery1935-53
KNA, AK/11/151 Nyanza Cotton Committee 1951-59
KNA, BV/6/628 Cotton Ginneries Nyanza Province General 1935-54
KNA, BV/14/203 Range management 1963-64
KNA, CS/8/11/134 Staff Housing Nyanza 1939-54
Central Kavirondo Annual Report 1934-51
KNA, HT/17/3 Annual Report District Commissioner Nyanza Region 1960-65
KNA, HT/17/5 Annual Report Nyanza Province 1960-68
KNA, HT/17/3 Annual Report Central Nyanza District 1961
KNA, HT/17/5 Annual Report Nyanza Province 1964
KNA, HT/17/16 Publications, and Records Annual Report Central Nyanza 1955-59
KNA, HT/17/22 Kisumu District Annual Report 1968
KNA, HT/17/16 Publications, and Records Annual Report Central Nyanza 1955-59
KNA, HT/17/19 Kisumu District Annual Report 1967

KNA, NHC/1/152 Housing Asian Scheme 1961
KNA, TP/5/29 Cotton Production and Marketing 1971-77
KNA, TR/18/59 Publications –Survey of Cotton Industry Nyanza Province in Siaya, Kisumu, South Nyanza 1973

Magazines
E.A.S East African Standard April 22 1969
East African Standard August 17, 1978, June, 13 1978, 10/10/69, 11/12/69
DN Daily Nation 10/10/1969, 9/1/70, 25/9/95
Finance May 13-26 1997
KT Kenya Timess 17/10/95, 1/6/89
WR Weekly Review, 6/10/78 March 6 1981, 26/2/82, 10/9/82,   January 1983, 21/1/83, 15/4/83, August 1983, 14/12/84 1986, 1987,   November 28, 1988, January 1992, 14/10/1994, 24/5/1996, 13, December 1996

Books

Abuor, C.O., (1972). *White Highlands No More*, Nairobi: Pan African Researchers

Ahluwalia, P., (2001). *Politics and Postcolonial Theory African Inflections*; London:

Ahluwalia, P., (1996*). Post colonialism and The politics of Kenya*, New York: Nova Science Publishers.

Andrew, A., (1976). 'Race and Politics in South Africa' in G. Bowker (ed*) Race and Ethnic ,* London: Hutchison and company A.

Ashcroft Bill, Griffins Gareth et al (1995) *The Postcolonial Studies Reader,* London: Routledge Publishers.

Atieno Odhiambo, E. S., (1981). Siasa*: Politics and Nationalism in East Africa 1905 – 1939*, Nairobi: Kenya Literature Bureau.

Atieno Odhiambo, E., (1995). 'The Formative Years 1945-1955' in Ogot B.A and Ochieng W.R., (ed) *Decolonisation and Independence in Kenya 1940-1993*, Nairobi: East African Educational Publishers.

Ochieng W.R., (1975). *First Word Essays on Kenya History,* Nairobi: East African Literature Bureau.

Atieno Odhiambo (1976). 'Seek Ye First The Economic Kingdom' A history of The Luo Thrift and Trading Corporation (LUTATCO)1945-1956 in Ogot B.A (ed) *Economic History and Social History of East Africa,* Nairobi: Kenya Literature Bureau.

Ayres, R., (1995). *Schools of Development Thought,* Dartford: Greenwich University Press.

Baker, D.G., (1983). *Race, Ethnicity and Power*, London: Routledge and Kegan Paul.

Barker, E. (1958). *A Short History of Nyanza*, Nairobi: East African Literature Bureau.

Baran, P., (1957). *The Political Economy of Growth*, New York: Monthly Review Press.

Barley, C., (1989). *Atlas of the British Empire*, Hamlya Publishing Group Amazon L.T.D

Bell, C. R., (1964) *The Road to Independence*, Nairobi: Longmans of Kenya.

Bennet,G., (1966) *Kenya A Political History: The Colonial Period*, Nairobi: Oxford University Press

Bennet G., and Rosberg C., (1961). *The Kenyatta Election: Kenya 1960-1961* London: Oxford University Press.

Berman, B., (1990). *Control and Crisis in Colonial Kenya: The Dialectic of Domination,* Nairobi: East African Educational Publishers.

Bhabha, H., (1994*). The Location of Culture,* London: Routledge.

Bhabha, H., (2006). Homi Bhabha, www.en.wakipedia.org/wiki/homi bhabha 2006:2

Bharati, A., (1972). The *Asians in East Africa. Jayhind and Uhuru.* Chicago: Nelson Hall Company.

Burgman.H., (1990). *The Way the Catholic Church Started in Western Kenya.* Nairobi: Mission Book Service.

Chanan, S., (1972). 'Later Asian Protest Movements' in Ogot, B.A (ed) *Politics and Nationalism in Colonial Kenya,* Nairobi: East Africa Publishing House.

Chilcote, R.H., (1974). '*Alternative Perspectives on Development and Underdevelopment in Latin America: The Struggle with Dependency and Beyond*, Cambridge Mass: Schenkman Publishing Co, Inc.

Chittick, N., (1974). 'The Coast Before the Arrival of the Portuguese', in Ogot, B.A. (ed) *Zamani: A Survey of East African History,* Nairobi: East African Publishing House.

Churchill, W., (1908). *My African Journey.* London:

Clayton, C., and Savage, D., (1974) *Government and Labour in Kenya* 1895-1963, London: Frank Cass

Das, M.R., (1975). *O Level Revision History Paper 1 History of East Africa*, Nairobi: Success Publication.

284

Delf, G., (1963). *Asians in East Africa*, Nairobi: Oxford University Press

Dilley, M.P (1966). *British Policy in Kenya Colony*, London: Frank Case and Company Limited

Dirlik, A., (1994*). The Postcolonial Aura; The World Critism in The Age of Global Capitalism*, Critical Inquiry, 29.

Ehrlich, C., (1965). 'The Uganda Economy, 1903-1945' in V.Harlow (eds) *History of East Africa,* Oxford: Clarendon Press.

Fanon, F., (1967) *The Wretched of the Earth*, Middlesex: Penguin Books

Farson, N., (1949). *Last Chance in Africa*, London: Victor Gollanz Limited.

Fearn, H., (1961*). An African Economy: A study of the Economic Development of The Nyanza Province of Kenya 1903-1953*, London: Oxford University Press.

Frank, A.G., (1967). *Capitalism and Underdevelopment in Latin America*, New York Monthly Review Press.

Frost, R., (1978*) Race Against Time*, Nairobi: Trans Africa Press.

Ghai, D. P., (1965*). Portrait of a Minority: Asians in East Africa*, London: Oxford University Press.

Ghai, Y. P., (1971). *The Asian Minorities of East and Central Africa Upto 1971*, London: Minority Right Group.

Giddens, A., (1971). *Capitalist and Modern Social Theory: An Analysis of the Writing of Marx, Durkheim and Max Weber*: New York Cambridge University Press

Gottlieb, S., (1992). *Marxism 1844-1990: Origins, Betrayal, Rebirth* New York: Routledge.

Gregory, R., (1971). *India and East Africa: A History of Race Relations Within The British Empire 1890-1939.* London: Oxford University Press.

Gregory, R., (1971). *India and East Africa: A history of Race Relations Within The British Empire 1890-1939.,* London: Oxford University Press

Gregory R.P., (1984). *Bear Banquets From Boston to Bombay Santa Barbara* California: Woodbridge Press.

Gunther, J. (1995). *Inside Africa*, Hamilton Publications

Himbara, D., (1994). *Kenya Capitalists, the State and Development* Nairobi: East African Educational Publishers.

Hurd, G., (1973*). Human Societies: An Introduction to Sociology*, London: Routledge and Kegan Paul.

Hollingsworth, L.W., (1960). *The Asians of East Africa,* London Macmillan and Company

Hoogvelt Ankie,M., (1978). *The Sociology of Developing Societies*, London: Macmillan Publishers L.T.D

Ingham, K., (1966). *A History of East Africa*, London: Longmans Green and Company.

JanMohammed Abdul, R., (1985) *Manchean Aesthetics: The Politics of Literature in Colonial Africa,* Amherst: The Masssachussetts University Press.

Kalaine, C., (1998). *The Indians Role In The Development of East Africa 1890-1920* School of Archival Studies, National Archives of India, New Delhi.

Kanogo, T., (1989). 'Kenya and the Depression, 1929-1939' in Ochieng', W.R (ed) *A Modern History of Kenya 1895-1980,* Nairobi: Evans Brothers (Kenya) Limited .

Kaplan (1967). *Area Handbook for Kenya*, Washington.

Kerner, Commission (1968). 'Report of The National Advisory Commission on Civil Disorders' in Baker, D. G. (ed*) Race Ethnicity and Power*, London: Routledge and Kegan Paul.

Kenyanchui, S.S., (1992). 'European Settler Agriculture' in Ochieng,W.R (ed)*An Economic History of Kenya,* Nairobi: East African Educational Publishers.

Kitching,G., (1980). *Class and Economic Change in Kenya: The Making of an African Petite Bourgeousie 1905-1970*, London: Yale University Press.

Kovel, J., (1971). *White Racism: A psychohistory*, New York: Vintage.

Kwame, A.A., (1992) *In My Father's House: Africa in the Philosophy of Culture*, Oxford: Oxford University Press

Larimore A., (1969). *The Africanisation of Colonial Cities in East Africa*. East Lake Geographers.

Lofchie, M., (1973). 'The Plural Society in Zanzibar' *in* Bowker, G. (ed) *Race and Ethnic Relations*, London: Hutchinson and company.

Loomba, A., (1998*). Colonialism/Post colonialism*. London: Routledge

Lye, J.,(1998*)*Some Issues in Postcolonial Theory. Http// brocku.ca/English/course/4f70/postcol.htlm

Makhan, S., (1972). 'The East African Trade Union Congress 1949- 1950' in Ogot B.A (ed*) Hadith 4: Politics and Nationalism in Colonial Kenya*, Nairobi: East African Publishing House.

Makhan , S., (1969). *History of Trade Union Movement to 1952,* Nairobi: East Africa Publishing House.

Maloba W.O., (1995). 'Decolonisation: ATheoretical Perspective' in Ogot, B.A (ed) *Decolonisation and Independence in Kenya 1940-93,* Nairobi: East African Educational Publishers

Mamdani, M., (1996). *Citizen and Subject: Contemporary Africa and the Legacy of Late Colonialism,* London: James Curry.

Mangat, J., (1969). *A History of Asians in East Africa C 1886- 1945*, New York: Oxford University Press.

Mangat, J., (1975). *'The Indian Office and East Africa 1889- 1903'* in B.A Ogot (ed) Hadith 2 Nairobi: East African Publishing House.

Mangat, N.S., (1956). *The Presidential Address Delivered at the 24th (open session) Kenya Indian Congress* Nakuru, 4,5,6 Aug 1956. Nairobi Printer.

Marx, K and Engels, F., (1954). *The Communist Manifesto*, Chicago: Gateway Publishers

Maxon R.M., (1980). *John Ainsworth and the Making of Kenya* Washington: University Press of America.

Maxon,R., (1992). 'The Establishment of Colonial Economy' in Ochieng, W (ed) *An Economic History of Kenya*, Nairobi: East African Educational Publishers.

287

Maxon, R., (1995). 'Social and Cultural Changes' in Ochieng W. R and Ogot B.A (ed). *Decolonisation and Independence in Kenya 1940-93,* Nairobi: East African Educational Publishers.

Maxon, R., (2002). 'Economic and Social Change Since 1963', in Ochieng W.R (ed). *Historical Studies and Social Change in Western Kenya*, Kampala: East African Publishing House

Mazrui, A., (1972). *Cultural Engineering and Nation Building in East Africa*, Illinois: Northwestern University Press.

Mbembe, A., (2001). *On the Postcolony*, Berkeley: University of California Press.

Memon, P.A., (1975). 'Some Geographical Aspects of the History of urban development in Kenya', in Ogot, B.A (ed) *Economic and Social History of East Africa,* Nairobi: Kenya Literature Bureau

Morris, H., (1968) *The Indians In Uganda*, London:Garden City Press

Mungeam, G.H., (1966). *British Rule in Kenya 1895-1912: The Establishment of Administration in the East Africa Protectorate,* Oxford: Oxford University Press

Myers, G.A., (2003). *Verandahs of Power: Colonialism and Space in Urban African*, Syracuse: Syracuse University Press.

Myrdal, G et al., (1968). *Asian Drama* Vol I-111. New York: Pantheon.

Nanjira, D., (1976). *The Status of Aliens in East Africa: Asians and Europeans in Tanzania, Uganda and* Kenya. New York: Praeger Publishers.

Ndege, P., (1992). 'Internal Trade in Kenya 1895-1963' in Ochieng W., and Maxon R., (ed) *An Economic History of Kenya,* Nairobi: East African Educational Publishers.

O' Donnel, G., (1978*). The Human Web*, London: Butler and Tanner Ltd.

Obudho, R.A., (1976). *Periodic Markets Urbanisation and Regional Planning: A Case Study from Western Kenya,* London: Greenwood Press.

Ochieng', W.R., (1974*). An Outline History of Nyanza Up to 1914*, Nairobi: East African Literature Bureau.

Ochieng, W.R., (1989). 'Independent Kenya 1963-1986' in Ochieng, RW (ed). *A Modern History of Kenya,* Nairobi: Evans Brothers Limited

Ochieng W.R., (1995). 'Structural and Political changes' in Ogot, B.A(ed) *Decolonisation and Independence in Kenya 1940-93, Nairobi: East African Educational Publishers*

Odinga, O., (1967) *Not Yet Uhuru,* London: Heinemann

Ogot B.A., (1968) 'Kenya under The British, 1895- 1963' *in Ogot B.A (ed) Zamani: A survey of East African History,Nairobi: East African Publishing House.*

Ogot, B.A., (1995). 'The Politics of Populism' in Ogot, B.A(ed). *Decolonisation and Independence in Kenya 1940-93,* Nairobi: East African Educational Publishers

Ogot, B.A., (1999). 'British Administration in Central Nyanza District of Kenya, 1900-1960' in Ogot, B.A (ed). *Reintroducing Man into the African World: Selected Essays 1961-1980.*

Ogot B.A., (2003). *My Footprints on The Sands of Time: An Autobiography,* Kisumu: Anyange Press limited.

Okaro-Kojwang K.M., (1969). 'Origins and Establishment of Kavirondo Taxpayers Welfare Association' in McIntosh, B.G (ed). *NGANO,* Nairobi: East African Publishing House

Onimode, B., (1985). *An Introduction to Marxist Political Economy,* London: Zed Books L.T.D

Osogo, J.N., (1969). 'Education Development in Kenya, 1911-1924' in Ogot, B.A (ed). *Hadithi 3,* Nairobi: East Africa Publishing House.

Polo, M., (1948). *The Travels of Marco Polo, the Venetian,* Marsden, Williams (ed and trans.) New York: Doubleday and Company Inc.

Rabaka, R., (2003). *'Deliberately using the Word Colonial in a Much Broader Sense' W.E.B Dubois Concept of Semi colonialism as a Critique of and Contribution to Post colonialism. Http//social. chase. ncsu.edu/jouvert/v712/rabaka.htlm*

Rai, K., (1979*). Indians and British Colonialism in East Africa 1863- 1939,* Delhi: Associated Book Agency.

Rex, J., (1970). *Race Relations in Sociological Theory,* London: Routledge and Kegan

Rex, j., (1973). Race, *Colonialism and The City*, London: Routledge and Kegan Paul Publishers.

Rodney, W., (1989). *How Europe Underdeveloped Africa*, Nairobi: East African Educational Publishers

Ross, W.M., (1968). *Kenya From Within: A short Political History'*, London: Frank Cass and Company Limited

Rostow, W.W., (1960). *The Stage of Economic Growth,* Cambridge: Cambridge Universty Press

Rothchild, D., (1973*). Racial Bargaining in Independent Kenya: A study of Minorities and Decolonisation*, London: Oxford University Press.

Rushdie, S., (1990). *In Good Faith*, London: Granta

Said, E., (1994*).* 'From Orientalism' *in Williams Pand L.Chrisman (ed). Colonial discourse and Postcolonial theory, a Reader. New York: Columbia University Press.*

Said, E., (1978*). Orientalism*, London: Routledge and Kegan Paul Ltd.

Salvadori .C., (1983). *Through Open Doors, A view of Asian Cultures in Kenya.* Nairobi: Kenways Publications Ltd.

Salvadori, C., (1996). *We Came in Dhows Vol 1-3,* Nairobi : Paperchase Limited

Seidenberg, A., (1996). *Mercantile Adventures: The World of East African Asians 1750-1985*, New Delhi: New Age International (P) Limited Publishers.

Shivji, I., (1976). *Law, State and the Working Class in Tanzania C 1920-1964,* London: James Curry.

Smith, M.G., (1965). *The Plural Society in British West Indies*, Berkley: University of California Press.

Stitcher, S., (1975). 'The Formation of Working Class in Kenya' in Sandbrook, R and Cohen R (ed). *The Development of an African Working Class: Studies in Class Formation and Action,* London: Longman

Tandon, Y., (1973). *The Future of the Asians in East Africa*, London:Rex Collings Ltd

290

Toye, J., (1995). 'Is the Third World still There' in Ayres, R (ed). *Development Studies: An Introduction Through Selected Readings,* Dartford: Greenwich University Press.

Van Zwanenberg and Anne, King (1975). *An Economic History of Kenya and Uganda 1800*-1970 Narobi: Macmillan Press Ltd.

Webster, A., (1995). 'Modernization Theory', in Ayres R (ed). *Development Studies: An Introduction Through Selected Readings,* Dartford : Greenwhich University Press.

Wolff, D. R., (1974). *Britain and Kenya, 1870-1930, The Economic of Colonialism,* Nairobi: TransAfrica Publishers Ltd.

Zeleza, T., (1989) 'Kenya and The Second World War, 1939-1950' in Ochieng' W.R (ed) *A Modern History of Kenya: 1895-1980,* Nairobi: Evans Brothers Limited

Zeleza, T., (1989). 'The Establishment of Colonial rule 1905-1920' in Ochieng' W.R (ed). *A Modern History of Kenya: 1895-1980,* Nairobi: Evans Brothers Limited.

Journals.

Bindra, S., (2005). 'We are Kenya Damu', *Journal of Kenyan South Asian History Awaaz edition Issue 1.*

Chege, M., (2004). 'EAST vs EAST: The role of Minorities in Business, East Asia and East Africa Compared.' *in Journal of Kenyan South Asian History Awaaz edition, Issue 111*

Fearn, H., (1956). 'Cotton Production in the Nyanza Province of Kenya Colony' *The Empire Cotton Growing Review 33 p 126-7.*

Furedi, F, (1974), 'The Development of Anti-Asian Opinion Among Africans in Nakuru District', *African Affairs Vol 73 No 292.*

Glassman, J., (2004). 'Slower than a Massacre: The Multiple Sources of Racial Thought in Colonial Africa', *The American Historical Review Vol 109 No 3.*

Honwana, A., (1999), 'Negotiating Post-War Identities: Child Soldiers in Mozambique and Angola'. CODESRIA Bulletin.

Hutcheon, L., (1995). 'Introduction: Complexities Abounding' in PMIA

Lemoosa, P.L., (1996). 'The Asians in The Kenyan Colonial Economy' *The East African Journal of Historical and Social Sciences Research Vol 1 No 1*

Mbae, N., (1996). 'Asians in Kenya Colonial Politics' *The East African Journal of Historical and Social Sciences Research Vol 1 No 1.*

Mbembe, A., (1992), 'Provisional Notes on the Postcolony '. *Journal of The International African Institute AFRICA Vol 62 No 1.*

Mbembe, A., (1999), 'The Civil Status of The state in Africa: Mamadou Diouf, Harris Memel Fote and Achille mbembe'. CODESRIA bulletin No 1

Mbembe, A., (2002) 'African Modes of Self-Writing' CODESRIA Bulletin No. 1

Memon, P., (1976), Colonial Marketing, and Urban Development in the African Reserves, *Journal of Eastern Africa Research and Development. Vol 6,2.*

Musalia, W., (1996). 'Asians and Africans in Kenya Post Colonial Economy' *The East African Journal of Historical and Social Sciences Research Vol 1 No 1.*

Mwangi, W., (2002). 'Race and Identity in Africa: Concept paper. CODESRIA bulletin.

Nabende, J., (1996). ' The Political Economy of Education for Asians in Kenya' *The East African Journal of Historical and Social Sciences Research Vol 1 No 1.*

Ngari, L., (1996). 'The Indian Question' *The East African Journal of Historical and Social Sciences Research* Vol 1 No 1.

Nyanchoga, S., (1996). ' 'The Role of Asians in Post Colonial Kenya' *The East African Journal of Historical and Social Sciences Research Vol 1No 1.*

O'Connor, A., (1965). New Railway Construction and the Pattern of Economic Development in East Africa, *Transaction Institute of British Geographers, 36.*

Ogot, B.A., (1963). 'British Administration in The Central Nyanza District of Kenya, 1900-1960'. *Journal of African History Vol. 2.*

Ojwang, D., (2005). 'The Bad Baniani Sports Good Shoes; Asian Stereotypes and the Problem of Modernity in East Africa'. *African Insight Vol 35 No 2 AISA.*

Xie S., (1997). 'Rethinking Problem of Postcolonialism' *New Literary History* No 28.1.

Rampersad, S., (2007). 'Indian –African Relations in the English – Speaking Caribean' , *Journal of Kenyan South Asian History, Awaaz Issue1* May –July.

Rattansi, P.M., (2004). 'Rebel With a Cause' *Journal of Kenyan South Asian History Awaaz Issue 1.*

Siddique, J., (2004). 'Haunts of Uganda 30 years of Old Past' *Journal of Kenyan South Asian History Awaaz, Issue 1.*

Sofer, C., (1954), 'Working Groups in a Plural Society', *Industrial and Labou Relations Review,* Vol 8 No. 5 pp 68-78.

Theroux, P., (1967). 'Hating The Asians', *Transition No. 33 pp 46-51*

Zarina, P., (2004). 'I am A Kenyan South Asian' *Journal of Kenyan South Asian History Awaaz Issue 11.*

Zeleza, P.T., (1997). *Fictions of The Postcolonial: A review article,* CODESRIA bulletin.

Theses

Anyumba, G., (1995) *Kisumu Town: History of The Built Form, Planning and Environment 1890- 1990.* Ph.D. Thesis, Moi University.

Aseka, E.M., (1989). *A Political Economy of Buluyia 1900-1964* Ph.D Dissertation, Kenyatta University.

Berman, B., (1974). *Administration and Politics in Colonial Kenya* Ph.D Thesis,Yale University.

293

Bhatt, P.M., (1976*). A History of Asians in Kenya 1900 –1970* Ph.D Thesis, Howard University.

Kalaine, C.N., (1998). *The Indians Role in The Development of East Africa 1890-1920,* Project Dissertation, School of Archival Studies National Archives of India, New Delhi.

King'oria, G., (1980). *Policy Impacts on Urban Land Use Patterns in Nairobi Kenya, 1899-1979* Ph.D Thesis, Indiana State University Indiana.

Kinyanjui, K., (1979). *The Political Economy of Educational Inequality: A study of the Roots of Educational inequality in Colonial Kenya and Postcolonial Kenya*, Ed Dissertation, Harvard University.

Kipkorir, B.E., (1969). *The Alliance High School and the Origins of the Kenya African Elite 1926-1962,* Ph.D , Cambridge University.

Kisiang'ani, E., (2003). *Rethinking Frantz Fanon in the concept of Kenya Decolonisation Experience, 1895-1992* Ph.D thesis, Kenyatta University.

Lonsdale, J.M., (1964). *A Political History of Nyanza 1883-1945* Ph.D Thesis, Trinity College Cambridge.

Murunga, G., (1998). *The Evolution of Mumias Settlement Into an Urban Centre to Circa 1940* M.A. Dissertation, Kenyatta University.

Ndeda, M.A.J., (1991), *The Impact of male labour Migration on Rural Women: A Case Study of Siaya District, C1894-1963*, Ph.D Thesis, Kenyatta University

Ngesa, P., (1996). *A History of African Women Traders in Nairobi, 1899-195,* M.A Thesis, University of Nairobi.

Odwako, E., (1973). *The Contribution of The Church Missionary Society to Education in Western Kenya 1905-1963,* M.A Thesis, University of Nairobi.

Ogutu G.E.M., (1981). *Origins and Growth of The Roman Catholic Church in Western Kenya 1895-1952 Ph.D* Thesis University of Nairobi.

294

Okuro, S.O., (2003). *The Impact of The Colonial Socio- Economic Policies and Practices on Female Headed Households in Kenya: The Case of Kombewa Division, Kisumu District, 1894-1963,* M.A Thesis, Kenyatta University.

Olima, W.H.A., (1993). *The Land Use Planning in Provincial Towns of Kenya: A case Study of Kisumu and Eldoret Town* Dr Ing. Dissertation Degree of Dortmund University

Olumwullah, O.A.L.A., (1986). *A history of African Housing in Nairobi C1900-1960, A study of Urban Conditions and Colonial Policies*, M.A Thesis, Nairobi University

Ongile, G., (1988). *Determinants of Female Labour Force Participation in Kenyan Urban areas,* M.A Thesis, University of Nairobi.

Opondo, M., (1989). *The Spatio-Structural Characteristic of Small Scale Industries in Kisumu Municpality* M.A thesis, Kenyatta University

Reed, H.A., (1975). *Cotton Growing in Central Nyanza Province, Kenya 1901-1939: An Appraisal of African Reactions to Imposed Government Policy* Ph.D Thesis, Michigan State University.

Seidenberg, D .A., (1979). *The Asians and Uhuru: The Role of a Minority Community in Kenya Politics 1939- 1963'* Ph.D Thesis, Syracuse University.

Schiller, L.D., (1982). *Gem and Kano: A Comparative Study of Two Luo Political Systems Under Stress, C 1880-1914*, Ph.D Thesis, Northwestern University.

Wafula P.W., (2000). *Politics and Nationalism in Colonial Kenya: The Case of the Babukusu of Bungoma District C1894-1963* M.A Thesis, Kenyatta University.

Zeleza, T.P., (1982). *Dependent Capitalism and the Making of the Kenyan Working Class During the Colonial Period* Ph.D Thesis, Dalhousie University

Papers and Articles

Desai, R.H., (1965). *The Family and Business Among The Asian in East Africa.* A paper presented at a conference of East Africa Institute of Social Researrch-Kampala Makerere College.

Holmquist, F., (2002). *'Business and Politics in Kenya in the 1990s'* Paper presented at the Centre of African Studies, University of Copenhagen on 2nd October 2001

Kisumu District Development Plan (2002-2008), Nirobi: Government printer

Ministry of Education (1967). *Triennial Survey 1964-66,* Nairobi: Government Printer.

Murunga,G., (2007). *Segregationist Town Planning and the Indian Bazaar in Colonial Nairobi, 1899-1923,* A Staff Seminar Paper Presented in the Department of History, Kenyatta University, Nairobi on 15th March 2007

Rachuonyo District Development Plan (1997-2001), Nairobi: Government Printer

Siaya District Development Plan (2002-8008),Nairobi: Government Printer

Printed by
Schaltungsdienst Lange o.H.G., Berlin